A BROAD ABROAD
IN THAILAND

*To Maline!
Enjoy!
Dudie
2007*

Do Good - Get Good
Do Evil - Get Evil

Thai Proverb

A BROAD ABROAD IN THAILAND

An Expat's Misadventures in the Land of Smiles

CrossRoads-FourWaysWest Publications

Printed in the United States of America

ISBN: 1-885614-75-6

Published by:
CrossRoads-FourWaysWest, 2007

Printed by:
Axess Book Printing
Cumming, Georgia 30041

Cover and Interior Design by: Joseph W. Shine

Illustrations by: Ernie Towler

To order additional copies of this book please go to:

www.abroadinthailand.com
or www.amazon.com

For my Buddy, Liz Miller
1938-2006

For her faith in me. For her love. For her friendship.
Who said: "Promise me you'll finish your book."
I'm a little late, Liz,
but you can get a copy from St. Peter.

Perseverance

Perseverance is a word that's widely used today,
Tho' rarely put to practice, I've only this to say:
That nothing ventured, nothing gained is my philosophy,
And tho' my luck may be detained I'm sure it's there for me.
So if you'd realize your dream, I think it's now quite clear,
There's just one course for you my friend,
and that's to persevere.

By: Pauline Baker

My first order of thanks will be to my poet and songwriter mother who authored the poem, *Perseverance*. I have definitely persevered to write this book and I wish to acknowledge and thank all the others who helped me along the way: Ardie Davis, my Palm Desert buddy, the first person to read my story said she laughed till she cried (I hope I got that right). She read it for content and pushed me onward; my wonderful sister, Margie McArthur, herself a talented author and editor, for giving me her time and patience; my writer's critique group in Palm Desert, friends in Washington, Jane Lloyd and Carl Komor; two knowledgeable expats living in Thailand, John Lyman and Duncan Stearn, who furnished essential information on the socioeconomic facts of Thailand; Patty Byrne, for offering her time and suggestions in reviewing my manuscript.

Multiple kudos to the talented artist, Ernie Towler, for his incredible illustrations. He had people laughing harder at his drawings than at my story.

Heaps of loving gratitude to my ever-patient husband, Ray Norwood, who read my manuscript but never really laughed out loud (I think I did hear a chuckle once), but without whose patience and menu planning/cooking, this book would never have come to fruition. He generously gave me all the time I needed, along with a multitude of synonyms that refused to reveal themselves to me.

Lastly, I would like to thank my publisher, Joe Shine and his wife, Gail, for their selfless help and commitment to make this book the answer to my *Perseverance*.

Of course, I can't finish this page without mentioning the many people who kept asking: "When is your book coming out?" They drove me crazy and they know who they are.

Welcome to My World!

PROLOGUE

Pattaya Beach, Thailand
September, 1991

I'm running away from a marriage that's about to implode. I have stuffed essentials into my carry-on. What won't fit I leave behind. I need to hurry before my husband returns.

There is one last thing I must do before I leave this house forever. I walk outside and try to burn the scene into my memory: the limitless blue sky, the wild-grass jungles with their shimmering, waving fronds, the kaleidoscope of vibrant flowers that never fail to take my breath away by their sheer beauty, the humid summer air that carries a promise of rain and wind in a smooth and seamless way. I must never forget them.

My loyal maid, Pon, has asked her nephew to drive me to Bangkok. I cry as we hug our goodbyes. We both know we'll not meet again. She hired on as a maid, but so effortlessly endeared herself to me that she became my confidante and friend. Many a day I cried on her shoulder. "Men, *mai dii,"*— no good—she'd murmur as she consoled me.

Pon gives her nephew last minute instructions and tells him to find a cheap hotel close to the airport. I'm praying that he understands c*heap* and *close.* We hug once more as her nephew stands by, head lowered in respect to the emotions he's witnessing.

"You goot?" he queries as I step into the taxi.

"I'm fine. Please hurry."

I fret about the long drive to Bangkok as we pull away from the curb. I know too well the congestion and fender-benders we'll encounter, adding to the gridlock. I'm beyond exhaustion as I lean back against the hard vinyl seat. My eyes feel grainy, my tongue sticks to my teeth. I find it hard to swallow. I feel like ten miles of bad road. The driver chatters to me in Pidgin English—most of which I don't understand—as his garlic breath and cigarette smoke permeates every molecule of air. I ask him to please open the windows. Moist heat slams me in the face from all four windows as he careens through town hitting speeds of 120 kilometers an hour entering the deadly Sukhumvit Highway. I ask him to please close the windows, which he does after giving me a questioning look through his rear-view mirror.

I close my eyes and try to escape my thoughts. Sleep is an illusion; I've been without it for too many hours, too many late nights of arguing and crying, and chest pain. I want to drop into a sound sleep, which becomes difficult as the driver tears around other cars, hits his brakes and honks his horn in a learned gesture of the Thai version of driving.

Near midnight I feel the car slow to a stop. From my window I see a run-down motel and wonder why he's stopped here. Pon told her nephew to find a cheap place, but this is way below cheap. He hurries around the car to unload my bag. My body sags as I step from the taxi. "Isn't there someplace else that's not so run down?"

"Too mut *baht*,"—Thai currency. He hands me my carry-on.

"Sokay, Madame."

Sure, it's "sokay" with him; he's not staying in this dive. I dig through my purse as I search for some stray *baht* to pay him. My throat constricts as tears well up in my eyes. He waves my money away. "*Mai pen lai*, Madame."

How many times have I heard that soothing phrase. The Thais live by its meaning: *never mind, no problem, it's okay.* It's part of their Buddhist belief that nothing matters in *this* life. You play with the cards you're dealt. If you're kind and honest, and don't kill, you will be reborn into a higher station in the *next* life. I like that idea.

"*Khap khun kha,*"—I thank him, and then watch him speed off.

I step into the hotel lobby and I'm amazed that it could look worse than the outside. Two old Caucasian hippy-types, each with long braided grey hair and shaggy beards, are deep in conversation with two adolescent-looking Asian girls. *Perverts!* Those girls are much too young for the old geezers and shouldn't even be out this time of night. One of the hippies drops his cigarette butt on the floor and grinds it into the shabby carpet with the toe of his boot.

The floor is littered with newspapers. A few paper cups are scattered helter-skelter around the room as if a party had taken place and no one stayed to clean up. The room reeks of tobacco, booze and bodies in need of deodorant soap.

The reception desk is littered with magazines featuring Asian girls in various stages of undress. The bullwhip-thin clerk leans on a torn vinyl counter, squinting at a fuzzy TV screen and lost in a fog of smoke. He looks up at me through Coke-bottle glasses smudged with fingerprints. I fight the urge to grab them and submerge them in Windex. He squints as he tries to focus on me. "Yeth?"

"*Sawatdee kha,*" I greet him in the traditional Thai way, hoping to sound un-touristy. "I'd like a room for four hours. How much would that cost?"

He scans my disheveled appearance. With the heat and humidity I know I look like an unmade bed. My hair droops across my skull, damp and flat. My clothes—unquestionably not the Perma Press variety— hang limp on my clammy body. Maybe he'll take pity on a down-on-

A Broad Abroad in Thailand

her-luck old gal. He smiles as he wedges a toothpick between yellowed teeth and probes for the last vestiges of dinner. "No can do. You pay foh all day, twenny dollah."

"What?" I croak, "I think that's a bit much …" I glance around the lobby, "…for a place like this." I know he's upped the price due to my white skin. I know the normal price for a three-star hotel in Bangkok is close to forty dollars but this has to be a minus ten on the Hotel Star ratings.

His eyes disappear into a practiced squint as he assesses what he can get away with. "How long you stay?"

"I'll only be here until four. I have to be at the airport by five."

His eyes trail to my left hand and stop when he spots my wedding ring. He gives me a wicked leer. "Wheh you husband?"

"I'm alone," I answer, wincing at the implication. "Look, there's no one else with me. I just need a place to sleep for a few hours before my flight. You know your price is too high. Can't you drop the rate a little?"

He scratches his head and looks off into space as if he's dealing in high finance. "Sokay, you pay foh half day. Ten dollah. No man stay. You pay moh if man stay."

"I said I'm alone," I repeat through clenched teeth. Does he think I'd have a tryst in this place? With the way I look?

I can't get too irate with him; he's my one hope before I collapse. I place my Visa card on the dirty counter as I say a silent prayer that my husband hasn't cancelled it yet.

He stares at the card and shakes his head. "No can do. Take *baht* oh dollah. No Wisa."

Oh please, Buddha, help me. I'd assumed my Visa would get me through any snags when I'd changed what little *baht* I had into dollars. But while Pon helped me pack, I realized she hadn't been paid her month's salary. I knew my husband would fire her, assuming her complicity, and didn't want her cheated out of her last wages. After paying her, I had only forty dollars to get me half a world away.

I dig through my purse and wonder how many taxis and porters I'll have to tip before I reach my final destination. I hand him two five-dollar bills.

He counts the money with tobacco-stained fingers. "You wan me get taxi foh airpoht?"

"*Khap khun kha.*" Maybe he's not so bad after all.

"Two dollah moh."

"What! To call a taxi?"

"One foh phone, one foh me."

"Never mind." I turn away. "I'll call the taxi from my room."

"No phone in loom."

"Oh. Okay, I'll use the lobby phone. You *do* have a phone down here, don't you?"

"Two dollah foh lobby phone."

I can't believe it! This place is a flophouse, not the Royal Thai Palace. What a racket he has going. "Okay, fine. Please call a taxi and have it here at 4:00 a.m. sharp." I put two more dollars on the counter. His eyesight improves to 20/20 as he scoops up my money.

I find my way through a dank, depressing hallway. It has to be 120 degrees in this place and the humidity lies on my chest as heavy as an x-ray apron. The hall is littered with bits and scraps of detritus, like ticker tape after a St. Paddy's Day parade. The walls are dingy and prison-grey. What little carpet left is beyond dirty and should've been removed after Genghis Khan and his boys ran amok here. The odor is overwhelming; a mixture of mildew and mold with years of neglect, and a smattering of BO thrown into the mix. I've heard that when someone is desperate, a hovel can seem like the Trump Towers—I'm waiting.

The dim lights in the hall reveal cracks along the floorboards, dotted with huge Asian roaches like shiny black dirigibles awaiting take-off. They squat there, lurking in fetid corners as they wave their glistening antennae at me. I look away in disgust as the hairs on my arms and neck stand on end. I must not think about all this. I'm here, I have a few hours to rest and then I'm homeward bound.

I scope out the room as I step inside. Dear God! He should've paid *me* to stay here. On a bedside table I see the remains of half-smoked cigarettes floating in a bowl of yellow liquid. Next to that lay two empty beer bottles, like dead horses. *Don't they have maid service here?* No way am I staying in this pig sty. I rush back to the front desk. The clerk has not moved from his grainy TV. "Excuse me," I say softly, trying not to sound like The Ugly American, "I need another room. The one you gave me hasn't been cleaned yet."

He turns to me as a slow grin creases his face. "You say you need foh haf day. No clean foh haf day. You take oh leave."

"But you can't expect me to pay for a room that's not been cleaned, I…"

He turns his back on me. "Take oh leave," he calls over his shoulder as he disappears behind a swaying curtain of grimy beads.

My skin erupts into multiple tiny goose bumps as I creep back into the room. The humidity is debilitating. There are no windows, just the drowsy movement of a ceiling fan that has seen better days. I'm afraid to touch anything; I feel just being here makes me susceptible to an STD of some kind.

In the bathroom I take a quick peek in the trashcan and recoil as I see its contents of used condoms and wrappers. In the sink I see a few suspicious-looking short curly hairs clinging to a small bar of hotel soap. I shriek as it dawns on me: *Oh my God! I've rented a one-hour special.* Then I remember the two young girls with the old geezers in the lobby. Why didn't I see this before I gave the clerk my money? It's too late to be walking the streets looking for a place to sleep. I have no choice.

I take a quick inventory of the bathroom. There's not even a fresh bar of soap to wash my face, no wash cloths, just a used towel thrown across the stained and grimy bathtub. I drag myself toward the bed. I have to sleep. Oh God, the bedspread! I know it hasn't been cleaned since dirt was invented. The last occupants didn't even bother to throw it back. I can see two body imprints. My imagination runs wild. Yuk!

I find a blanket in the closet. It's still folded and looks to be unused. I give it the sniff test—it passes. I throw it over the dirty bedspread and flop down. My eyes close. Just as I feel the last wisp of energy escape my body and begin to drift off, the parchment-thin wall behind my bed begins to vibrate as groans of pleasure are carried on the humid airwaves. I don't want to hear this. I cover my ears. I want to bury my head under a pillow but they're on the floor, too disgusting to touch. I bang on the wall. The vibrating stops. Giggles ensue, then the vibrating commences again. My bed is moving with the tempo of the wall.

Okay, I tell myself, it's just for a few hours. I can't think about it now. I'll just close my eyes and…

There's someone banging on my door…

A BROAD ABROAD
IN THAILAND

WELCOME TO BANGKOK

1

Thailand: August, 1990

The flight to Thailand was miserable. I was frazzled, cranky, and a full-scale gas war had been roiling inside my gut for hours, as though I'd eaten a boxcar of popcorn and drunk a keg of beer. My stomach was rolling and bucking like two wild cats in a burlap sack.

Flying has always caused me terrible gas. I know it and it's embarrassing. But what can I do? The atmospheric conditions didn't help either. Turbulence bounced our plane around for over an hour, and with each bounce I produced another gas bubble. I knew I'd better get to the lavatory or I'd explode. The man in front of me, snoring loudly, had his seat laid back into my thorax. I waited, trying to come up with a way to ease out of my seat while my eyes bored holes in the flashing seat belt sign. I sat very still and tried to visualize the gas bubbles evaporating into oblivion. After ten minutes of meditating and emitting tiny bubbles into the cabin, I couldn't wait any longer. I looked behind me and saw the flight attendant preparing her beverage cart and knew I'd better make my move. The second the seat belt sign blinked off I stood and tried to wriggle between the snorer's head-rest and the three inches allotted me by the stingy engineers who designed the seats.

I'd waited too long. There comes a time when your bodily functions have their way—without any warning—and detonate!

Well, I'm sooorry! Geez, I didn't do it on purpose. It ticks me off the way some people get that "What the hell was that?" look on their face. It's just a part of being human. Everyone does it. So, sue me. *Sheesh!*

After twenty-one hours in the air, we landed in Bangkok, Thailand. I stepped from the jet-way and thought I'd entered a sauna. *Where the hell were the air conditioners?* No AC, no Muzak, no helpful porters wending their way toward us with eager smiles. It had to be over 100 degrees and so humid I began to slide inside my shoes. My husband and I staggered toward the baggage carousel, pushed along by hundreds of cranky travelers.

I could see it might be a challenge getting ten pieces of luggage off a carousel with 300-plus people clamoring to do the same, without getting bruised. It seemed as though Dick and I were the only two people who queued for a spot next to the carousel; the Asians pushed in whether there was an opening or not. *Geez, you'd think they lived here.*

Airport personnel, assigned to remove large boxes and duffel bags from the carousel, grabbed and flung them onto the floor at various spots. "You stand here and watch for our stuff," Dick ordered as we got close enough to see the bags, "I'm gonna check the floor on the other side."

Trying to spot our luggage was next to impossible, as clumps of suitcases, boxes and bags came flip-flopping by. I dared not move to another spot as everyone had already claimed their territory. I also had the responsibility of hanging on to my carry-on and huge purse. I placed them between my legs and tried to straddle them—no easy feat—hoping to foil the ever-present airport thief. Heaven help me if he decided to grab them and run. There I stood, bow-legged, concerned about my balance—and my gas—as people pushed and shoved by me.

I began by checking the carousel, then the pile of boxes and duffel bags on the floor, then the baggage carousel again, and then back to the pile on the floor. But as I surveyed the heap on the floor, then turned to check the carousel, the workers might have thrown a dozen more duffel bags on the ever-expanding floor mound. Frustrated with the whole thing, I decided to just relax and let it happen. I yelled to Dick across the frenzy, "Hey, I have an idea. Why don't we go find a chair and just relax? After everyone's claimed their stuff, ours will be all that's left." It seemed like a simple matter of logic to me: ten unclaimed bags would be in a pile just waiting for us. He didn't like my idea.

"Don't be dumb," he yelled back. "Someone could walk away with our stuff and we'd never see it again." That did it. My eyes were riveted. After more than forty-five minutes of this search and recover mission I managed to find one oversize suitcase, one huge duffel bag— the kind you could smuggle a 49ers halfback in—and my golf bag. So along with my carry-on and humongous purse, it all ended up piled on a cart designed to hold three petite pieces of luggage at best.

Dick, loaded down with the remainder, found a porter and offered him a five dollar bill to push our huge pieces to the Customs counter. We were told later that five dollars is more than they might make in tips for a month. Well good for him, I thought, I hope he buys his buddies a round of beer.

Dick followed the porter toward Customs, attempting to wend his way around the cluster of humanity and somehow escape the mess on the floor. Luggage lay piled on the carts helter-skelter, high above our heads, making it difficult to see anything in front of us. Dick is not a tall man, so he had to jump up every so often to get a clear view of what lay in his path. He turned once to check on me and as I peeked around my mountain of luggage I saw a rather strained look on his reddened face. His carotid artery stood out like a garden hose, which I attributed to the humidity and change of altitude. We'd just passed an airport sign showing the temperature at 100 degrees. Without needing a sign I knew the humidity was off the charts; this alone was enough to make anyone's carotid bulge.

With his usual pronouncement of "Let me take care of this," we lined up at the Customs counter where we tried to affect innocuous expressions, fearing they might want to search our bags, which could take at least two hours. I'd heard rumors that you could be fined for bringing new appliances into the country, and we did have a few such items stowed between towels, sheets, tablecloths and some of my undies. But some people love to warn you about things they know very little about, so we chose to ignore the warning. I could now picture the Customs officer grabbing us by the ear and marching us to a small interrogation room where the militia would deal with us.

The Customs agents were preoccupied as we stepped up to the counter. The object of their attention was a turban-headed gentleman with scores of boxes—all wrapped with twine that I imagined were new goods going to a 7-Eleven store. Our innocuous looks must have worked as the agents gave a cursory glance at our passports and visas, and waved us on our way, turning their attention back to the turbaned guy. We scooted by as unobtrusively as possible with a sigh of relief.

Another long walk! After leaving Customs we still had miles to go. *Can't anyone build a small airport anymore?* I began to feel a melt-down. Temptation urged me to abandon this stubborn beast—the cart, not Dick—well maybe him too—and run away. But where would I run? Certainly not back to the plane. *What was I doing here?*

With fatigue draining my spirits and strong thoughts of divorce proceedings flitting through my mind, I spotted a gentleman with a broad smile holding a sign that read: *HEADE PARTY.* A company limo driver had been dispatched to meet us and deliver us to our hotel. I waved at him as he approached and offered a humid smile. He gave me a short bow, and then grabbed Dick's cart. I couldn't believe it! Before

I collapsed on the ground and caused a scene, I thought I'd give Dick a chance to clear this up. I raised one eyebrow as high as possible, glowering in the process.

"What?" he asked, feigning innocence.

"You've got to be kidding me. You're not going to let me push this while you walk empty-handed, are you?"

Dick stopped. I could feel his discomfort as he tried to weigh his options. I'm sure he didn't want to insult Thai culture the first day in-country, but on the other hand...

I kept on with the eyebrow thing.

He hung back a few more seconds, brows joining in one long hairy line of concentration. As the young Thai pushed Dick's cart toward the exit, Dick made a very wise decision; Thai culture be damned, he *sleeps* with me. "Let go," he growled, as he pried my cramped fingers from the cart handle. And, off we went, following this smiling Thai to our new destiny.

As I stepped out into the steaming, throbbing streets of Bangkok, I wondered—again—what had possessed me to marry this man and come to this miserably hot place.

I thought back to how it all started...

THE START OF A FATEFUL AFFAIR

2

California: January, 1990

Most women are suckers for men who carry the feminine-energy gene. I was one of them.

A widow of five years, I was also recovering from a close friend's recent suicide when I met Dick. I worked part-time in customer service at a golf course near my home, where he was the golf instructor. We talked now and then and eventually he asked me to have coffee with him after work. That led to a glass of wine, occasional dinners and movies. He told me he was going through a messy divorce and looking to move closer to his job. After I'd worked with him a couple of months I felt reasonably assured he wasn't Ted Bundy incarnate and suggested he might like to rent a room from me, helping us both financially.

Dick seemed sincere, very attentive, oozing with compassion, even tearing-up when I told him of my losses. He gave me the tea and sympathy I needed, and I gave him the opportunity to work his way into my life. Dick had been rent/sharing my home for close to three months when we did the "excitement"— as Frank McCourt terms the sex act in *Angela's Ashes*—and began a committed relationship.

He wasn't "my type" as my friends often reminded me. I normally went for the tall, dark types, which also included good dressers, educated and classy. Dick was about 0-for-4 in the batting averages. He dressed like the quintessential hippie who didn't like that the 60s and 70s were over and had taken their fashion statement with them. He was short and painfully thin, with a black ponytail and sideburns that smacked of circa 1960. When he wasn't wearing the traditional golf garb, he preferred to lounge in Nehru shirts, ratty jeans, and feet complimented by run-down Birkenstocks.

Dick seemed entirely committed to me. I loved his enthusiasm, impulsiveness and ability to put my friends at ease. They all thought he was great. We went on trips with them, out to shows and dinners. He wowed them with his attentiveness. However, I worried that some of this attentiveness—to them and to me—might be a subtle form of control. There never seemed to be a minute when he wasn't doing something *for* me that I was ready and willing to do for myself. I thought perhaps it was just a "first impression" kind of thing that guys do. It was flattering at first, but over time it became annoying. *Hey, I can do that for myself.* But, that was the least of the problems.

Dick's testosterone tank never hit empty. I guess *insatiable* is as good a word as any to describe him. At sixty he was incredibly virile. Even though I was ten years his junior, I didn't seem to have the hormones to match his libido. He'd come to bed with a bottle of massage oil, offering to give me a massage to relax me and help me sleep, saying he cared so much for me he couldn't bear to see me so stressed out.

I was? Working an office job for eight hours and then another four hours at the golf course, maybe I was a bit stressed. But by the time he'd massaged my body—giving special attention to all the nooks and crannies—I'd be titillated and he'd be there to accommodate me. The next night, here he'd come again with his bottle of massage oil.

While all this may sound wonderful to some women who'd give their right areola for this kind of treatment from a man, the inevitability of it wore a little thin night after night. Lord knows, sometimes a woman just wants to throw on a ratty old T-shirt, not shower, or remove her make-up, but flop into bed spread-eagled on her belly, stretch out and drift off to sleep—unencumbered by hands, arms or penises.

It soon became obvious that Dick had ulterior motives to all of his caring. My sleep and relaxation had *nothing* to do with it. His relaxation, stress reduction and release had *everything* to do with it. We had numerous small squabbles about this routine of his, which was now happening every night, and these gradually grew into huge arguments. I'd say "No!" after two consecutive nights of this hot body stuff, and then have to put up with his pouting, sullenness and cold shoulder most of the next day. But as bedtime approached, miraculously his moodiness would lift and in its place were smiles, back rubs and "anything I can do for you?" questions. Many times I gave in just to quell an argument. Then of course the whole cycle would begin again.

"Don't bother putting on your nightgown," he'd call to me while I showered, a sure sign that his T-level was near overflowing. We talked about it during the day, when his level had waned a bit. He'd admit he did have a high libido, but claimed that I brought it about with my sexiness. *Right!* He would do anything for me, he said, but unsaid was the inflexible reward of sex. But, come on! How many rewards does a woman have to dole out every week? I never had the opportunity to initiate sex, which I might have given the opportunity, but he always seemed to be hovering close by, like an eager kid who's just finished his chores and waits for his allowance.

I know that sex is a big part of the human condition, but sometimes I wondered: If no sex were forthcoming, would men even come around? Would they even call us, cuddle with us, hold the door for us, pull out the chair for us, or put the toilet seat down? I think the Almighty realized this in Her infinite wisdom and came up with the solution. I can see it being planned: "Alright," She'd say. "They're as different as seaweed and sorghum so I must find something that will make them tolerate each other. Oh, I've got it! Sex!"

Don't get me wrong. I like sex as much as the next woman—depending on her age, of course, and realize it's part and parcel of how we're created; love, fulfillment, the old primordial instinct that pushes for the reproduction of the species, but I just didn't see it happening every night—and I was way beyond my reproductive years.

Out of frustration I made an appointment with a therapist. After a few sessions she came up with a regimen for us. We were to plan our evenings for sex. Dick looked pleased as she began to lay out our schedule, but his grin sagged when he heard that sex should be only three nights a week. And, she said, we were not to alter the schedule. My grin sagged as well; two nights a week would have been my choice.

The therapist saw the look on Dick's face and quickly added that there could be no pouting or moodiness, either. *"Both* people must be agreeable to this plan for it to work." She looked at Dick and frowned. "If one person forces himself on the other it then becomes a job—an unpleasant job that must be endured.

"Try to make a party of it. Take the phone off the hook, turn on soft music, light some candles, get in a bubble bath with a bottle of champagne, and enjoy each other."

I looked over at Dick, with his shoulders slouched and a pained expression, and I wondered if he was getting any of this. How much was hitting home, or how much he thought was pure psychobabble. He straightened up when she addressed him sternly. She told him if what she had heard from him so far was true, he might be what the textbooks refer to as a "Sexual Addict." She admonished him to be very careful because it surely would end our relationship. That got his attention. He looked chastised and reached for my hand. "This'll all work out," he whispered to me.

The therapist asked Dick why he felt the need to pout to get what he wanted. While he tried to come up with a clever answer, I remembered something he'd told me when we first met. I wondered if his closeness with his mother in his early years had been the cause of his constant craving for physical comfort. He told me his father left the family when he was very young, and his mother would take him to her bed to comfort him. She would massage his back until he fell asleep, he said, which made him feel safe and loved. But when she tried to put him in his bed he would cry and beg until she'd give in and let him sleep with her all night. He said this massage and comfort from his mother's bed had continued way into his teens. I wondered if he could change after years of crying and pouting to get what he wanted.

We left the therapist office vowing to work on the relationship.

I began to prepare for our three evenings with a different attitude. I even anticipated them instead of being irritated. We'd shower together then get into a warm tub filled with lavender bath oils and candles on every flat surface. I'd put on some soft music and seductive cologne—he'd come to bed with the massage oil.

It worked—for a while.

THE CARROT

3

What sounded like a great employment opportunity materialized for Dick about six months into our relationship when he was offered a two-year assignment in Thailand.

I'd been working at a large company when a casual detour in my morning run for coffee found me walking right into the path of a man swinging a pitching wedge as he strolled the halls. I'd seen him before and knew he was some sort of VIP, but seeing the golf club was something I had to comment on. I smiled.

He waggled the club at me. "How do?"

"Hey," I said, "you're out of bounds."

He looked at the club and grinned. "Right! You play golf?"

"I play at it. But I'm getting better. My boyfriend's a golf instructor and he's cut a few strokes off my game."

"Yeah? He's good, huh? Been lookin' for a good teacher. Where's he teach? Me and the wife could use some help."

And that's how *Mr. Jelly Belly* and his wife, *Mrs. Anorexia* (names changed to protect the guilty) came to play a key role in our lives.

Mr. JB was long in the jowls, short on looks, but tall with a long stride as he patrolled the halls of the company. He had a few strands of grey hair haphazardly clinging to a freckled pate, but an otherwise friendly face. True to his word, the *JBs* signed up with Dick for private lessons. A couple weeks later, *Mr. JB* stopped me in the hall to tell me how impressed he and his wife were with their new golf instructor. He said his wife was shooting better than she ever had. "Great instructor. Gotta keep that boy close by."

During his lessons, *Mr. JB* discovered that Dick's background had been in construction. He questioned him about his field of experience, saying he needed a good man on his up-and-coming project in Thailand. Would Dick be interested? Dick and I discussed the possibility, but he had some reservations. He'd left construction because of the stress, which his doctor attributed to the heart attack he'd suffered five years earlier. He'd always been a good golfer, so it seemed obvious that he might pursue his passion as a golf instructor and leave the stress-filled environment of construction.

At his next lesson *Mr. JB* questioned Dick again. He assured Dick that if he'd come to work on this Thailand project he could make enough money to retire. And, as a supervisor, he wouldn't have the stress. "That's why we get some good men under you, let them do the stressin', you just do the paper work."

The offer sounded good. But when Dick inquired about taking me along, *Mr. JB* told him we'd have to be married for the company to pay for my trip. He said Dick would then go as "Married Status" and everything would be paid for. We'd be treated royally, fly to Thailand in First Class splendor, live in a new two-story house with a pool, have the services of a maid, a car and driver at our disposal, plus extra pay for me as a dependent. How could we turn this down?

It made me a tad nervous. I asked Dick why we couldn't just go as POSLQs (people of opposite sex sharing living quarters). No deal could be made, he said. Either we get married or he'd have to pay my way and his salary would reflect single status without all the perks.

But Dick still worried about the stress factor of the job. Why would he want to give up the great job he had working outdoors and doing something he loved? Why tempt fate?

When *Mr. JB* saw that Dick seemed hesitant, he began to work on me. Sometime during our conversations in the hall I'd mentioned that my son, Dale, was in construction, had worked overseas with his dad, and would give his eye teeth to work abroad again. Armed with this ammunition, *Mr. JB* came into my office every day shooting the breeze, and then asked if Dick and I had talked over his job offer yet. When I said that Dick was still mulling it over, *Mr. JB* shifted to a new tack. "Ya know, I got a foreman position open on the site that Dick would run. I might be able to use your boy in that spot." Leaving my office, he added, "Ahm tellin' you girl, you'd better tell Dick to think about this long and hard. It's a great opportunity."

With thoughts of living in a paradise like Thailand *and* my son and his family having a chance to build a nest egg, I secretly hoped that Dick might change his mind.

When I brought up *Mr. JB's* offer of Dale working on the project, Dick wavered. "Yeah," he said, "he mentioned it, but I'm still not convinced. He could be just using that as a carrot to get us to go. He knows you'll push me if your kid has a chance for an overseas job."

"But what if it's true? What if it is a possibility?"

"Yeah, but that's not the bottom line. We still haven't talked about the marriage bit. What're you thinking?"

"I don't know. We'll have to see where this goes." Secretly, I was mentally packed and ready to go. I felt sure we could find a way to get around this without marriage mucking things up. If he wanted Dick badly enough then he could probably sweep the marriage thing under the rug.

At work the next day *Mr. JB* called me into his office. "Step over here, little lady," he said, "I want y'all to look at this." He held his index finger on an organizational chart. A yellow highlighter line ran across my son's name, under the title of "Foreman."

This must be the infamous carrot Dick had mentioned—the one that would push me to push Dick. Mother's are suckers for grabbing at carrots when it might help their kids. "No way! Can you really use him?" I blurted out

"I don't see why not. If he's got the experience you say he has, I could use a good foreman in that spot."

Okay, I admit it. I wanted to grab the carrot.

Mr. JB made several more calls to Dick at work and at home. "We could use Dodie's boy on the jobsite, too," he'd throw in. "And he'd be workin' right under you."

Dick eventually met with *Mr. JB* and the contract was spelled out. When he returned home he was hyped. He liked the job description, perks, and especially the money. He said in two years we'd have a good nest egg, maybe even buy me that new Cadillac I'd always wanted. I couldn't help but think how ecstatic my son and his wife would be with a nest egg of their own. Dale had had a taste of working overseas, and as with most expats, he would love another chance at it. I called my son. He was ready to sign on the dotted line before we even hung up. "Hell, yes, I'll go. When do we leave?"

At *Mr. JB's* next golf lesson he threw in: "Y'all probably'll spend more time on the golf course than on the job site. Ya gotta' keep the clients happy, ya'know." At the end of the lesson *Mr. JB* got right down to business. "If y'all want to go Married Status and take Dodie along, then marry her and get it over with; ya' ain't got that long. Take your choice. Sleep with her over there or sleep with a bunch of guys."

It was now crunch time. "Well?" Dick asked when he returned. "What about it?"

Marriage? Me? Dick and I were not what you might call entirely simpatico. We were both old enough to have our own ideas how things should be done. "Set in our ways" is the expression that comes to mind.

We were what statisticians refer to as middle-aged and not about to change our personalities. We were who we were and the life experiences that shaped us could not be changed in a few short months. We would really have to try to make this work.

We did have our good times. Bedtime dating seemed to be under control and we were cruising along without any pouting. But, what were my options if things got nasty over there? I'd be stuck in a foreign country—not an easy place to run away from. It wasn't as if I'd be able to run to a girlfriend's house, or tell *him* to pack and leave my house at once—it wouldn't be *my* house. It would be company housing.

Also, with two husbands deceased, I wasn't eager to try marriage again. I thought maybe our relationship would improve living in a paradise like Thailand. Not having money worries is a great incentive for getting along. And, surely in time his sexual needs would wane. A free trip to Thailand was not a reason to marry someone, and I certainly didn't like the idea of adding another marriage to my resume, but I loved the idea of going to Thailand.

I called my daughter.

"What are you waiting for, Mom? He's good to you, he's good to your grandkids and we all like him. What's the problem?"

How do you tell your daughter that the man she wants you to marry has some sex-addiction problems? She was right, he was good, caring; the things a woman looks for in a husband. But sometimes I felt that it was only because of his final reward—Sex. When it wasn't forthcoming, his caring, thoughtfulness and goodness dissolved into a sullen soggy mass.

I wasn't a bit nervous about picking up and traipsing across the world—quite the contrary. I'd been carted from place to place as a child, always the new girl in the class, out-of-sync, and always the unwanted interloper in the group. By the time I met Dick I'd moved forty times in my life. My mother and I were nomads. She had been abandoned by my father, then forced to put me in an orphanage for three years while she worked to support us. Weekends were our only time together, spent in the tiny room of her boarding house. When I turned six she gathered me up and found various room-and-board homes for the two of us until she remarried when I was ten years old. And for the first time in my life I had a permanent home.

Over the years I'd moved many times. Until I met the man I was to be married to for twenty-five years. But he had his fair share of wanderlust, too. I had no problems as he accepted far-flung assignments: Iran, Alaska, and Louisiana—to infinity and beyond! Moving became just another adventure for me; a new place, new friends—things that I guess, after years of moving around as a child, had become ordinary for me.

But this time I wasn't moving with a caring mother or a loving husband. I would be moving half way around the world with someone I really didn't know that well—and had niggling doubts about. Not having $5,000 for my airfare lying around in an old purse had a lot to do with my decision.

I've never been one to listen to my instincts and this time was no exception. So, with the cockeyed optimist attitude that I'm famous for, I walked into it with my eyes "half-open" and prepared for another moving adventure in my life. We were married in a quickie ceremony at a Las Vegas chapel the following week. Walking down that short aisle together, every nerve in my body was on red alert:

What are you doing, you crazy lady?

PACKIN' IT IN

4

Before getting into the actual job of packing, we had to create an inventory of what to put into storage, what to ship overseas, and what to bring with us in our luggage. It did not go smoothly. I wanted to take everything I owned. Dick wanted me to leave ninety percent of it behind. "Why do you need to take all that crap with you?"

"Crap? Look at all the golf stuff on your list. Three pairs of golf shoes? Isn't that a bit excessive? And do you need ten pairs of shorts and ten golf shirts?"

"I'm not takin' any chances. What if they don't have decent golf clothes or regulation golf shoes? Good golf shoes are part of your equipment. Besides, the old man is bankin' on my teachin' skills so's he can win money from the rich Thais and I'll be sittin' in the same cart with him. I can't go lookin' like a slob."

We got a call mid-week from the company's relocation department, complicating my packing even further. We were now told to take *any* creature comforts we could stuff into our luggage. They said it might be difficult to find what we needed in a third-world country. And, *if* we did manage to find what we needed, it would probably have been imported and the cost could be exorbitant. I guess if they were paying for this flotilla, I could accommodate them.

I have always over-packed. I admit it. I can't help myself. I once called Over-Packers Anonymous as an intervention for myself, but promptly ruled it out when they told me I was only allowed one small bag for the weekend program. *How Rude!* You never know when you might need a heating pad, an ice pack or two, and a Yoga mat. I have to admit, I do know my way around a suitcase or two.

Relocation also informed us we might be without our shipment for perhaps two months or longer because of the Customs back-up in Thailand. Also, the house we were to occupy in Pattaya Beach—still under construction—might not be completed for two months or more.

"Two months? Does that mean we need to pack enough stuff to get us by for two months?" My packing addiction only went so far. However, that's probably what I'd pack for a one week trip, but I didn't want to have to haul all that stuff around for two months.

"You got it."

"And take it with us on the plane?"

"Yup."

"Wait!" I had just experienced a eureka moment. "You're only allowed two suitcases per person on the plane. Who's going to pay for the overweight charges?"

"We are."

"But why?" I whined. "It's not our fault that the shipment's late or that our house might not be ready on time."

"Yeah, but it's not the company's fault either. If you didn't need seven changes of clothes a day and as many shoes and purses, we'd probably get it all into two suitcases. Whatever! They won't pay. So, pack what you will *have to have* for two months and we'll ship the rest."

I was not happy. All you packers out there think about it. If you were told to pack two months' worth of stuff that you'd need day in and day out, would you be able to think of everything? Maybe so. But could you find a warehouse *big* enough to hold it all? Before I began the packing I tried to envision how much we'd need for a day, then multiplied it by sixty: shaving cream (his and hers), aftershave, deodorant, (his and hers) toothpaste, mouthwash, miscellaneous first-aid necessities such as hormone pills, vitamins, band-aids, Alka-Seltzer, Pepto-Bismol, Lomotil, Imodium, Milk of Magnesia, Gas-X— I think I might have had some fears of stomach upset. Also, Neutrogena bar soap (for delicate skin), razors, (his and hers), shampoo and rinse, (his and hers), hair spray, (his and hers), body lotion, sun-screen, lip-saver, a blow dryer and curling iron—and the list also had to include clothes for two months.

In the end, after bickering throughout the whole wretched job, we headed for the airport with ten pieces of luggage: three large suitcases each, one refrigerator-sized cardboard box, two sets of golf clubs, one body-bag-sized duffle bag filled to overflowing with sheets, blankets, towels and pillows (down-filled of course), a mere pittance of what our shipment held. I had made a decision to take my own bedding in case the shipment hadn't arrived before we had to move into the new house. Dick groaned on that one. Okay, okay, so I'm an over-packer, I already admitted it. I prayed that the house we were to occupy would have twelve closets and fifty cupboards.

Will wonders never cease? When we got to Thailand I found that after lugging all that baggage halfway around the world, through airports, Customs, in and out of transport vans for the trip to our final destination, and then living out of them for close to two months, the *only* thing that I could not find in Thailand was a curling iron. Proof positive why you should *never* listen to anyone who has *never* been to the places they claim to be experts on.

I did find that some imported things were expensive. But for the hassle of dragging them halfway around the world, paying hundreds of dollars in excess baggage charges, tipping everyone and their brother,

I could have come to Thailand with a knapsack over my shoulder, a curling iron stuck in a side pouch, a pack of Kleenex in my pocket— and done without the rotator cuff tear, tennis elbow, neck and back strain.

THE ROYAL PALACE

5

nce outside the Bangkok Airport, I thought I'd faint from the oppressive heat and debilitating humidity; it felt like trudging through neck-deep cement. Our driver steered us to his waiting van. Dick flopped back against the seat and groaned about the heat. After the long flight and the debacle at the luggage carousel, I melted into the soft leather seats and closed my eyes—but not for long. A cacophony of horns, shrill and constant, filled the air and followed us on our drive. "Are we in the middle of an air attack, or what?" I asked the driver. "Why is everyone honking?"

"No wolly, Madame."

Well, that explains everything. "Is it some sort of Thai holiday, maybe?"

"No, jut honk."

Later I learned that honking is part of the driving experience in Thailand. I imagined that "When to Honk" might be one of the questions on the DMV written exam. I watched in amazement as our driver indiscriminately honked his way across town; whether a car was close or not had no bearing on his honkyness. It was sort of a "Hey, I'm here" type of signal, not aggressive, just happy to be out there driving.

Strange odors wafted in and out of my consciousness as we flew along with all four windows open. With my eyes closed, I tried to identify them but the smells eluded me. Most were indescribable, some delicious, some downright unpleasant. Sounds of rock and roll blared out of boom boxes, interspersed with laughing, yelling, honking horns and a few tire screeches thrown in for good measure. We flip-flopped back and forth as our driver made heart-racing stops, starts, dodges and turns. I was terrified. This was not the place I wanted to die. My kids would never find my body. And even if they did, there wouldn't be much left to identify after I'd been splattered all over the highway. Finally, the driver braked and slid to a stop. I opened my eyes and checked to see that all my body parts were still attached. He stepped from the car and proudly announced, "Bet palat in Thailand."

I looked out to a spectacular sight. "Look at this place. It does look like a palace. Are you sure we're staying here?"

Dick rolled his eyes. "We're here, let's act like we belong."

"I don't know. Maybe we should call someone in Relocation before we check in. I'd hate to get settled in this gorgeous place and then find out they made a mistake."

We struggled out of the car and stepped into Fantasy Land. The courtyard was an extravaganza of dancing water and lights aglow in constantly changing colors of crimson, topaz blue and purple, all focused on a fountain that soared ten feet into the air. In the pond at the base of the waterfall, six-foot high sculptures of fierce-looking horses reared on hind legs, as leering gargoyles and majestic dragon sculptures frolicked with each other in a wonderfully exciting panorama. Then we walked inside.

Inside, the lobby was massive with cavernous gold ceilings that seemed to soar into infinity. Smells of incense, teak and flowers filled the air. Vast wall mirrors reflected five enormous chandeliers overhead, adorned with hundreds of globes etched in gold filigree, and reflecting the lustrous marble floors. I could see my reflection in those mirrors—a sight that didn't fit in with all this opulence. Filling the lobby were elegantly carved rosewood and teak furniture in all the regalia of the Thai culture, with carved angels and devils cavorting together and evil looking gargoyles skulking in the periphery. I reverently touched one of the tables just to feel its beauty. The smells of the teakwood and incense made me want to swoon.

A huge portrait of the King and Queen of Thailand was the focal point of the lobby, with a profusion of colorful flowers encircling it. (The King and Queen are adored by the Thais, as I learned later, evidenced by their pictures in every shop window, street and Thai home.)

We followed our driver with open-mouthed awe, looking like country bumpkins arriving in the big city. He stopped as we approached two oversized velvet armchairs, motioned for us to sit and *waiied* as he backed away. (The wai is accomplished by putting hands together, as in prayer, and lifting them to your face—or higher— depending on whom you're waiing.) I'd done my homework before leaving the States and learned that the *wai*—a sign of greeting—was also done as a sign of respect to an elder. *Thanks a lot.* It's also given to persons above your station in life, so I knew we weren't supposed to return the driver's *wai.* However Dick was *waiing* his little heart out until I nudged him. "What?" he whispered, looking pissed that I'd interrupted his practiced *wai.*

"You're only supposed to return the *wai* if the person is higher ranking than yourself."

His face flushed. "I knew that. I was just practicing."

We sat. The chairs engulfed us. I felt I could die of happiness right there in that velvet cocoon. I closed my eyes and wondered why they wanted us to sit. Were they going to call a cab to take us to our rightful destination? Did Bangkok have a *Motel 6?*

I had just begun to sink into a REM state when a young man approached holding a tray with two sterling silver goblets filled with champagne. He handed a goblet to each of us, bowed and backed away. I did not want this dream to end.

"Do you think we should drink this?"

"Why not? We might die tomorrow. Let's live tonight."

"I don't know." I said, "If this isn't the place we're supposed to be, they might charge us for the bubbly."

"It's worth whatever they charge. Drink up!"

We drank. Then waited expectantly for someone to grab us by the nape of the neck and toss us out the door. After a tactful amount of time an elegantly dressed gentleman in colorful full-parade dress-blues approached. He bowed and handed Dick a registration form. "Please sigh name." Dick asked if he was sure the forms were for the Heade party. He nodded. Wow! This was truly going to happen. What a pleasure. This was the only way to register after a hard day's flight. No lines to stand in—first drink, then work. What a great country. I knew immediately that I'd be happy here.

Our suite on the tenth floor looked to be nearly 900 square feet, and from our eight-foot wide windows we had an expansive view of downtown Bangkok. Hundreds of headlights lit up the sky, along with a jungle of colorful neon lights. The city looked incredibly exciting. I stood hypnotized by the ever-changing spectacle of colors. I tore myself away from the view to check out the rest of the suite. This was more elegant than any hotel suite I'd ever occupied.

I peeked into the bathroom and saw a phone, desk, bureau, bidet, and a Jacuzzi bathtub large enough for four people. Deliciously decadent hot towels and robes were neatly hung within arms' reach of the pampered guests. The shower was floor to ceiling glass, but I was surprised that it didn't have a door. The least they could have in this fancy schmancy joint would be a shower door, I mumbled to myself as I walked over to check it out, when WHAM! I found the shower door.

In my exhaustion—and a tad of presbyopia—I'd walked smack into the door and was thrown back two feet. It was virtually invisible. The shower was floor to ceiling glass with a glass handle and no visible hardware. I guess that's what the wealthy expect in these upscale hotels. Maybe a cute little card on your pillow or a sticky on the glass door would've been nice: CAUTION: WATCH HEAD ON INVISIBLE SHOWER DOOR.

While I could still stand upright I felt I'd better take a shower and began to undress. Two seconds after I'd turned on the shower, Dick sidled in with the dreaded words: "How about a massage?" I stopped undressing. "I'm exhausted. I can't imagine you're not! We've been traveling over twenty-four hours and on the highway from hell for another hour. How could you even think about sex tonight?" The minute the words left my lips I knew it was a ridiculous question. Dick could think of sex 24/7. I didn't want a full-fledged fight on our first night in Thailand, but I wasn't going to take his pouting either. He stomped out of the bathroom and I could hear his answer, "Welcome to Thailand" then the hotel door slammed for punctuation. Good! Go have a drink and numb your loins. Please!

Dawn arrived and with it sore muscles, an aching back—and one lumpy forehead that didn't make for a good night's sleep. Ah, did I say sleep? My introduction to the Thai mattress didn't lend itself to a restful night either. Picture sleeping on a concrete bench with a few pebbles thrown in for good measure. I had no idea what time Dick returned to our room that night, but in the morning he didn't mention his trip to the bar, and I was not about to bring it up. I checked out his face for any signs of impending sullenness.

After a pseudo-American breakfast of runny eggs, UFOs floating in our orange juice and strange-tasting bacon, we decided to take a walk and check things out. The debilitating heat of yesterday was still present, but I was determined to do it all in the short time we would have in Bangkok. Rounding the corner of our hotel, we were hit in the face by a disgusting odor. The stench took my breath away. I searched my purse for an oxygen mask but had to settle for a tissue over my nose. The offender soon came into view; an innocent looking grating over the sidewalk, happily emitting the fumes from Bangkok's over-worked sewage system. The alleyway, awash with every conceivable type of trash, invited passersby to drop anything they needed to dispose of: rubbish, decaying food, even unwanted furniture. I suspected there was no City Beautiful Committee as the refuse lay there patiently waiting to be tomorrow's compost.

Dick grabbed my arm. "Walk faster. Christ! I can't breathe. Let's get out of here."

**ROBINSON'S
AND THE ILLUSIVE SKIVVIES**

6

fter a short hot walk we returned to our hotel room and Dick headed for the shower. "Hey, bring me some underwear, would ya?"

"Sure." I yelled back. "Where are they?"

"How would I know? You packed 'em."

Silence.

"Didn't you?"

After rummaging through all the bags, I realized that Dick's underwear had not been included in our packing. Either they were put in the duffel bag marked for shipment or went to storage. Not his T-shirts, handkerchiefs, work socks, dress socks, golf socks or skivvies. I called the front desk before he could get out of the shower and strangle me.

"Jut sic brock," the helpful concierge responded when I inquired as to the nearest clothing store. "You go Lobinson's, take *tuk-tuk.*"

Robinson's. Wow! I couldn't believe it—in downtown Bangkok. How lucky could I get? Not knowing the Thai word for what Dick needed, I assumed that Robinson's, being a world-wide chain, would be the obvious place to understand English. With the temperature over 100 degrees and the humidity nearing monsoon proportions, we set out. I suggested we take the concierge's advice and flag down a *tuk-tuk.*

After standing in the crushing heat for over fifteen minutes, we finally stopped a *Tuk-tuk*.

Ah, the *tuk-tuk*. I like to think of it as an underdeveloped motorcycle with an attitude. It has a motorcycle frame with a little surrey on top for shade, a bench seat that holds two unsuspecting tourists, and sounds like a chain saw having its way with a tin roof. The *tuk-tuk* is the fastest mode of transportation in Bangkok. It can squeeze between lines of cars that are stalled in gridlock; although at times the cars were so close their side-view mirrors nearly touched.

Only six blocks the concierge had said, but the trip took nearly fifteen minutes, with the driver charging full speed ahead, dodging and squeezing between other *tuk-tuks* in an attempt to get ahead. Ahead to where? There was nothing but a parking lot ahead of us. But it didn't stop our driver as he happily scrunched his way past other cars and *tuk-tuks*; at times so close I could see their passengers' nose hairs. I'd find myself sucking in air as we came precariously close to parked or moving cars. Cars on either side of us held children waving and smiling. Old ladies squatting curbside on their haunches, held umbrellas over their thinning hair, and raised spindly arms to wave at us; the two *farang*s who had neither hat nor umbrella to protect their pumpkin heads. Thais use the word "*farang*" to refer to any fair-skinned, round-eyed foreigners who are not Asian. I had a feeling that the synonym for *farang* might be *idiot*.

Danger lurked in every molecule of oxygen. I imagined that the fumes from the lack of catalytic converters on the hundreds of cars, motorcycles and busses, combined with the leaded gas, could easily inflict an unsuspecting passenger with emphysema in one innocent-seeming six-block ride. Dick found himself in the throes of an acute asthma attack. His convulsive fits of coughing and wheezing sounded like an overweight rhino in a mating frenzy. Our *tuk-tuk* driver, on hearing these alarming sounds, would turn to look nervously at Dick, hoping his passenger would live long enough to pay his fare. "I can't take much more of this," Dick wheezed. "Where'd all this traffic come from?"

I told him what I'd read before leaving the States: that Bangkok was the home of the five-hour gridlock, with stalled traffic in never-ending bumper-to-bumper formations. I could now understand why the traffic cops wore surgical masks—a deterrent to Workmen's Comp claims I would guess.

"Why don't we get out and walk?" Dick grumbled. "It'd be a lot faster."

Why didn't we get out and walk? Well, I did consider jumping ship but we had no clue where we were. We'd been moving in traffic for what seemed like hours, our driver cutting in and out, around and back. We had no idea where our hotel was—or Robinson's. At least, I thought, the *tuk-tuk* would be a place to sleep if we never got back to our hotel.

Just when I thought I'd surely die in the *tuk-tuk*, I spotted a huge sign on the roof of a building: Robinsons—Bangkok's Premier Shopping Center. Dick let out a wheezy shriek as we staggered out of our chariot, brushed the road dust and invisible caustic fumes from our clothes, and stepped inside. The air conditioning hit us broadside. I'm sure we looked like survivors from a Grade IV hurricane. People passed us and respectfully looked away, or down at the floor.

The store was immaculate, filled with wonderful fragrances all blending together in one large mystical aroma. The floors were polished to a brilliant sheen. The counters were neat and spotless. I reached out and touched the shirts on display; I could see no visible pins holding them in such precision. All were stacked by color, then size, then price. I wanted to keep touching. I'd never seen such a display of neatness in a department store, and crawling with shoppers. It was as antiseptic as a contact lens lab. I looked around expecting to see salespeople wearing white lab coats.

The first salesgirl we encountered touched Dick's arm and giggled, "You vely sma', jut like Thai man."

Dick *waiied*—wrong again—and grinned the grin he always grins when he doesn't have a clue what someone's just said. Knowing he wouldn't like the interpretation, I thought it best not to translate. "Sorry," I said, when he looked at me with his What-the-hell-was-that-all-about look. "I haven't a clue what she said. Let's see if she can lead us to the men's underwear.

"*Sawatdee kha,* can you tell me where the Men's department is?" I asked amid her *waiing* and smiling. Robinson's or not, I could see by her nonplussed look it was not going to be easy. "Underwear!" we said in unison. "You know, like this." Dick reached inside his waistband and pulled up the elastic on his shorts. The salesgirl continued to smile behind her dainty hand but made no move. I had the feeling she thought he might be offering stud service.

We reluctantly struck out on our own and soon found ourselves in the underwear section of the Women's department. Dick pointed excitedly to the silk panties on display, pantomiming to the next confused clerk that he needed "These." She gave a knowing smile to the other clerks and asked, "Wat sigh, suh?"

"No! No! You don't understand," Dick pleaded. "Not women's! Men's!"

"Oh, solly suh," she demurred, "no haf."

We spent another ten minutes going from one department to another, up and down the escalators. Every time we asked—pantomimed—we were pointed in a different direction. We rounded a corner and there they were. We had finally found a display of *Fruit of the Loom* men's jockey shorts. Yes! Funny, what makes some people happy. We had done the impossible. We had found skivvies in Never-Never Land—but paid three times the U.S. price. We had accomplished the first of many such victories.

I left Dick in the Men's department hunting for white socks and T-shirts while I sauntered through the store, savoring every solitary minute. After noticing nothing other than petite women and trim salesgirls gliding about, I thought perhaps a new outfit might lift my dampened spirits. I'd look for some cutesy little sundress that would make me look petite with my 38DD bust and 30 inch waistline. All these teensy clothes and weensy women led me to an inexorable truth: not only were they perfectly groomed and beautiful, they were all positively svelte. I mean, how many attributes do they get? I felt like Gulliver in the land of the Lilliputians.

Women's dresses shouldn't be that hard to find. Everywhere I looked seemed to be ladies clothes. I spotted a rounder of what I thought were women's dresses and headed for the racks. I stopped short when I saw how small they were. Wait! These had to be Teens Wear. But on the top of the rounder was a cardboard cutout of a woman wearing a smart little outfit. Well, it looked like a woman but when I pulled out a few dresses I was flummoxed. Where was I—in the Barbie and Ken Department? Size 2? Who wears a size 2? I couldn't get these styles around my thighs, much less my butt. Ok! I had gained a little weight. There now seemed to be more tension in my waistband than in the Middle East. But, please! These sizes were for Munchkins.

I turned away from the rude display of petite-ness and saw a young girl walking toward me. From a distance she appeared to be a child, lost in this huge store. But when I turned to look for a salesperson she stepped in front of me. "Goosmoanin."

"Oh." I felt my face get hot. She wasn't a little girl after all. She was at least in her 20s and obviously the salesperson in this department.

"Uh, I…is there a Women's department in this store? You know, like my size?"

"Yeth." She smiled and waited expectantly.

"Oh. Well, could you point me to it?"

She didn't understand. More smiles.

We were getting nowhere, fast. I pointed to my well-fed body and then yanked on the waistline of my dress. "Dress. For me."

She smiled shyly while looking at her feet, "Please come."

I followed her to an area, clearly removed from the other departments, where a few ample tourists were grazing about. She *waiied* and backed away, as if leaving me to my sorrow. Sidling up to a rather rotund shopper, I asked her why we were in this segregated area. "Is it because we're foreigners?"

She screwed up her face like she'd just bit into a sour gumball. "Yeah, honey, we're foreigners all right. Larger-than-life foreigners." At that she had a good guffaw at her own cleverness.

"Huh?"

"The only sizes they carry out there are twos and fours, and honey, that ain't us." Once again she chortled and slapped my back for emphasis. I snuck a peek around the room while she enjoyed her witty repartee and saw that these people were years past those proportions.

I grasped that I wasn't going to like these svelte Thai women. They must be bulimic—that's it! Binge, purge, binge, purge—they weren't fooling me. But for the, ahem, larger sizes, anything non-Thai was deplorably pricey. An imported name brand in Thailand was three times higher than one would pay in the States. Paradoxically, Thai clothes were very inexpensive and quite stylish. However, you had to be less than five feet tall and weigh between seventy and ninety pounds to wear them.

The salespeople at Robinson's had the perfect solution for us larger sizes. It was called "Won Sigh." You entered the clothing department, and unless you were built like Twiggy, the sweet, smiling, ever-helpful pre-pubescent looking salesgirls would steer you toward the "Won Sigh Department." There you could find the loose-fitting, baggy, beachy, gauzy, hippie-looking outfits all claiming to be One-Size-Fits-All. The range went from size six all the way up to Mama Cass. This was their way of saving face—*yours*. They would never dream to insinuate you were large, fat, obese or chubby. You just happened to fall into the category of "Won Sigh."

Okay. I realized then that some drastic measures had to be taken. I'd gained a bit of weight, from the 120s of maidenhood to the 140s of motherhood. Now my weight seemed to be slowly heading toward the 150s of matronhood. Nothing is more demoralizing than stepping on a scale and seeing the digital readout: *One at a time, please*.

I made a decision then and there. I would diet, fast, quit eating, quit breathing; whatever it took to look as good as these svelte Thai women.

I left the Won Sigh department in a cute little number that I *just knew* made me look adorable—that is until I passed a wall mirror and caught a glimpse of my reflection. Yikes! The gauzy muumuu I'd bought wasn't doing a thing for me. Picture Hilo Hattie in strappy sandals.

Maybe I'd go back and try to find one with a little more shape to it. But for right now, I needed to find a restroom. Fast!

THE UBIQUITOUS EASTERN TOILET

7

When nature called, I listened. I'd been having some bladder problems and as many women in their fifties know, we don't turn a deaf ear when Mother Nature bellows. Logic told me I should wait to use my hotel toilet, but with thoughts of the *tuk-tuk* ride still vivid in my memory, I decided on the store restroom. I mean, how bad could it be? This was Robinson's.

I spotted the unisex sign for "Toilet" and peeked inside. I wanted to turn and flee. I gagged. Think Kansas City Stock Yard meets Los Angeles County Landfill. I held my breath until I felt faint. I thought about trying to breathe through my mouth but decided it might be better to smell than to taste.

There it sat, the ubiquitous Eastern toilet, waiting for the next feeble foreigner. I swore I could hear voices calling for help, possibly ghosts of tourists who'd fallen in. The inside of the hole was porcelain, trying hard to resemble a Western toilet, but that's where the similarity ended. The hole was oval, about two feet in circumference, its depth I would leave to the ghosts. Encircling the hole was a porcelain ring with indentations on either side for very small feet. (I later learned that the Eastern squat toilet is sometimes just a hole cut in a dirt floor, depending on whether you're in a nice department store or a little shack on a country road.) It was dirty and disgusting, foul smelling, and slimy, and when I graduate from my Toastmaster's class, I'll be able to describe it more effectively.

Why does the elimination process have to be so difficult for women? It's a cakewalk for men. They have it way too easy. In my years of wandering the globe I'd learned an undeniable fact: the world is a man's toilet. They seem to be comfortable anywhere the urge to purge hits them—behind a car, on the golf course, in an alley, wherever, while the disadvantage of indoor plumbing is that we females are forced to find a sit-down area for release.

However, all toilets are not created equal and herein lies the rub: the Eastern squat toilet is discriminatory against females. For my lady friends who've never traveled to a foreign country that offers these contortion contraptions, let my story serve as a high-level travel alert.

How was I going to do this? I studied this enigma and tried to decide on the best point of entry. I walked closer, faced it and forced myself not to look down. I stepped up closer still to the beast and panicked. How is a woman supposed to squat on this thing? If you're wearing slacks, they need to be pulled down, along with your undies. To where do you pull them? If you just pull them down a little, you'll pee on them. So, you have to pull them down just over your butt, squat, then while still squatting, pull them down a little more and tuck them under your knees, hoping that they stay put. And what if you have on a full skirt or muumuu? You have to pull the front of the skirt up and wad it under your chin, then take the back of the skirt, lift it up, wrap it around your waist and pray it stays there. While you're trying to maneuver yourself into position you realize you can't see what your feet are doing, what with all the clothes piled up on your waist.

You look around for the toilet paper roll—noticeably absent—and begin to panic. Here, as in all Asian countries, water is the cleanser of choice, with the pail and hose standing at the ready to use for the fanny lavage. Thus, water surrounds the hole making the porcelain quite slippery, which adds to the problem of balance. You now have to do the job you came here to do. You're trying for an Olympic score of ten on your mount, praying you'll hit the sides of the target and not the center. The porcelain and floor are wet. There is no paper. You start to pray. You make the jump, your score is a minus ten but that's okay. Now you're in the squatting position. You wonder if you can keep your balance long enough to do the job. Your back hurts, your thighs are screaming and your hamstrings are losing ground. You've got your purse between your teeth as you try to dig out your tissue; hopefully it's in the little side pocket where you last saw it. You're searching with one hand only as the other is waving in the air for balance. One wrong move, one slight error and you could do a pratfall onto the filthy, wet floor, or, the unthinkable—the hole.

You're finished now but how do you dismount? You realize you have to get up, and you must do it *before* the store closes. There's nothing to hang on to. Your arms are flailing about trying to keep your balance, your purse is between your teeth and your clothes are tucked into your wrinkles. You must now prepare for your Olympic ten dismount by giving a giant heave and flinging yourself up and out of the crouched position, praying your feet hit a dry spot on the floor.

Recovering from the squatting position is the true test of your mettle and you'll have no help from your atrophied thigh muscles. There is no chrome bar thoughtfully placed nearby to aid in pulling you to a standing position. Nope. Just you and Mother Nature! After you've landed your dismount, don't think you're home free. These babies don't flush. Next to this thingamabob is a small spigot with a hose attached, along with a pitcher and scoop to accessorize the ensemble. You must fill the pitcher with water, pour it into the hole and hope gravity helps everything go down. It may not. The person before you may have been in a hurry, over-parked, had to catch a bus. Whatever! Now you must take care of his and yours, so the person next in line doesn't think *you* left that awful mess.

The Eastern squat toilet is, without a doubt, a great idea when it comes to the physiology of elimination. That is, if you're twenty years old and practice yoga every day. I missed these criteria by about thirty years. Suffice it to say I wouldn't want to be caught with my knickers around my ankles when Alan Funt and his Candid Camera crew were hovering in the wings.

Dick had been standing outside the restroom waiting for me. He said that he—and everyone in the store—knew I'd successfully landed my dismount when they heard me yell, "Thank you, Jayzus!"

With my thigh muscles taut and painful and my body in need of sleep, we left Robinson's in search of a *tuk-tuk*—a motorcycle, a camel, anything to get us back to the hotel. We stood in the scorching heat for ten minutes, then thought it best to keep moving in hopes that someone would stop for us, the two bedraggled foreigners. After getting directions from different bystanders—and no *tuk-tuks* in sight—we took our chances and set off on our own. I could see the newspaper's headlines: *"TWO AMERICANS STILL MISSING. LAST SEEN TRUDGING THROUGH THE STREETS OF BANGKOK IN SEARCH OF THEIR HOTEL."*

We eventually found our hotel, albeit in a roundabout way, and flopped into bed. Arising hours later, and hungry, we managed to find our way to the hotel dining room and ate a light, uninspiring meal of rice, chicken and tea. With no strength to go any further we headed back to our room and fell into bed, spending yet another restless, jet-lagged night trying to get comfortable on the concrete-slab mattress.

THE EXOTIC STREETS OF BANGKOK

8

After catching up on lost sleep, I was now ready to do some sight-seeing. I dressed in shorts and T-shirt, and carried a towel and a bottle of ice water to pour over my head to ward off heat stroke. I wasn't going to let a little monsoon keep me inside.

The sights and smells of Bangkok cannot be adequately described by a mere mortal such as I—but I'll try. Bangkok is a mish-mash of elegance, squalor, delicious aromas, and putrid smells—from an overworked, under-built sewer system. Sightseeing was going to be a problem, I could tell. I had to keep my head down and a wary eye on the pavement to avoid various bricks and rocks strewn here and there. An unsteady obstacle course awaited the hapless toe. I'd heard that archeological excavations revealed civilization was alive and well in Thailand over 4,000 years ago. Could these bricks be the remnants of their digs?

Melting asphalt stuck to my shoes as I tried to pick my way across the steaming streets. Dirt, grime and debris cluttered the sidewalks, buildings and alleyways. Scurrying tourists and expatriates from all over the world filled the streets, along with the wonderful smiling Thais. Bangkok, I'd read, is truly an international city and one of the largest ethnic mixes in the world, with people shopping, selling, buying and trading, cooking and eating. I found myself caught up in the frenzy and excitement.

Stores, stores, and more stores, selling leather goods, ready-made clothing of wools and silks made by artistic Thai and Chinese tailors, genuine Ralph Lauren shirts, jewelry, paintings, footwear, and household goods. Carts with fruit sellers and fortune tellers squeezed into small stalls dotted the area. My eyes could not keep up with my thoughts as I surveyed the excitement surrounding me. Whatever Madame's heart desired could be produced, and all you had to do was ask! I loved this place. The gracious vendors smile, *wai* and disappear, returning a few minutes later with just what Madame requested. And tailor shops were everywhere, each offering ready-to-wear in twenty-four hours. If you had a favorite outfit purchased at, say, Nordstrom's, and wanted it duplicated, all you had to do was give it to the tailor and two more would be ready for you the next day at one-third the price paid for the original.

In fact, if you stood still long enough, you might find them coming up to you with their measuring tapes at the ready. On one such encounter I stood peering in a shop window when I felt someone touching me. I whirled around. "What are you doing?" I shrieked at the startled man beside me. I was worried he might be one of those pickpocket experts I'd been warned about.

"Sokay Madame, I jut fit you foh new cloths. We make what you like foh goot *baht*."

"What kind of clothes?" I asked, not quite so worried.

"Genuine copy, Madame."

Having something tailor-made, plus a "genuine copy" was exciting, but I had nothing with me at the moment to give him. "Maybe I'll come back and bring something."

"Sokay, sokay, you come back latah, yeth?"

"Probably not today, but maybe…"

Dick had been checking out some western boots in a shop window when he heard the transaction take place. "Christ, don't start. You already have more clothes than you can wear and no closets to put them in."

"No mattah," the vendor said, pointing to my slacks. "I make copy foh you now."

"Well, I do like these…"

"Jesus H. Christ!" Dick was now mad enough to give Jesus a middle initial. "Don't you have enough to wear? Come on, let's go." He grabbed me by the arm and started walking away. The vendor looked startled at Dick's outburst. I learned later that it's out of character for Thais to raise their voice or show any kind of aggressive behavior in public. It's fundamentally against their nature and their Buddhist beliefs. To witness this kind of behavior was not acceptable. He looked down at his shoes.

"Excuse me?" I threw Dick a hateful look. "Could you be any more rude?"

"Yeah, well, I know you when it comes to shoppin'. Say goodbye, let's go."

I gave the vendor an apologetic look as I turned to leave, but made a mental note of his area. I would return—*sans* husband.

I noted dozens of these vendors milling about. They didn't have a specific area where they did business but rather walked around drumming it up, sort of like a tailor's rep. If they found any live ones they'd drag them to the shop, drop them off to be fitted and then leave to find another customer. I assumed they received a commission for all the bodies they brought in. I was sure I'd find just the right place when I returned.

Dick grumbled that he was hungry, a euphemism used to drag me away from shopping. We followed our noses toward the food smells, but as we approached the area he slowed his pace. "What?"

"Maybe we should wait 'til we get back to the hotel."

I could hear the fear in his voice. "Come on! What're you afraid of? I don't see any tourists bent over with signs of botulism."

"Maybe they've been here a while. They're used to the food. We've got USA stomachs. That stuff might give us the runs."

"We have to get used to it sooner or later, we're going to be here for a while and I plan on eating like the natives, not the tourists."

"And in the meantime, we suffer?"

Geez, what a wuss! "We'll build antibodies."

I strode off ahead of him, wondering what I would do if I got a case of the runs right here in downtown Bangkok. I should have put some Lomotil in my purse before I left the hotel, a purse that was now heavier than a pallet of bricks as I kept adding all the things that I felt would keep me from getting all the things that everyone said I'd get.

With cauldrons of boiled chicken—feathers floating in the water—frying fish and oysters, coupled with the noxious fumes from the cars and sewers, it was easy to understand how a newbie could get nauseous. I strolled and sniffed. Oh the smells; some good, some disgusting, rancid, flowery, spicy, fishy and others unnamable.

A bit further down we found the origin of the odors. Natives were hawking their foods and wares on card tables, pushcarts, wooden tables, concrete-blocks, showing and selling their treasures and serving their food. One cart might have *Rolex* wannabes and genuine look-alike pearls and rubies, while the next might sell fish—cooked or raw—while ravenous flies were no doubt dropping their larvae as they hovered above the food. With a wave of the hand to disburse the flies, and an exchange of *baht*, off went the food to the Thai's iron-clad digestive system; curried chicken, noodles, shrimp, squid, and the all-important staple—rice.

Next to the food were tables with T-shirts, shorts, "genuine" *Gucci* purses, leather pants, more watches and "No Copy" *Dior* perfume. The next cart might be laden with kettles of boiling squid, noodles or shrimp soup, sending their tempting aromas to the heavens. I took a quick peek inside the pots. I could have sworn I saw some very dubious looking characters bearing an uncanny resemblance to octopi, bats, snakes, and strange looking mushrooms. Maybe I'd pass on the soup. The next cart could be *moo* (pork) or *gai* (chicken) and *mee grob*, the Thai national favorite of fried noodles.

Standing at the ready, beneath the food carts, were the ever-present ravenous dogs, waiting for a tidbit to fall their way. This was one of the most pathetic sights I'd ever seen. Literally dozens of dogs roamed the city, the majority of them looking sick and emaciated, fur coming out in large patches. Some were bleeding from mange with flea-infested scabs invading most of their ravaged bodies. With their hind legs in constant motion as they scratched, they appeared to be permanently standing on three legs. Years of inbreeding and lack of care left them looking more like canine caricatures than real dogs. Some appeared to have begun their lineage from a large breed with perhaps a smaller one infiltrating the love nest. Many had at least one of their legs broken and twisted from either a head-on with a motorcycle or a car.

The Thais didn't seem to notice the pitiful creatures as they walked around or stepped over them. But they never seemed to be upset by the sight of them and most didn't even bother to shoo them away. They seemed to tolerate them—as they did the *farangs*—without showing animosity.

The number of dogs running loose without a home saddened me. In the span of a few blocks, we saw, and nearly tripped over, dozens of them. Some were mating, some looky-loos wishing they were mating, very few were fighting, and some were just cooling their heels by a rubbish heap waiting for a juicy morsel to unearth itself. The dogs seemed to have the same kicked-back personalities as the Thais, lying outstretched in the middle of a street or highway or just dozing under food carts.

Adding to this carnival-type excitement, on the sidewalks and streets, were the merchants who pushed or drove their portable kitchens on what appeared to be old Schwinn bicycles with sidecars attached. On top of the sidecar stood a shelf with a butane burner, which kept the food tongue-scorching hot. Down the street they'd peddle—fires burning, kettles boiling and pots swaying to and fro.

Further along I saw frail little pushcarts on spindly wheels with pots hanging from wires over a small butane burner, brimming over with boiling delicacies. Ten to twelve plucked chickens, open eyes staring, dangling limply on wires stretched across the cart. The seller, after shooing away the flies, would grab a handful of chickens and toss them into the steaming cauldrons, along with boiled corn on the cob and fresh veggies to finish off the well-rounded meal. Next to these pushcart, and stacked high on blocks, were a profusion of tape recorders, cassette tapes, candy bars melting in the heat, and Buddha statues. All this seemed quite unsanitary by American standards, in fact, an inspector from the Health Department might drop with apoplexy, but I said damn the fly larvae and ate with abandon. I ordered what I thought looked edible but dumped the little wiggly things that appeared to be treading water. Dick opted for corn on the cob and rice.

I had made up my mind that if I was going to live in this country, I'd better learn to like their food. And like it I did. In fact, I can close my eyes today and fondly recall the smell and taste of Bangkok.

Following us as we walked along during the day, and well into the night, was the constant noise; blaring horns, screeching tires, revving motorcycles, roaring buses, Thai music, chatter and laughter. I found it stimulating and exhausting all at once. After a busy day of shopping, walking and eating, I slept like the dead—concrete-slab mattress and all.

The next morning, after breakfast in the hotel, I struck out alone. I knew I was beginning to acclimate when I could walk for more than fifteen minutes without emptying my water bottle over my head.

Downtown I saw something I hadn't noticed before. Small children seemed to be much too close to the dangerous streets. Some were sitting on curbs with their feet in the gutter, oblivious to the dangers around them. Others were playing tag in and out of the suicidal gutters where buses flew by at menacing speeds. The parents who worked the carts and shops would occasionally check on them and then walk back to their wares. I supposed they preferred to have them nearby where they could check on them. I tried to picture my young grandchildren running loose in this chaos and shuddered at the thought. I couldn't fathom what kept these little ones from rushing into the path of one of the monstrous buses or being snatched by some slimy pedophile.

Buddha must have a long, protective arm.

TEMPLES, KLONGS AND TOUR BUSES

9

The next day we signed up for the temple tour. In the sunlight, Bangkok's skyline glistened with ornate Buddhist temples and palaces. The whole city seemed to be drowning in gold and jewels and I wanted to actually touch them. The first temple we visited was the immense *Wat Arun*—Temple of Dawn—towering over the waterways seventy-nine meters high, unrivaled in its majesty. The *Wat Pho*, another amazing temple, housed the reclining gold-plated Buddha, forty-six meters long and fifteen meters high with inlaid mother of pearl soles. Bangkok boasts of more temples than anywhere in Thailand and I was looking forward to seeing them all. We were allowed to enter most of them if accompanied by a guide, but were asked to remove our shoes before entering; a sign of respect and a must in Thai culture. Tourists could be seen staring in open-mouthed wonder at the incredible architecture of years gone by, amazed at the craftsmanship and what they'd built without our modern-day tools.

Along the Chao Phraya River, a labyrinth of canals that bisect Bangkok, tourist long-boat rides were a favorite and always filled to capacity as they slowly made their way up the *Klongs*—rivers. On these waterways we had an unobstructed view of the skyline that highlighted the many Buddhist temples in Bangkok, standing as bejeweled sentinels over the city.

Dotting the waterways were rundown box-like structures made of wood, sitting on stilts, and accessible only by boat, each one looked as though a gust of wind might flatten them. Most had no doors—the front and back of the house opened to the river. Our guide informed us that many of these river dwellers never left their homes, born on the water—and died there. The occupants made their living by making and selling souvenirs to the tourists. Our boat glided silently by the shacks. I was appalled at what I saw happening at these homes: a young woman knelt on the porch and rinsed her dishes in the river, a ways down a man emptied a squat-pot into the water, and beyond this I saw young children swimming in this same contaminated water. It was putrid and unquestionably bacteria-ridden. With my Virgo-sense of sterility, I was repulsed. I had to believe that after years of building antibodies, the children were resistant to most bacteria.

The tourist boats made frequent stops at these homes, allowing us to buy jewelry or clothing from the artisans—their only means of income. I did my share to support them. Cruising down-river we encountered many small, single-seated long-boats as they traversed the water. The boats were propelled by small outboard engines, each emitting the ever-present foul-smelling fumes that hung over the river like a lacy grey shawl. Most were driven by ancient females selling their wares to tourists. With thinning grey hair straggling beneath huge straw hats, blood-red eyes half-hidden under a brim, they offered wide, toothless grins. The old ladies sold everything from fruit to flowers and soup to nuts. Who could say no to a sweet-looking grandma type? They saw me coming with their opaque cataract-filled eyes and managed to steer straight for my boat. Dick, notorious for walking me away from vendors, had a definite problem while being held captive in a boat. "Okay, enough of this. We have everything we need. Look the other way."

"Oh stop! These poor people could use some help."

"So could we at the rate you're spendin' money."

Of course I knew this would happen. "This beautiful country is rife with treasures. I buy because it helps their economy and keeps them from begging on the street. How can you be so insensitive?"

"What's the difference? Street? Water? They're still beggin'."

"They are not begging. Far from it! They're selling things made with their own hands. Souvenirs we can take home as gifts."

"Right! Where else can you find a tambourine with starched Thai noodles hangin' from it? Or a straw beach pad with seashells woven through it. But don't try to lie on it."

"Blah, blah, blah," I chanted as he carried on with his no-buy mantra. "Why did you even come today? You could've stayed at the hotel and watched golf on TV." He turned away, ignoring me and the old lady. Why he had to accompany me on these outings, I had no idea. Did he think I'd buy a townhouse on the water?

We also took three bus tours while in Bangkok. These caused a few stomach ulcers for Dick, as every bus driver knew precisely where to stop so the *farang* could spend his *baht*. On one such trip, "The Ancient Architecture Tour," the bus driver had seen fit to stop at three jewelry stores just in case any of us might want to buy some jewelry (and he could collect his commission). The stores were alive with sparkling bursts of topaz, garnet, lapis, tiger's eye, rubies, sapphire and diamonds. Enough to make a woman's heart burst with excitement. Enough to a make a husband's heart go into dysrhythmia and stop beating. By the time we got to the third store Dick was worn down and bought me a beautiful topaz ring. *What a softy.*

Then there were the bathroom stops. The tour bus driver, knowing that the tourists would surely need to use the bathroom, didn't let this opportunity pass. And he knew just where to find them. We were of course told that this was the only store in town that had the "Western" toilet, conveniently located, surprise, surprise, all the way to the back of a huge gem store. We all had to pass through a brilliantly lit warehouse-sized room filled wall to wall with sparkling gems to get to the bathroom. Most of us were agog with the dazzling jewels before us and the jewelers were happy to oblige the disheveled *farangs.*

The next day we were off to the crocodile farm, the cultural theme park and the zoo. Unbelievably, the driver didn't stop at any jewelry stores. I think he knew we'd bought out all of Bangkok.

Thailand is world renowned for its fine jewels. If a tourist travels to Thailand for the express purpose of purchasing fine jewelry, he would not be disappointed. Every kind imaginable is displayed in brilliantly lit glass cases, the lights inside giving off heat and majesty, making it almost impossible to resist. Cases full of tiny diamond stud earrings or gemstone rings the size of bowling balls for your pinky. Most are authentic. But to make sure the traveler gets the finest gems, we were told they would be wise to either ask for guidance at a bank or from their hotel manager. These gentlemen know the city and are happy to point you in the direction of a reputable jeweler. But, on the streets? *Caveat emptor*, as they say in Rome.

MOVIES AND MARAUDING MEESES

10

I did manage to catch an American-made movie while in Bangkok—with Thai language dubbed in. We went in mainly because it boasted air conditioning and we were both drained from the heat. The movie entertained us and kept me busy as I tried to translate, which also kept me off the streets, so Dick was happy.

During the movie I was startled when I heard a scratching noise coming from the floor near my feet. It was too dark to see but it had me on edge.

"What?" Dick asked as I squirmed and brought my knees up to my chest.

"I just heard a strange noise under my seat."

"Gas, maybe?"

"No, I'm serious! It sounded like scratching. Like little feet scratching."

"Oh, Christ, don't start with the detective stuff. It's probably the guy next to you."

"I know what I heard and I heard little feet, damnit!"

"Can't you just relax and enjoy the movie?" he hissed.

"Well, I guess I could if I had an interpreter's mic in my ear. Can you understand any of it?"

"Sure. We've seen this movie in English. Just remember it and you'll understand it."

"Okay, tell me what the Thai word for 'HELP' is." I wanted to believe that it might be the gent sitting next to me. Then again, maybe it was just my overactive imagination. When the lights came on at the end of the movie, we stood along with everyone else and turned to file out. We were stopped short. No one moved. They all stood and faced forward while a huge picture of the King and Queen of Thailand appeared on the screen. Music began and the throngs sang along to a hymn of homage to the King, followed by their national anthem. *How patriotic.*

While the crowd sang, I lowered my gaze to the floor, hoping I wouldn't see what I thought I might see. My hopes were dashed. Vermin! A shriek erupted from my throat. I had no control over it. People turned to look at me with disapproval scrolled between furrowed brows. "Christ! What now?" Dick hissed.

"Look!" I pointed downward.

"Look at what?" he asked, not looking down. "You're gonna get us thrown out of here."

"Look down, damnit!"

Dick slowly lowered his eyes so as not to attract attention from the already focused crowd in front and behind us. He made eye contact with a couple rats and roaches as they had their way with bits and morsels dropped from the enraptured crowd.

"Christ!"

It took all the willpower I could muster to keep from jumping up on my seat and shrieking, which would have been highly irreverent by anyone, much less a *farang*. How could I do this when they were giving honor to their King and Queen? I gritted my teeth and squeezed my eyes shut. I just knew that some of those vermin had made it to my shoes and were headed to parts north. I picked up one leg and gave it a violent shake to dislodge any traveling vermin then banged it against Dick's leg. I then shook the other leg, hitting the gentleman next to me.

He turned and looked at me with annoyance. I kept my eyes on the screen, hoping he'd think it was a roach that had attacked him. I shook my legs a few more times until I felt him move over one seat; I'm sure he thought I was in the midst of a seizure. I wanted to run screaming from the theater, knocking people over in front of me, but I held on until the pomp and ceremony had ended. Once outside I had Dick check every inch of my clothes to make sure I had no hitch-hikers.

Back at the hotel, I ran into the bathroom, locked the door and ripped off my clothes. I jumped into the shower and scrubbed my skin until it glowed pink. The rest of the night I imagined creepy-crawlies all over me as I scratched my way into the wee hours of the morning.

I made a decision to forego any more movie-going adventures.

SHOPPING WITHOUT GUYS

11

Before we left for Pattaya, I wanted to make sure Dick got the western boots he'd admired in a store window a few days earlier. I talked him into a quick stroll and casually walked in that direction. "Wait!" he called to me as I pulled ahead of him. "Where're you headed?"

"Just to check out something you might be interested in." I could feel him hanging back. "Oh, stop. It won't hurt to have a look. You did say you wanted a pair of boots, didn't you?"

"Okay, but I'm just gonna look. Don't pull any crap about me buyin' 'em. I can always come back and get 'em some other time." He defiantly dragged his feet.

A sharp-eyed vendor stepped out from his store. "You come back foh boot, yeth?"

I could feel Dick's irritation. "Maybe. I'm just lookin'. If I did buy how long does it take?"

"Sokay, I do foh you now," he said as he motioned us inside the store.

"Okay! But I'm still just gonna look," Dick proclaimed a bit too loud.

A huge assortment of boots were on display, filling the store with the comforting smell of new leather. Elephant, ostrich, alligator and boa constrictor boots were on shelves and cured skins were hanging from rafters. Dick's irritation began to fade from his face as he looked around. He actually looked impressed. The sharp vendor saw this and asked Dick to please sit and remove his shoes. He then spread some blank papers on the floor in front of Dick. "Put you foot on papah, Suh." Dick reluctantly removed his shoes and stepped onto the paper. We watched as the vendor squatted and traced each foot with his shop-worn pencil, taking a quick measurement over the instep and under the arch, making squiggly lines on a notepad. He told us to return the next day for the boots. Dick regained the normal irritated look he wears for shopping, as if this was a colossal waste of his time. Just humoring the little lady, ha-ha. Fine! Wait until he sees the finished product.

The next morning we returned to the shop. Dick tried to look bored while waiting for the vendor to bring out his boots. His eyes widened when he saw the boots. They were exquisite; highly burnished ostrich leather in rich tans and browns. When he stepped into them a look of utter contentment came over him; a look I didn't see too often. He took a quick walk around the store while a smile curved his otherwise flat expression. "They're the best fit I've ever had."

The cost for these stunning handmade boots was nowhere near their worth. In the States he would have paid $500, and they would not have been hand-made. Here they were $150. Incredible! The bonus was that the workmanship was top-quality. He walked out of the store looking down at the boots. With each step he remarked on their comfort. He wore them the rest of the day, and I think he might have worn them to bed had I not been there to witness it.

For the next two days we did the normal tourist trips with constant complaints from Dick about the cost of everything; the heat, the humidity, the state of the nation and the national debt. Why didn't I insist he just stay at the hotel? I made a mental note to return—alone.

The day before we were to leave for Pattaya, Dick complained of a stomach ache. He swore it was something he'd eaten, but I'd had the same food and felt fine. *Well, damn! I'd have to go shopping without him. Who said there wasn't a Shopping God?*

When you really think about it, why would any woman want to drag a man along on a shopping trip anyway? If you want to shop without a care in the world, leave the guy at home. Set him up with a sports broadcast on TV, a six pack of Bud, a copy of *Sports Illustrated* in one hand and the TV remote in the other. You could go to Europe and back and he'd never know you were gone.

I told Dick I'd look for some sort of stomach medicine while I was out. "Be back soon."

"Where you goin'?"

"I won't be gone long. I'll check at the desk for something for your stomach. Then I'll probably run over to that wonderful computer store I saw the other day and then…"

"Christ!"

That said, I was on my way.

I ran by the front desk and asked if they had any type of medicine for a stomach ache. The receptionist looked at me rather quizzically so I held my stomach and looked pained. She got it. She returned in a few minutes with a small bottle of pink liquid with Thai writing. She assured me it was "Goot foh you" and rubbed her stomach. *Okay*, I thought, *goot enough for her, then goot enough for Dick.* I asked her to have it delivered to our room and was on my way.

I flagged down a *tuk-tuk* and pointed straight ahead toward the computer mall. If I carried a wet wash cloth to hold over my mouth and one to place on the back of my neck, as well as a bottle of water to pour over my head, I could better handle the heat and smog; but, hey, what's a little lung congestion when your goal is shopping?

Dozens of stores filled this enormous mall, all selling computers, programs, manuals and offering repairs and training. I also found a tech who was delighted to copy a program for me while I waited—throwing the manual in for free. Cost of the program stateside would be $200 or more; cost in this lovely computer mall, "Tweni sree dollah."

After leaving the mall, I thought I'd check out a store I'd heard about, modestly named The World Trade Center. It was the largest building in Bangkok at the time and housed some of the world's most famous chain stores such as Nieman Marcus, Sogos, Saks Fifth Avenue and many others I'd never heard of. I was in heaven as I sauntered from store to store, trying on clothes and twirling in front of mirrors with never a thought of a sour-faced spouse standing nearby to quash my fun. I didn't buy anything that day but I knew I'd be back to Bangkok in the near future. I could wait.

When I arrived back at the hotel, Dick opened the door for me. "Where ya been so long?"

"I told you I'd be a while. Did you get the medicine?"

"What medicine?"

"For your stomach. I asked the receptionist to send it up to you. Didn't you get it?"

"Oh, you mean that pink crap? I wasn't about to drink somethin' I couldn't even read."

"So what did you do about your stomach pain?"

"I started feelin' better about an hour after you left so I opened a beer, found an old *Sport Illustrated* magazine in my briefcase, turned on a great golf match and just kicked back. Why?"

I rest my case.

CUBBYHOLES AND CURLING IRONS

12

After spending six exciting and busy days in Bangkok, it was time to move on. A company van had arrived to take us to our hotel in Pattaya Beach—the resort city we would live in for the two-year duration of Dick's contract. I hated to leave Bangkok but knew I'd be back often to see my friend the tailor, visit the malls and walk the city.

The first thing I spotted when I settled into the van was a hand-grip that hung from the headliner above the driver's shoulder. With his left hand on the wheel and his right hand holding tight to the grip, he sped off. I grabbed the door handle as the driver tore headlong into traffic— without so much as a peek over his shoulder to check for approaching cars. I began searching the seat pockets for a barf bag. It's terrifying enough that the Thais drive on the *wrong* side of the road but they also drive on the *wrong* side of the car. Everything was bass-ackwards, and I became more disoriented and nauseous by the second. "Dick, don't you think this guy's going a bit too fast considering these horrible roads?"

"I have a feelin' this is how they all drive. Sit back and think of somethin' to get your mind off it—like shoppin'." He then leaned forward and patted the driver on the shoulder. "Say, fella, could you maybe slow down just a skosh?"

"Skosh, Suh?"

"Well, I mean, could you drive a little slower maybe?"

"Oh," he answered, now getting the gist of the conversation. "No wolly, cah not tip ovah."

"That's encouraging."

Dick glowered at me again. "Relax! He's used to this type of speed. I'm sure he knows where every pothole is."

Was he trying to beat the land-speed record? I saw potholes large enough to swallow a tire, but our expert driver managed to swerve and miss every one, bless his heart. Death-defying was one of the better adjectives that came to mind. I counted eighteen separate instances where we should have been creamed as cars pulled out of their lanes and into ours. In the back seat, Dick drove surreptitiously. His eyes never leaving the road as though he could stop an impending collision. After an hour of this I told him to stop; he was driving himself—and me—nuts. And hadn't he told me to sit back and relax? I had yet to learn about the Buddhist logic of acceptance. I just hung on and tried to appear nonchalant. I laid my head back on the headrest, closed my eyes and tried to recall if I'd updated my Last Will and Testament before leaving the States.

We arrived four shaky hours later in Pattaya, a beachside resort on the gulf of Siam. Our hotel was not nearly the majestic place we'd experienced in Bangkok, and the VIP status was abysmally lacking?*What? No bubbly?* We were given a pen to register, handed our room keys and directed toward the elevator, with a bellman following at a respectful distance. Judging by the load he had to push, he must have thought we would be staying for a few years. I did feel relieved that I'd be stationary for at least two months or until our new house was finished and ready for occupancy.

We opened the door to the perfect suite—perfect if you planned to stay maybe one weekend. The thought of possibly two months in this cubbyhole made me claustrophobic. I walked around in disbelief. "Oh my God! How can we bring all our stuff into this overgrown closet?"

Dick shot me a look that smacked of: I told you not to pack so damn much.

"What?

"What, what?"

What was that look for?"

"It's small, Okay? So we'll just have to make do, that's all. So get over it." He grumbled something that I didn't hear as he walked out to bring in more bags. He was right, but a bit late to change my packing habits.

I wandered around looking over my temporary digs. Two closets; one was three feet by three with the top half used for hanging shirts and the bottom half reserved for a safe and a shoe shelf. The other closet was about three feet by four with the bottom half reserved for a mini-bar. The sole dresser had four drawers, about the size of large shoe boxes. I shuddered at the thought of unpacking and trying to find a place for two months of necessities.

Two bathrooms were allotted us, both only large enough for a tub enclosure, shower, sink and toilet. The counter space was abysmally small, without the room for all the important tchotchkes that women need. I have to believe that most hotel bathrooms were designed by eunuch engineers. "Okay," I can hear them say as they lean over their drafting boards, "all we need is a three inch wide counter for deodorant, razor, and jock-itch powder."

My plan was to fit some of our clothes into the small closets and tiny dressers, leaving the rest in the suitcases. I couldn't bitch and moan too much as I'd been warned of this. *Why did I bring so much?* "Hey," I yelled to Dick, who was busy surfing the TV stations. "I just figured out what I can do with all the clothes."

"Throw 'em away so you can buy new ones?"

"Not a bad idea, but listen. We have two bathrooms. Why not use the second for storing the clothes that don't fit in the closets?"

"Do what you like," he answered, not a bit into my storage problems. "I'm goin' down to the bar for a cool one."

"While you're there, how about ordering a larger room."

"Yeah, right! I'll check to see if they have one we can rent for your clothes."

The door closed.

I walked into the other bathroom. Hmmm. I checked around for hangers and found dozens in each closet, crammed in so tight I broke three nails trying to pry them off the rods. That really pissed me off. I had no idea if or where I could find a nail salon. I was dismayed to find the hangers so tiny and misshapen. How in the world could I hang anything on these baby-clothes hangers?

After filling the closet to the hilt, I grabbed some of my clothes from the suitcase and headed for the second bathroom. I plopped some in the tub, hung some on hangers on the shower curtain rod and piled the rest in the sink. There, that'll work. I had to back out slowly to keep from dislodging the piles of clothes.

When I'd finished shoving clothes in every empty cubbyhole, I decided it might be a good time to shower and wash my hair. While in Bangkok I hadn't wanted to search for my blow dryer and curling iron, so I had it styled in the hotel. I'd been sporting the bed-head look for a couple days and thought I'd better get it done while Dick was out. I locked the bathroom door. Sometimes a woman just likes to shower alone, ya know? Stand in front of the spray without being mauled, let the ole stomach relax and not have to stand there sucking in my gut so I look like a hard-belly. No hands groping me when I have soap in my eyes, not knowing what's going to be groped next. Normally when Dick hears the shower start, he comes running like a cat that's heard the electric can opener whirring.

After a leisurely shower and shampoo, I thought I'd do a quickie blow-dry, then use my curling iron. Above the sink I saw an outlet, obviously marked for youthful eyes. I squinted and did the circled-fingers-in-front-of-the-eye thing but I still couldn't read the small print. I thought I could see three holes in the wall so how hard could it be to shove in two prongs?

I plugged my *only* curling iron, 110 volt, into a 220 outlet. I could swear it screamed "Nooo!" But it was too late. It crackled, melted into a mutated version of plastic and metal, curled into a fetal position and died. My reflection in the mirror was not a pretty picture. The humidity made my hair frizz due to a recent perm and the blow-drying caused it to splay out in a halo. Picture the offspring of Gene Wilder and Diana Ross. I dressed, grabbed my dead curling iron and headed for the front desk. In the elevator a kindly tourist spotted my hair and the mangled curling iron. She said she'd be leaving for the States the next day and kindly offered me the use of her converter. She'd have it sent up to my room. Even though the plastic and tip of my curling iron was melted and twisted, I managed to plug it into the converter, then into the wall, and voila! It heated up just enough to partially ease my Diana Ross look.

After hitting most of the stores in Pattaya searching for a curling iron, I finally got it: with such beautiful, thick, straight black hair, Thai women needed curling irons like I needed chopsticks.

**PATTAYA BEACH
DRUG CONNECTION**

13

Our hotel room was on the 14th floor, with an over-sized window in the center of the suite. I loved to look out over the immense Gulf of Siam—a symphony of topaz and indigo; a magnificent view during the day—if you looked straight ahead. But looking down to the left and right presented another view. The perimeter of the hotel was strewn with all matter of debris. I discovered later that it is quite natural to see a beautiful hotel, as well as Thai homes, shops, and restaurants, with rubbish piled along the boundaries. When something's unwanted it is simply discarded alongside the closest building available and left there until someone sets a match to it.

When it was too hot to venture out, I often curled up on the sofa for some non-stimulating TV. The hotel television offered the Asian version of MTV, which played rock and roll most of the day. The only English-speaking programs were the *BBC* and *MASH*. After five weeks of this I began to speak with a veddy British awksent and could sing *"Lowlin, lowlin, lowlin on the liwer*—Creedence Clearwater please forgive me.

Eight Thai-language channels filled the screen; three showing American movies with Thai language dubbed in. It was a hoot to see Michael Douglas in *Falling Down*, cursing two Mexican gang members in Thai, and to see *My Cousin Vinney* arguing his case in court. How does a Thai say "Youtz?"

Our sex life was still on the three-nights-a-week schedule, but Dick was having a rough time hiding his pouting on the other four. I was turned off by his childish behavior and three nights a week was more than I wanted to partake of. When we did have sex, it was as though he had to make up for the nights he'd missed. He became more forceful, more aggressive and I had to push him away as a familiar onset of pain returned. *Was he punishing me for holding back?*

Into our new quarters for just a few days, the pain worsened and I began to feel the all too familiar signs of a recurring problem. "Oh-oh!"

"Mmm." my husband grunted, never taking his eyes off the European golf match on the tube.

"I'm pregnant," I said, knowing he wasn't listening.

"Umm," he said, while staring straight ahead. "Do we have any beer left in the fridge?"

"I think my bladder infection is back."

"I think I put a couple bottles in yesterday. Check to see if we still have any, will ya?" Eyes still glued to the TV.

I couldn't bear his outpouring of sympathy. I swept past him, sighing heavily. "I'm going into the bedroom now to kill myself."

"Umm," was my worried husband's reply. Then, "WHAT A SHOT!"

I don't know why I even bother talking to him when he's watching a golf game. Might as well empty his wallet and bank account and leave; he'd never know it until the match was over, the beer gone—and the bed empty.

I have suffered from recurring bouts of bladder infections on and off for over ten years. It's a condition well-known to women. Another name for it is "Honeymoon Cystitis" and as the name infers, it's overuse of a female's female parts. The pain is excruciating. At the first niggling symptoms, as the sneaky little bacteria begin to rear their ugly heads, I know I need help—fast. The drugs my stateside doctors had prescribed were Bactrim for the inflammation and Pyridium for the spasms. Presto—gone in three days.

I began to frantically search through the myriad of suitcases and boxes for my cystitis medication. Where could they be? I treated them like my American Express Card—I never left home without them. Living in this small resort town of Pattaya, a three to four hour drive to the more cosmopolitan city of Bangkok, I felt sure no doctor would understand my symptoms and admit me straightaway to a hospital. How could they understand me when most Thais found it impossible to even comprehend my name. Not excited about getting into the froggy position for a doctor, I asked our driver to find the nearest drugstore, hoping for a miracle. "I need to go for medicine."

"Yeth," he answered politely.

"Do you know med-a-sin?"

"Yeth." More politely.

I'd been told by old-timer expats that the Thais are so accommodating that the first thing out of their mouths is "Yes" when a foreigner asks them a question.

"Farm-a-see," I said slowly, hoping this word was more familiar.

"Oh, yeth, can do."

Thank you, Buddha. Let's go. The pain was now a plus-nine on a scale of one to ten. I crawled in the back of the car and into the fetal position as the driver sped away. He pulled to the curb of a ramshackle building not far from our hotel. It looked rather seedy, but with my pain, I'd have gone into a lion's den and wrestled a lioness if she had my meds nestled between her bicuspids.

I gingerly stepped around boxes lying helter-skelter in the doorway and aisles as I entered the store. Mystical smells of herbs and potions engulfed me as Asian music blared from speakers. Every nook and cranny in this minuscule store was filled to overflowing with boxes and bodies. It looked like Social Security Check-day at the bank.

I observed from a respectable distance as the man behind the counter dispensed multiple little odd-shaped pills to multiple little odd-shaped ladies. No sterile measures here—just dust, dirty hands and smiles. He was an elderly gentleman with thinning gray hair and walked with a slight limp. His movements were slow and deliberate. I tentatively stepped up to the counter, hoping he was an English-speaking pharmacist and not just a store clerk. He looked up and gave a short bow. "Goosmonin."

Okay, it was now or never. *"Sawatdee kha,"* I said with my most learned Thai accent. "Do you have any Bactrim?" I held my breath.

He looked nonplused as he shoved a scrap of soiled paper and a well chewed pencil in front of me and ordered: "You lite, please."

Unobtrusively, or maybe not, I wiped the pencil with the ever-ready piece of tissue I kept stuffed in my pocket for just such encounters. You can't be too careful what with germs and diseases running amok. In over-sized third-grade characters I printed: B-A-C-T-R-I-M and slid the paper to his side of the counter. He glanced at the paper and turned his back on me. *Oh God. Does that mean no?* I watched him limp away, disappearing behind a wall of boxes. I didn't know whether to cry or run after him, pleading, begging and throwing myself at his feet. The line was now growing behind me and snaking out the door. My pain jumped to an eleven. What should I do? I didn't want to lose my place in line. I might not get another chance to plead my case. I could hear murmurs behind me. I tried to locate him over the boxes and heads in this jam-packed room, bending over as spasms of pain had their way with me.

Then he reappeared. He carried a dilapidated wooden stepladder, with more rungs missing than present, and placed it against a wall behind the counter. He gave it a push to test it then started up, deftly missing the gaping holes as he climbed to the top rung. The entire wall was miniature drawers from floor-to-ceiling. My pulse quickened as I saw him reach to the highest shelf and pull out a drawer. He scooped up a handful of something white and dropped it into his jacket pocket. He then slowly and deliberately descended the ladder. With every step he took my pain intensified. He then took the time to return the ladder to its original resting place before heading back to the counter. A huge smile lit his face as he scooped the pills from his pocket and plopped them down on the counter in front of me—in a puff of white dust.

Dust or no, I was ecstatic. The pills looked identical to the Bactrim I used in the States. I wanted to grab them and throw them down my gullet. *Oh Buddha, thank you! How could I get this lucky?* He scooped the pills into a wrinkled paper bag and handed them to me with a grin.

"Umm, is there an expiration date?" I asked.

He looked a bit irritated by my question. *Did he understand me?*

"Uh, I just said it's an excellent day." *Don't press your luck, goofy.* He bowed.

Okay, here's the clincher. Could I be this lucky—twice? "Do you have any Per-id-de-uummm?" I drug it out hoping if I enunciated each syllable he'd miraculously understand me.

He pushed the scrap of paper in front of me again. "You lite, please."

With my best Catholic school training I printed: P-Y-R-I-D-I-U-M. I felt damp beneath the underwire of my bra—the height of excitement for me, a non-sweater.

He looked at the paper, then back at me, his face creasing in a huge grin. In a booming voice he proclaimed for the entire world: "OH YETH, FOH PEE-PEE PAIN!"

Well, fine! Now my reputation was tarnished here in Pattaya. Did

I imagine it or was everyone looking at me as a tainted woman? I flushed bright red and felt a trickle of sweat drip down from my underwire.

The pharmacist returned with the Pyridium and dropped a handful of pills into the same bag. He handed it to me with a knowing smile— *I felt*— and waited for my gratitude. *"Khap khun kha,"* I mumbled as I dropped a fist full of *baht* on the counter and ran for the safety of my waiting car. I grabbed my water bottle and gulped down the pills in one swallow.

How embarrassing was that? I wondered if any of those little old ladies had ever suffered with Honeymoon Cystitis. Nah!

From that day on, *Lady with Pee-Pee Pain* was a regular customer of the good pharmacist. I could purchase my hormones, anti-inflammatories, penicillin, cortisone cream and *KY Jelly*—I'm still surprised he didn't do his Town Crier bit on that one.

Total cost for sulfa and pain pills: 60 *baht*-($2.40); enough pills to last me seven days; twenty-five days worth of estrogen: 75 *baht*-($3.00). Love this country.

MASSAGES FOR MADAME OW-OW

14

My pain was gradually abating with the meds, but Dick was not a happy camper being kept from his three-nights-a-week action. He walked around with a black cloud over his head, and I knew it wouldn't be long before a huge fight ensued. The problem was, when these fights ensued they were always followed by chest pains. I tried to be away when he was home, and vice versa, until I was completely recovered. The thing about cystitis is that when it returns after a bout, it does so with a vengeance. I had to make sure I was over it before I let Dick near me. He watched me like a cat watches a grasshopper with a broken leg, waiting for his chance to pounce.

Then I was introduced to a real stress-reliever. A most amazing practice I found while in Thailand, and one that all new expats come to love, was the wonderful Thai massage. It is usually performed by strong young girls, however I did notice a few males in the trade. One hour of this relaxing massage and most women would be able to negotiate with a terrorist. What a warm and muscle-stimulating practice it is—for most people. I have a problem with pain. I admit it. I have no tolerance for pain and don't try to hide it.

After a few trips to the massage parlors around town, I'd earned a reputation as Madame Ow-Ow. The tiny massage girls all seemed to be amazed that I could be so sensitive. As soon as I appeared in the waiting room, I'd hear the giggles start. *Fine, giggle all you want—just don't hurt my body.* Like it or not, they had to use a little less muscle with me. One of the little power-houses literally left her fingerprints on my arms and legs in the form of purple circles. I warned her about my condition before she started on me; in fact, I showed her some old bruises that the last girl had left on my rump. She obviously had no clue why I was pointing to four round dots on my butt, but as was the norm in this land of smiles, she giggled and began leaving her own marks. Giggling I later learned, can also be the Thai way of hiding embarrassment. Bruises or no, I kept going back—possibly because it felt so good when they stopped. Okay, I admit it, I'm a masochist.

Seeing all the massage parlors in town brought back memories of an earlier visit to Thailand. I had to laugh as I remembered being introduced to the words: "Physical Massage." It was in the 70s and we were expats living in Iran. My husband, feeling we had earned this treat just by living in that hotbed, had surprised us with a week of R&R at Pattaya Beach. On our first day there we decided to let the kids enjoy the pool while we read and soaked up the sun. We were half asleep when my youngest son, about ten years old at the time, came running up to us. "Dad! Can I have ten bucks?"

"Whaa for?" my half-asleep husband asked.

"That lady over there said to bring ten bucks and she'd give me a good massage."

At these not so soft-spoken words, we both sat up—as well as most of the people around the pool—and looked in the direction my son pointed. And there she was, a beautiful Thai girl who looked to be no more than sixteen, standing in her shimmering red gown, leaning seductively against the massage parlor door, smiling the sweet Thai smile and motioning for my son to come to her.

"Uh, I think not, son," I said.

"But, why?" he whined in his usual "you love her more than me" voice while pointing to his sister. "You give her money all the time. Can't I just have ten bucks?"

"Honey," I whispered, "she's not a nice lady. She'll take your money and God knows what she'll do to you. Besides, massages are for grown-ups. Wait until you're older, then *you* can pay for it."

"Paaaleeez," he cried plaintively.

By now the male population around the pool was sitting upright, awaiting our decision.

"No! And that's final," said my husband in a not-so-final voice. This was not the answer my son wanted to hear. He was the kind of kid who never would accept the word "No" and could argue you to the ground until you cried "Uncle!"

"She said it was good for me," he yelled in his outdoor voice. "How could she hurt me, Mom? Dad could go along with me to make sure I got my ten bucks' worth."

"No." I said, this time in my outdoor voice. "No more talk of massages." I turned to my husband for reinforcement, but he was busy putting a bookmark in his novel. "Go back to sleep," I said, "you're not going anywhere either."

Now, two decades later, I was happy to see so many massage parlors in Pattaya; the kind of massage my body needed. A friend called me one day to tell me about a new parlor just outside of town. "If you like ambiance, honey, you must try it." Instead of just the ordinary plain trappings, she said, this place was very high class.

On a whim, I invited Dick to join me for a massage. I felt that it might ease the sexual tension that seemed to be weighing him down. The massage parlor was very upscale, softly aglow with candlelight, mirrors, and statues of Buddha on gold-gilded altars surrounded by bouquets of fragrant flowers. We were put in cubicles across from each other while we waited for our masseuse to come for us. The cubicle was enveloped in wondrous aromas of lilac and lavender and other mystifying, but marvelous scents. I felt an immediate release of tension. The whole experience was warm and seductive.

I looked up in time to see a miniscule young nymph, who appeared as though she didn't have the strength to blow a kiss, glide by me with tiny delicate steps to match her under-developed size-two bare feet. Dick's eyes lit up like two keg lights as she approached. He definitely lost the battle as he tried to hide his excitement. I wanted to reach out and slap the sappy look off his face. When he'd wiped the drool from his chin he turned my way. His face became swathed in nonchalance as he shrugged his shoulders as if to say: *Geez, what's a guy to do?* then got up and stumbled behind her to the massage room.

Men!

I wasn't as lucky as Dick. I think I got a cross-dresser. She could not have weighed more than sixty-five pounds but she looked a tad masculine, not at all like the typical Thai girls I'd seen. I even detected some fine black fuzz on her upper lip, and her eyebrows were definitely unisex. Great! He gets the Geisha, I get the transvestite. She opened the door to the massage room and motioned for me to disrobe to my underwear. She handed me a towel to cover with, then busied herself with her mysterious oils as I undressed and crawled up on the table. When she had her potions mixed, she pulled a small stool to the edge of the table, nimbly hopped up on it and within seconds was literally sitting on top of me. She positioned her body over my upper torso—with her knees on the table—and began to knead. Oh, my, what a wonderful feeling. I was prepared to give my customary "Not too hard, please," but she was so light-handed I assumed I'd been given a trainee. I didn't know this was her warm-up phase. After she'd kneaded for about five minutes, she began to pummel—well it felt like pummeling; push, pull, twist, shove, bat, smack; all sorts of noises. My skin felt twisted in twelve different directions. I craned my neck around and stopped her mid pummel: "Ow!" I yelped.

She stopped and looked around, as though she had no idea where that noise came from. "Ow," I repeated, a little softer this time. *"Kao jai kha?*—Do you understand me?" I asked, a bit too harsh. I softened my voice when I saw her look of confusion. "Please, please, not so hard." I forced a smile. Sweet thing that she was, she smiled back, giggled softly, and went back to her pummeling. I'd hoped for a miracle, to get the only Thai in the place who might understand me.

Again with the pummeling. "OW!" It jumped out of me again. *"Mai kâo jai kha?"* She still didn't understand me.

I sat up to illustrate my problem. I took her arm and squeezed my fingers around her minuscule wrist, overlapping them with my thumb. *Sheesh, how does one stay so tiny?* I put some pressure on her wrist to emphasize the meaning of pain, hence "Ow!" She didn't flinch. Okay, now she must think I'm nuts. "No *jep* —pain, *Kao jai kha?"*

She smiled again. No! Please, not with the smiles again. That's the thing about these people. They giggle when they're amused, and giggle when they're embarrassed. It's hard to know which is which. If I ever wanted to get this over with I thought I'd better just shut up. That is until such time as I saw blood on the sheet, then I'd have to buck her off, grab my clothes and run.

She continued. Now I felt some chiropractic moves. I assumed after she'd dislocated my body she thought it best to put it back together, stretching and kneading. I felt like a ball of dough being readied for the oven. She finally slacked off a bit—I assumed out of exhaustion— and just when I was starting to enjoy it, the timer went off.

Dick stood by the car with a scowl on his face. Limping up to him I asked what was wrong. He couldn't possibly be unhappy with *Ms. Glides on Water.* I'd had *Ms. Masked Marvel* and I had a limp to prove it. "What? You didn't like your girl? Your skin is tough as cow hide."

Don't tell me she hurt you."

"No, she was just a bit over-zealous, is all."

"Really! What happened?"

"Well," he said, feigning indignation. "She nearly pinched off my gonads."

I looked at him in utter amazement. "Your gonads? What were they doing flapping about? You were supposed to keep your underwear on."

"Oh!" A look of innocence. "I thought I was supposed to strip all the way."

Sure you did, Dick.

What is it with men, anyway? They can't get their skivvies off fast enough. Yet every woman's prayer in the doctor's office is: *Please don't make me take off my undies. Please, please, please.* Men can parade through Times Square with everything jangling about—and with a smile on their face to boot. I don't get it. They have more to hide than we do, what with all the outdoor plumbing and all.

I'm beginning to realize that ole' Eve in her Garden really screwed things up for us gals. Why the shame, the modesty, the embarrassment? Why the worry about getting naked? Why can't we just flop around like men do? What's the big deal, after all? Babies can parade around without a stitch, totally unaware of their bodies, yet the minute they can understand English we have to push our insecurities and modesty off on them. Something's not right here.

One of the best massages I found was in an old run-down home outside of town. The Hilton Hotel Spa it was not, but you soon overlooked the lack of fluff for the wonderful treatment you received. The house was over 100 years old, with cracked windows, torn curtains, sagging sills, patches of linoleum missing here and there, and a musty smell that permeated the whole environment. The interior walls in the center of the house had been removed and the space had been converted to a large dormitory-type room, with mats laid out side-by-side on the floor. Much to my discomfort, air conditioning (or air-con as the Thais say) was sadly absent in this old house. The AC phenomenon was introduced to Thailand with the advent of the *farangs* invading their land. The Thais don't seem to feel the heat as the *farangs* do. When the temperature drops to eighty-five degrees, it might move them to put on a sweater.

Now, I could handle everything else in this place, but when the weather was at its worst, the massage room became one huge sauna and bordered on feral. I tried to get there early before it became too warm. Warm, as in 100 degrees F. The place lacked the niceties of Muzak and ambiance, but it was home to some wonderful girls.

The Blind Student Massage School, appropriately named, was home to young girls who were clinically blind, but who gave wonderful massages. The girls were mainly from poor villages where their parents were unable to get help for them. They were brought to Bangkok by Good Samaritans and schooled in the art of Thai massage. Once trained, they were sent to Pattaya and other towns to live with their benefactors, working to earn their keep. The Thai couple who owned this establishment gave the girls a home to live in, in exchange for their massage work and a small salary. They did very well on their tips and always thanked us profusely. We did wonder how they knew how much we tipped.

The routine went something like this: After check-in, you were given a towel and a pair of cotton PJs—designed to fit a ten-year-old— then escorted to individual vapor steam rooms the size of a small shower, with a bench seat for snoozing. After disrobing, you'd be saturated in wonderful mystical aromas of incense, eucalyptus steam and various other herbal delights. It took me five minutes of this heaven before I would doze off and dream I was Eve, lolling about the

Garden in my birthday suit. When you'd yell "Uncle" they'd scoop you out of the shower, help you on with your PJs, and lead you to the massage room and the assigned mat on the floor. What joy! You were clean, warm, snugly, and then the fun began.

The girls would first try to identify you—a game they all played with giggles and excitement. They'd begin by running their sensitive little fingers over your face and downward. By the time they reached your legs they could identify you. Of course, with me, as soon as I uttered "Ow-Ow" I was caught, and had to listen to a chorus of giggles wafting through the room. I still think it was unfair; when they couldn't immediately identify me, they'd give a pinch to hear my Ow-Ow.

After one hour of this heaven you were escorted to the co-ed shower room where you'd find the usual male opportunists— showering, changing clothes, urinating, or sitting and watching you do thr same. At first it was difficult, but over time I would envision myself as Raquel Welsh—loin cloth and all—and didn't feel quite as modest.

At this same establishment they offered haircuts, facials, manicures and pedicures—I asked for the sighted girls for these jobs— all for less than ten dollars. If you came in for a wash, you were put on what looked like a hospital gurney and rolled to the shampoo bowl. The first time I experienced this I was a tad apprehensive. *Okay, where's the operating room?* But it turned out to be another treat for the pampered *farang.* They had a very inventive way of preparing you for the shampoo by slipping one end of a rubber tray under your neck, while the other end drained into the shampoo bowl. *Why don't we have this technique stateside?* What a simple concept: the water doesn't drain down your neck, leaving a soggy blouse; no wet towels to deal with, and no concrete slab for your arthritic neck to balance on. You're in a lying position and soon you're fast asleep.

Along with these wonderful shampoos would come a head massage, neck and scalp massage, and anything else you wanted massaged. The shampoo was something all the expat ladies looked forward to; three washes, three rinses, and a twenty-minute head and neck massage.

Other pleasures to the senses were the trips that many of the ladies took to Bangkok for beauty treatments. The salon offered massages, hair and nail services, and pedicures. It was heaven to spend the day being pampered. If you were in a hurry it was the best place to go. To gain entrance you had to ring a buzzer, wherein the manager would greet you at the door and ask you three questions: (1) Are you in a hurry? (2) What services do you want? And (3) Whom would you like to have work on you? If the answer to number one was in the affirmative, the manager would assign as many girls to you as you had appendages; one girl for each hand for manicures, one girl for each foot for pedicures, one girl for cutting, curling and blow drying your hair. Watching all these girls working on me, I felt I was being prepared for a Thai barbecue.

It was marvelous if you needed to be in and out quickly, but made it quite difficult to read a book.

BEACH ROAD HAGGLING

15

Beach Road—famous for its nightlife—can be raunchy. As its name infers, Beach Road runs along the eastern coast of the Gulf of Siam and is home to some of Pattaya's famous tourist attractions. To the casual tourist on a short stay, Beach Road is fun and exciting. The road is lined with shops, open-air restaurants, bars, night clubs and hawkers with their food carts and tourist gimmicks.

In the 70s, when I vacationed in Pattaya, Beach Road was quite different. It offered over eight miles of sparkling white sandy beach and shimmering turquoise water, an invitation to swimmers. Now, in the 90s, signs were posted along the beach that read: NO SWIMMING—STAY OUT—TOXIC WATER. With hordes of tourists, sand erosion and a lack of quality sewer systems, waste obliterated the shoreline and the ocean smelled of raw sewage. This area was considered central Pattaya, where hundreds of tourists came to play, hitting the bars and night clubs, and leaving their trash behind. Swimming in the water was dangerous at best, and discouraged. A few natives did brave the toxic waters, but I never saw *farangs* get their feet wet. The local English-language newspaper ran articles about the problems of Beach Road and surmised that if the infrastructure wasn't improved, Pattaya would become another Bangkok, as far as the traffic and rubbish—and very soon.

In the 90s, amazingly pristine beaches lay to the north and south of Central Pattaya and I'm certain they remained so because there were no bars or bargirls, massage parlors or strip shows—ergo off the tourist's radar. Jomtien beach was one of those areas that had been saved from ravage. There was a lovely hotel at the time and apartments nearby.

The Strand, as we called it, was quite a shopping experience! Kaleidoscope flashes of colorful silk fabric glinted in the afternoon sun along the road. Bolts of red, green and yellow fabric lit up every cubbyhole of space. Ready-made and also tailor-made clothes hung haphazardly, piled six deep. A shopper's paradise. I bought goofy trinkets, silk fabric and ate from food carts with abandon—after checking for fly larvae.

I have always loved to haggle or argue as Dick called it. One of my Thai friends told me not to take the vendors' first price. She said they try to get as much as they can from *farangs*, so let them know you're ready, willing and able to haggle. It's a way of life for them." I had to agree. I couldn't imagine how boring it would be to stand there and sell things at the same old price, day after day and they did seem to love a good spirited haggle. She said to remember that the first price a vendor gives you is always two times higher than what they expect to get, so don't let them down. I did my best to comply. It did seem to me they perked up when they realized they had an able haggler.

When Dick was with me he didn't want any part of it. The first price out of the seller's mouth he'd whip out his wallet. I'd give him a frown and then step in. "Too much," I'd tell the vendor. Dick would look pissed and walk away shaking his head.

"Too much, too much," I'd say again, and then start to walk away. The vendor would then touch my arm, "Sokay, sokay" and drop the price a pittance. Thus it went until I got to the price it *should* have been and he *knew* he would sell it for.

Dick was amazed at my determination. He'd rather just hand over his money and get it over with. I tried to explain to him that haggling was an art but I think he just wanted to be done with shopping. What I did not share with Dick was, try as I might, even after they'd come down to half of what they'd first asked, I pictured the vendor's face morphing into a broad grin as I walked away, while he tucked my money into his trim little waistband and thought about the terrific deal he'd just made. *Oh, well, can't take it with you. Mai pen rai.*

While walking Beach Road I was again made aware of the dainty Thai women and their itsy-bitsy footwear. Dozens of open-air shops sold clothing and shoes along this road, each calling out to tourists as they strolled by: "Madame, you need goot shoe?" I decided the way to keep from being embarrassed was to pretend I didn't hear them, or get into a lively conversation with someone. I knew that these Barbie-sized shoes would never fit me—maybe back when I was in grade school. I never did understand why they sold those teensy-weensy things out where the big-foot tourists strolled. Why not reserve them for Thai specialty shops? Certainly, other than Asians, no *farangs* could ever fit into those baby shoes. *How embarrassing.*

"*Khap khun kha*, no shoes today," I'd call out to them if they caught me peeking.

"Madame, I haf goot shoe foh you, ditcount foh you sigh." *Well, how rude!* I'm pretty sure that once the vendors learned that the *farangs* loved "discounts," the word became part of their selling stratagem. It did get my attention a few times, but not with those little doll shoes.

After days of limping around this country in way too-tight, hot shoes, I tossed my old closed-toed shoes and opted for the ever-lovin' Asian sandal. I marveled at the ease in which the Thais walked around in those flimsy things. It took me hours to get used to wriggling flip-flops between my recalcitrant fat toes. In the States we called them

"Go-Aheads" a euphemism for "Go ahead and stub your toes"—which I knew would happen to me in this country where hunks of concrete were silently awaiting a foot to clobber. With constant toe-stubbing opportunities, rocks and debris lying about, holes to fall into and the unforeseen brick that could send your big toe screaming back under the other four, I was a bit leery to wear them.

I rarely saw an expat woman who'd been in Pattaya more than a month wearing closed-toed shoes. I had to try the flip-flops. It didn't take long to get accustomed to the heavenly freedom of toes and heels flapping in the breeze. On the few occasions I had to dress for a formal company function. I complained bitterly and whined all night about sore feet. It felt like my size eights were squeezed into size six vices.

In Thailand, as in most Asian countries, it's the custom to remove your shoes before entering a home. Piles of shoes could be seen lying about at the front and back doors of Asian homes: tiny size four sensible pumps from the office workers, gentlemen's loafers, and the ever-faithful sandals from the gardeners. Most Thais spend their life in these comfortable sandals. And that's fine for them, but what if your feet are socially unacceptable and you'd rather not share their disfigurement with the world? But, I caved. After living in this sandal-footed atmosphere for a short time I thought who gives a rat's arse? *Slip them on and let your bony outcroppings hang out and get some air.*

While I lived in Thailand I don't think I ever noticed an Asian woman with ugly feet. Maybe if they worked in a rice paddy from dawn to dusk they might be dirty, but even so, their feet were still well-shaped and attractive. The feet I saw in the malls or businesses were beautiful, daintily formed with no unsightly bunions poking permanent lumps into their shoes. Could it be because they grew up wearing sandals or open-toed shoes that didn't pinch or squash them? Also, maybe all five toes were allowed to point straight ahead, as opposed to those of us who've lived in ill-fitting and pointy high heeled shoes with space for no more than three toes, and constantly forced our feet to walk downhill. After all that torture, the toes seem to have found the point of least resistance—hiding under each other, thus the big toes look like they're supposed to curl under the other four while the others just lie there and play dead.

Oh, yes, and let's not forget the dainty callus—caused by ill-fitting shoes—that some of us carry along as baggage. Ever so pretty in summer sandals, while boring holes in our cute little espadrilles. And, how about the well-placed corn on the bottom of the foot that feels as though you're walking on a misplaced carpet nail?

Ladies! Why do we do this to our feet? They're supposed to be our best friends; they support us through thick and thin. Shouldn't we have some allegiance to them? I heard somewhere that high-heeled shoes were invented by men to hobble women. If that's true, isn't it about time to boycott high-heeled and closed-toed shoes?

And speaking of tiny…How do the Thais keep so trim? It seemed like everywhere I looked they were always eating. No matter what time I walked along Beach Road, early morning or late evening, I'd see Thais gathered around food carts. I did wonder if this was more of a social thing than fulfilling a hunger pang. How do they do it? Eat, eat, eat, and yet they stay so slim. To see an obese Thai was very rare.

Another scene in and around the streets of Pattaya that always caught my attention were men driving their wives to work on the back of motorcycles; the women riding side-saddle, sitting prim and proper, dressed in neat tailored suits, shapely little panty-hosed legs with smart sling-back pumps hanging to one side, while the husbands wore neat shorts and shirts and flip-flops toting the little missus to work. How nice. The military, police, guards and office personnel all looked spit-shined and crisp—even coming *from* work. In our shorts, sleeveless tops and flip-flops, some of us felt like slobs next to these tidy little people. I knew I could never live up to that neatness—through monsoons, humidity, heat and rain.

I thought about this contradiction in such an enchanting country. The people all seemed to be neat and precise about their appearance. The school children going and coming from school looked like they were just freshly scrubbed and pressed in their blue and white uniforms and shiny black shoes. The paradox was the natural beauty of this country—versus man's despoiling imprint on the land—and the always neat and tidy Thai people.

VANITY AND ITS PRICE

16

A foolish thing I did in my frivolous past returned to bite me in Thailand and left me sitting in an Emergency Room. I had only been in Pattaya a few weeks when I noticed a familiar sharp pain in my left eye and knew the dreaded "anomaly" had returned. I then introduced the good Thai doctors to the Eyelash-Scratching-the-Cornea Syndrome.

In the 80s I had let vanity overpower my good sense and visited a dermatologist who specialized in Permanent Makeup Tattooing. The end result was to have my eyelids permanently lined, giving an effect of natural, full lashes and a dark, exotic frame to my eyes. To rationalize my vanity—and I must—many women have this procedure if they feel they're lacking in some areas of beauty that should have been bestowed by Mother Nature. I was short-changed by Mother— I got itsy-bitsy pale red lashes.

The doctor's ad read: "You too can be a Natural Beauty." How could I resist?

Eyelid tattooing is done in much the same manner as a standard tattoo, using a fine needle and permanent ink. Most of these guys will tattoo anything you want. If you're tired of applying lip-liner every two hours, they'd be glad to outline your lips. *Voila!* After you've demolished an ear of corn and wiped away the butter you still look eminently kissable. Let's say your preference is permanent eyebrows—

never having to use the dull eyebrow pencil again. The doctor will shape them to any style you prefer—from pencil-thin, à la Cyndi Lauper, to the Joan Rivers look of constant surprise. In general, if you don't like waking in the morning resembling an unmade bed, the doc's the man to see.

I've always envied women with long, thick lashes and arched brows. My daughter's are unbelievable. Her huge, chocolate-brown eyes are framed in gorgeous tendrils of thick black lashes, reaching out like so many mink slivers from her beautiful eyes, and her thick well-shaped brows would make Brooke Shields look like she has alopecia. And those ruby-red lips, full and sensuous! *Where did she get these?*

All things in my life being equal, I must tell you that I was the *only* person my doctor had seen whose "permanent eyeliner" was *not* permanent. What I did get, however, that *was* permanent, were damaged eyelash roots that caused my lashes to grow catawampus. Instead of growing out and down from the bottom lid as designed by our DNA, they grow up and into my eye—ergo the pain. It feels like a railroad tie is stuck in my eye. I know immediately when it's coming; my nose runs and eyes water, and every time I blink the little suckers scratch my cornea. Very painful!

The usual procedure for removal of these lashes entails an ophthalmologist using a slit-lamp; a contraption used to examine eyes for pathologic problems. It magnifies a bazillion times over and is perfect for viewing these miniscule lashes of mine. With surgical tweezers at the ready, the doc plucks the short, prickly little suckers from the offending root giving me immediate relief of pain. The medical name for this anomaly is trichiasis, which sounds like a sexually transmitted disease, but more painful—so I've heard. In the States this aggravation has sent me scurrying to emergency rooms at least eight times a year since 1985.

So there I was sitting in the emergency room in Pattaya wondering how in the world I could ever explain my problem to the docs when my Thai was as unintelligible as their English. I did a lot of loud talking as well as pantomiming. They finally got it when I pointed to my eyes, which were red and irritated. I then brought their attention to the fact that my eyes were awash with tears, taking my mascara on a slippery slide down my cheeks, and joining with the leakage from my nose as it made its way down my chin. "Eyelash. Poking into my eye."

"Yeth."

"Can you take out?"

"Yeth."

I spent two hours with a four-man team of doctors—one working on my eyelid with tweezers while three watched—trying to dislodge four minute eyelashes that were wreaking havoc on my cornea and my nerves.

Peek, peek, peek…. they all had to have a peek. They had never seen such a sight. Plunk. Plunk. Plunk. I felt the eyelashes being tweezed out one by one while six concerned eyes observed. No wonder they were all gaping at me; the Thais have such coarse black eyelashes and here's this *farang* with short, spindly red lashes causing her terrible pain. This was quite an anomaly for them.

After the last plunk the doctor smiled and waited for my gratitude.

"You bettah now, yeth?"

"Yeth. *Khob khun kha.*"

They bowed in unison: *"Mai pen rai."*

My ER team of docs became my best friends while living in Pattaya, and I secretly think they looked forward to seeing the redheaded lady with very odd eyelashes.

VISIT FROM STRANGERS

17

We'd been in Pattaya close to three weeks, sightseeing and meeting new friends. One evening while out to dinner one of the guys from Dick's job asked if we'd had our visit yet.

"Visit? What's that mean?" Dick asked.

"The Bosses just got back from the States and they'll probably drop by for a visit."

Bosses? We only knew of one boss that Dick had to answer to, and that was *Mr. JB,* the guy who'd hired him. "Is there more than one boss on the job?"

"They're a husband and wife tag team," he said. "And they always make a point to drop in on the newbies and run down the list of their rules."

"So? What's the big deal?"

"Well, if you break em', you could be sent packing."

Dick laughed at this bit of nonsense. "I don't think we need to worry about them sendin' us packin'. It's kinda late for that after they've spent a few bucks gettin' us here."

"Don't count on it."

Dick frowned. "What's with the *Bosses* thing? His wife's not employed by the company, is she?"

"Well, no," he said, "but you'd think so by the way she doles out rules to the wives."

I thought back to the first time we'd socialized with the boss and his wife. They'd invited us to dinner after Dick signed on for the project, and we'd played golf with them several times. We liked that *Mr. JB* would be Dick's boss. We enjoyed the personal relationship we had going on with them. He'd even given us a pre-wedding gift of $300, which he handed off to Dick and winked: "So, when's the big day? Not that I'm rushing you or anything. Ha-ha-ha."

Why should we now worry about a visit from them? We promptly dismissed this latest bit of rumor and went on with our lives. That is, until the phone call.

"Ah you going to be in the hotel today?"

A cold, ominous feeling wrapped around me like a shroud the minute *Mrs. Anorexia* set her royal size six shoes in our hotel room—followed at a respectful distance by her husband, *Mr. Jelly Belly.* They acted as if they'd never met us before. Our smiles of greeting soon morphed into serious, obedient faces. *Mr. JB and Mrs. A* thought it was time to make their presence felt. I could see the look of worry on Dick's face. He'd been working on the project for a couple of weeks and there didn't seem to be any problems—as far as he knew.

Mrs. A took a chair, regally crossing her long, reedy legs; one Gucci shoe swinging idly off her toes as she waited for our attention. Her posture was ramrod straight. Not a hair out of place in her well-coifed upsweep. She wore a champagne colored silk suit with alligator matching pumps, and a plastered-on smile that looked a bit tighter than the last time I'd seen it. I assumed by the look on their faces that this would not be a chatty visit but I thought I'd try to give it an air of civility. "Would either of you like something to drink?"

"That won't be necessary, my deah," she cooed in a deep southern accent—more southern than I'd remembered. "We-ah not heah for a social visit, just to go ov-ah a few rules."

Dick and I smiled at her like a couple of idiots. I took a seat next to him on the sofa as she reeled off the rules and conditions: what was expected of the wives, what we could do, what we couldn't do, and what times we could do them. Dick looked at me dumbfounded. Who were these people and what had they done with the other two we'd met in the States?

Something had to be wrong. First of all, she wasn't *my* boss but she kept cutting her eyes my way. Secondly, she sure as hell wasn't Dick's boss, but she also included him in her eye cut. Dick looked over at *Mr. JB*, thinking any minute he'd break out laughing: *Hey, this is all a joke. Funny, huh?* But the old man wasn't about to interrupt her.

I did manage to shake my head in agreement as she rattled off her rules; I *would* ride in the company van with the ladies on their grocery shopping runs, I *would* attend all her "ladies" meetings as directed by letters sent home from the jobsite. We *would* ask permission for anything and everything that had to do with our private lives. Whoa! She had to be kidding. My mind wandered back to the stories our informant had divulged about *The Bosses*. They had a reputation of taking over the lives of their employees when overseas, he'd said, and fired those who didn't follow *their* version of the rules. He also mentioned couples who'd sold their homes, put everything in storage, changed their whole lives to go overseas with the company, only to find that they didn't meet *The Bosses* requirements and were shipped home. Well, I reasoned, that couldn't happen to us—they liked us. I assumed that the people who'd been sent home had probably screwed up on the job. Sometimes jealousy begets gossip. Possibly the people passing these stories around had been turned down for a job overseas and were just being hateful. Who knew?

I thought back to the last dinner we'd had with them before we left for Thailand. That night we sat in awe as they told us of their importance, and regaled us with their tales of travel and money: Africa,

Japan, the Caribbean, Korea—they had done it all. *Stick with us baby, we're goin' places.* Were these two the same people? I sat there and looked at them from a different perspective now and wondered why the sudden change. And why was *she* calling the shots?

"Really dahlins," I heard her say as she brought me back from my reverie. "You'll see, it's all very simple." With that said she picked up her Gucci purse, ending the visit and any questions we might have had. *Mr. JB* jumped up to hold the door for her as she swept by me in a cloud of Chanel No.5. Stepping into the hall she called over her shoulder, "Awl you need do is follow owah rules and evra-thin will be fine."

I closed the door behind them and leaned against it. "Call me crazy, but I didn't get any of that. Were they kidding? Are they nuts? What?"

Dick looked bewildered. "What the hell was that all about?"

NEW HOME - NEW PROBLEMS

18

We heard no more from the *The Bosses* and as time passed we wondered if we had imagined the whole thing. No news is good news, as the saying goes, so we went on with our life.

"Get your shit together!" Dick strode into our hotel room yelling like the town-crier. He'd received word at work that the house was ready for occupancy. Oh joy of joys; I was more than ready! The hotel room felt like a tight girdle without an inch to spread. I couldn't wait to move into a 3,000 square foot house.

We grabbed some suitcases and boxes and headed for the complex. We'd visited the construction site many times but I couldn't picture it complete or imagine myself living there. Now as I stood in front of it, the whole area seemed totally different. It looked way too large and too sterile sitting there empty. Gone were all the trash and minutiae that accumulates on construction sites. It looked positively gargantuan.

I slowly walked through the large double doors. It was more than I'd dared hope for. I gaped at the cavernous rooms and knew I could fill them up in no time. I mentally unpacked everything and still knew I'd have room to spare.

"Ohmigod!" I yelped. No sooner had I hit the second syllable than the first came floating back to me, echoing through the great tiled rooms. I tried to take in the spaciousness of it. "Ohmigod," I yelled again, listening for that wonderful echo. Thank Buddha I'd have a maid. I knew I could never keep up this place.

The tiles on the downstairs floors glowed as if lit from above by klieg lights. Highly polished terracotta marble covered the kitchen, living and dining room floors. Everywhere I turned the house was radiant and alive with intensity. New electrical appliances graced the kitchen. All were strictly Thai, no GE or Frigidaire, no name brand I'd heard of, but hey, they were new and looked like top-of-the-line appliances to me after eating in restaurants for two months.

Upstairs the master suite was covered with exquisite hardwood flooring, varnished to a high sheen. For some reason the builder had seen fit to throw in three bathrooms as well, which seemed like overkill to me. When I walked in the first one, I wondered why they just didn't make two large bathrooms. They were tiled in multicolored Thai marble that started at the floor and ended at the ceiling, but much to my disappointment all three were less than four feet wide—the standard Thai bathroom.

Our master bedroom was sunny and bright, at least 400 square feet, but closets were at a minimum. Judging by Thai standards I should have no more than three dresses, two slacks and two pairs of shoes—size three—to fill this miniature closet. Okay, no problem. I'd find a carpenter to build me larger closets. I certainly had room for them. Wall-to-wall windows opened to breathtaking views. Palms, frangipani, and silvery swaying banana palms waved at me from all directions.

Two guard shacks could be seen above the six foot block wall that surrounded the complex. I was told that these men were hired to sit in the shack and look threatening. They were rotated every twenty-four hours with fresh guards, and I felt very safe with them sitting up there ready to take on the bad guys. I waved to them as I stepped onto my balcony. They waved back in shy unison. Hey, I'd already made new friends.

The complex comprised ten newly built two-story houses, which circled an over-sized pool. The houses looked like huge tan toads dropped in the middle of the jungle. The grounds, landscaped with spectacular flowering bushes, lush palm trees and multihued flower beds, were spacious and inviting. In front of each house and along the paths were flowers of every variety: bougainvillea in a riot of brilliant reds and pinks, frangipani in deep pinks and creams, while orchids and anthurium, hanging in pots graced the patios; quite an oasis from the surrounding dense jungle. Ten female gardeners were hired to tend the grounds and their tireless work was evident.

Our house sat at the edge of the complex next to the block wall, and was the only one with a side-yard. Dick had picked this lot when he'd first seen the plans in the States. He knew this extra space would be the perfect place to assemble his golf practice net and work on his game. He'd brought the net into the country tucked inside his golf bag. And *I* was given hell because I'd packed way too much "unnecessary shit." *What nerve!*

The pool was glorious. It was an artist's easel, reflecting the blue sky and the colorful surrounding shades of greens, purples and pinks. I pictured myself lying on a raft in the middle of that inviting water, face upturned to the cloud formations while my skin took on a mahogany sheen. I could hardly wait to move in, get out my trusted journal and start writing in this beautiful setting.

In the first few days before the kitchen and dining area were set up, we'd head out to one of our favorite places, an outdoor restaurant that catered to expats called Rancho Tejas. And, as the name implied, it had the ambiance of a Texas Ranch, sans cow manure, yet sported dozens of cats and dogs running amok throughout the eating areas leaving their own brand of manure. The Rancho sat in the middle of the jungle, off a rutted and narrow dirt road. The owner, Larry, hailed from Texas and proudly displayed an oversized Texas flag, along with a Thai flag, the Union Jack, the Maple Leaf, and Old Glory—all hanging precipitously over the buffet line—dotted with fly specs, cobwebs and various species of creepy crawlies living in profusion amongst the folds.

Larry oversaw the food preparation and prided himself for smoking his own imported hams and providing authentic Tex-Mex food, and just good ole' down-home cookin'. Many expats gathered here for the same reason: to commiserate about being homesick and raise one for their country. Tears would start to fall when the speakers thundered out Willie Nelson and the Boys, serenading us with Americana to make us homesick, and push us to perhaps buy another dozen rounds.

One night while dining at Rancho Tejas it hit home that it might be time to wear my "occasional" glasses on a full-time basis. I knew I had become a tad presbyopic, but who wasn't at my age? Walking through the buffet line I asked the Thai cooks: "*Allai?*"—what is this? I wasn't about to put on my glasses just to distinguish between soup and potatoes. People in line behind me let out a few chuckles when I pointed to an object and said "*Allai?*" It looked like a casserole of sorts to me, and I wanted to make sure before I dipped into it.

"It's the cutting board they slice the roast beef on, Dodie," sang a chorus of voices.

Well, how embarrassing! The secret was now out: I couldn't tell the difference between a theatre marquee and a house on fire. Okay, it was time. I just hated to wear glasses, but more than that I hated to admit I needed to wear them.

Now that we were ensconced in our new home, I began to schedule my pool time after morning walks when it was especially inviting. Our ten little gardeners were always hard at work and I felt terribly guilty as I walked past them in my swimsuit to while away the hours while they were bent over flower beds. I told myself that this was their karma. Someday they might return with *me* as their gardener. Good luck! I can't even keep a silk plant from wilting.

The serene pool called to me daily. It was the perfect spot for meditating. No one else in the complex seemed that entranced with the pool, and I secretly hoped they'd stay away. It lured me outside through all types of weather. The cool, calm water reflected the sky and clouds in ever-changing cycles. I spent many hours floating on my raft as I studied the cloud formations; thin clouds that took on the hues of their environment and produced pinks, greens and blues; cumulus clouds formed by the extreme heat, rising in tall peaks, feathery and white as doves' wings. When I closed my eyes I could still see the colors on the inside of my lids, all blending into the azure sky.

During the hot season I watched the horizon holding back blotches of heavy dark clouds, ever-lurking and trying to hide a resilient hot sun and make way for some much-needed rain. At that time the sky would actually take on an indigo hue, shading the pool in purplish-black, obscuring the bottom and sides. But as midday receded into evening, tropical breezes embraced us from the sea.

During the hottest part of the day, as the morning ebbed into midday, the changing colors of the clouds also became a welcome sight. Soon they would become heavier, darker and lower, creating a type of dusky-mist until they finally poured forth their bloated bellies, giving me a break from the increasing humidity and the tropical heat of the afternoon. During the rainy season, torrential downpours became the rule rather than the exception, and terrifying if you didn't expect them.

In the early evenings some of us in the complex would sit outside to enjoy the camaraderie, and delight in the cacophony of jungle noises. We watched the sun as it disappeared below the tall palms, leaving a greenish-red glow in its wake. As dusk began to creep in and obscure our vision, the ever-present mosquito population, knowing their dinnertime—our blood—was near, came out in droves to fill their empty bellies as we frantically ran for the safety of our sterile indoor environment.

I kept telling myself to drink all these wonderful sights into my senses because it wouldn't last forever. I had no way of knowing then—blithely going about my leisurely life—it would come sooner rather than later.

PON: THAILAND'S SECRET JEWEL

19

few weeks before our house was ready, I'd put the word out that I needed a full-time maid. The company paid for a housekeeper, but only for a twelve-hour shift. Having a maid for eight hours would be heaven, but to have her live on-site was more important to me. I felt that it would give her a sense of belonging and I wanted her to feel at home.

The drivers hired by our company to chauffeur the husbands to work and drive the ladies around in the vans, were quite willing to offer their wives for work. One of the van drivers asked me if I'd found a maid yet. When I told him no, he quickly offered his wife. "She do goot wok foh you."

"Oh no, *khab khun kha*," I said. "I'm looking for a live-in maid. She needs to move in. I need her full-time. *Kao jai kha?*"

"Sokay, sokay. She do foh you. She stay foh long time, *mai pen lai*, she no come home."

Amazed, I protested, "But, you don't want her to be gone all night, do you?"

"Sokay. She wok foh you at night." I thought I caught a lecherous smirk; putting wifey to work so hubby can play. *Mai pen lai.*

Word did indeed move fast. A week after we moved into the house Pon appeared at my door. She had a friend with her who would act as interpreter. I was a little nervous about dealing with an interpreter. How would we communicate when she left? I asked Pon: "Do you speak *any* English?"

"No too mut."

Well, at least she understood my question. That was a plus.

Pon looked to be in her sixties, but then I wasn't a good judge of age. She was tall and solid, uncommon for most Thai women, and walked with a slight limp. Her hair was still dark, with a corona of grey around her face. The only way I could describe her face was "peaceful." She looked satisfied in her skin. I loved her smile.

They had arrived on Pon's motorcycle. Her interpreter quickly assured me that I was very lucky as Pon could do all my marketing without needing to hire a taxi, which I would be expected to pay for. *Another plus.* I invited them inside to sit, but Pon declined, bowing, as if to sit in my presence would be rude, so I interviewed her standing on the porch. I learned that Pon had worked for expats for over twenty years and understood more English than most maids. She was divorced and had one son who lived in another city. She was reserved, yet I caught a look of amusement in her eyes as I yapped away about her duties. I worried that I might have sounded like a crony. I certainly didn't want her to think I was too easy. I asked her if she'd mind living here with us.

"Foh how long I wok?"

"Oh, you'll only have to work eight hours. It's just that I'd like you to live here so you're here in the morning." She turned to her interpreter with a questioning look. I prattled on. "And sometimes when I have guests I'd like you to cook and work a little later in the evening. Of course I'd pay you for the extra hours."

Her interpreter relayed my instructions, at which point Pon turned to me with a broad smile. "I wok foh you now."

Pon was back within an hour, suitcase strapped to the back of her rickety motorcycle, bags of groceries crammed in a tiny basket attached to the handlebars, tidy housedress modestly held down by a quick flick of the hand, and worn-down sneakers, scrubbed and clean. It was obvious that she was ready to work.

She entered my life that day, as well as my heart.

Our new house came equipped with a maid's room, as do most Thai homes in Pattaya. Even the middle-income Thais have maids' living quarters built into their homes. Pon's room was a mere six by four feet with a pull down single cot attached to the wall. I couldn't fathom how anyone could live in such small quarters, but Thai friends assured me that it's what the maids expect, and feel lucky to be employed.

A pathetically small corner was set aside for a shower, which was tiled from floor to ceiling. It also included a hand-held shower hose that hung from a ceiling pipe over a small floor drain. Obviously the builder felt the maids needed no privacy as the shower area had no enclosure. The infamous eastern squat toilet was tucked away in another corner of the tiled floor. I envisioned my poor Pon using this debilitating contraption day after day and wondered at her agility. I had to concede that since she'd been squatting on her haunches since childhood, she was head and shoulders above me when it came to flexibility.

The going wage for a live-in maid in Pattaya in the 90s was 3,000 *baht* a month, roughly $160 U.S. For that amount a maid was expected to work six days a week from seven in the morning to seven in the evening, stopping only for meals. I was curious about Pon's age and her ability to work such a demanding schedule. After much coaxing she told me her age and I was appalled. She was sixty-nine years old! How could I ask her to work so many hours at that age? During my working years I'd whine and complain if I had to work on Saturdays. I was half her age at that time and I was paid overtime. I raised her salary to 4,000 *baht* a month and gave her the weekends off. She showed her appreciation—by working longer hours.

Pon was untiring in her quest to be a good employee and to show me how lucky I was to have her. After she'd finished all the housework to her liking, she'd mosey outside and look for work in the yard. She'd hose down the patio and water the flowers—even though we had gardeners for that. She'd wash the car when she ran out of work, which thoroughly ticked off our driver. That was his car, his domain, and no pushy maid was supposed to mess with his car. I heard him grousing whenever she'd step outside and pick up the hose. It didn't stop her. She reminded me of the Energizer Bunny. "Sit down and take a load off," I'd tell her when I saw her working nonstop.

"Take leg off? *Mai dii!*"

"No, 'load' not 'leg.' It means just relax for a few minutes. Sit for awhile, have some tea."

She looked relieved. "*Mai pen lai,* Madame," she'd say with a giggle. "No goot."

This was Pon's universal answer. She was being paid to work so why would I tell her to sit? She'd throw me that "crazy *farang*" look she reserved for people she thought weren't too bright. I hated sitting and relaxing while she worked around me. I felt like a slug. When I'd see her moving some heavy piece of furniture I'd offer to help her, but she'd just give me that "crazy *farang*" look again. Even with her limp, she got around on that gimpy leg faster than I ever moved. Pon was overloaded with energy and I'd get exhausted just watching her. She made me look like I was in slow-mo. Through heat, humidity and endless hours she was always looking for something to do. Only when I'd firmly say "Sit!" in my employer-ish voice, would she submissively sigh, plop down and look put-upon. I'd bring her a glass of iced tea, which she'd sip delicately. I could see she hated every slothful minute of it. She'd sit a few minutes, fidgeting all the while, then stand and look around for something to do, as if she were doing me a terrible disservice by taking up my time. *Why can't we have such work ethics stateside?*

Sometimes I'd catch Pon furtively peeking at an English-language TV station while she worked in the front room. I knew she was determined to learn more English so I encouraged her to watch television. I caught her mouthing words once and asked if she'd like to learn more English. "No can do, Madame, too many woods."

"Pon, if you really want to learn I'll try to help you—and you can teach me Thai." I did attempt to tutor her but with neither of us knowing the other's language we ended up giggling throughout most of the lessons.

After a few months, Pon began to take charge and I let her go at it. What she did to my messy closet amazed me. She put my clothes in such perfect order that they looked like the clothing displays I'd seen in Bangkok stores. All items were ironed and separated by color and neatly hung—shorts, blouses, slacks and dresses. When she first began doing my laundry she'd put the folded clean clothes on top of my dresser. I wasn't sure why she didn't just put them in the drawers where they belonged, but I figured she had her reasons. Maybe it was a privacy thing. She'd fold them and lay them on top of my dresser where they stayed until I put them away. Then one day I guess it became too much for her—or she had nothing else to do—so she tidied my dresser drawers to look like department store displays. I opened my sock drawer and thought I was in the wrong house. It was usually in chaos with mismatched socks clinging together for dear life. I had to assume that Pon was disgusted with my cluttered drawers and decided to put them in order. Each sock had the mate inside and she'd shaped and pressed the little darlings until they looked as though they were stuffed with cardboard inserts. Drawer after drawer presented pressed, neatly folded knit tops all in order of color, from dark to light. How could I live an orderly life without her? After dropping my soiled clothes into the hamper, never to see their dirty little bodies again, I had but to open the closet or a dresser drawer to choose from freshly washed, ironed and starched whatevers.

The linen closet was also a sight to behold. Everything was folded with sharp, snap-to corners, pressed and squared off. She even put a sweet-smelling dryer sheet between the linens and stacked them to within a hairbreadth of perfection. I suppose I was a bit spoiled, but hey, I gave her job security by being such a slob. I often thought about how fate had brought Pon here, waiting on me while I sat reading in my comfy chair. The only way I could handle this was to focus on reincarnation. What a wonderful thought; get this over with, come back, do it better, and move on up.

In the kitchen Pon ruled supreme. She'd allow me to fry an occasional egg or cook a pot of oatmeal, which were non-starters for Thai cooks and way beneath her, but the kitchen was her domain and she let me know it. Occasionally she'd allow me to help her prepare a meal when I gave a dinner party. Pon prided herself on her Thai cooking and rightly so. After cooking for a large dinner party, she'd stand in the hall listening to the oohhs and aahhs of my guests as they delighted in her delectable culinary offerings. "Pon?" I'd call. "Come on out here."

"No, Madame, I jut see you wan anysing."

"Come in here for a minute, will you? We were just talking about the fantastic meal you prepared for us."

At this point my guests would chime in, praising her cooking and her incredible choice of spices. I could imagine her smiling and glowing in the hall. She'd then make her entrance, presumably to remove dirty dishes, enjoying the compliments and trying to look embarrassed by all the fuss.

"When are you going to teach me how to cook Thai food?" I asked her one day as she fussed about in the kitchen.

"No can do, Madame."

"Really. I want to learn. Can't you teach me?"

Pon's English was now much better than my Thai. I felt she understood quite a bit more than she let on. "Okay, I do foh you, *mai pen lai."*

When I wanted to cook something special for my dinner guests, I'd hop on Pon's motorcycle with her. She drove very cautiously for a Thai, but I had the distinct feeling it was because she didn't want to kill the boss that laid the golden egg, so to speak.

"I buy food, you cook."

"Great. No Thai chili though, I don't do Thai chili." In fact I didn't do any kind of chili. It burned my mouth, tongue and esophagus, and my intestines screamed loud and clear that they were in accord with my mouth.

"Mut do Thai chili foh goot Thai food."

We had a minor battle over this one but she eventually caved. Oftentimes I'd have to push my weight around so she'd let me do more cooking. I'd stand around with a hang-dog look until she'd finally agree to teach me the art of Thai cooking, but only once a week. I figured that was about all she could handle with a *farang* in her kitchen. She was a good teacher, patient most of the time, except when I'd do a stir fry and not stir as much as she'd like me to. At that point she'd grab the spatula out of my hand and do it the "Thai" way.

I also took a five-day course in Thai cooking at a nearby restaurant and tried several of their famous dishes: cashew chicken, pork fried rice and Thai noodle soup. But I had to admit, Pon's always tasted more Thai-ish, even though we used the same ingredients. When she did allow me in the kitchen, she was right at my heels letting me know she knew the "Thai way" to do it better. I knew she was right but I did have to show her who was boss, didn't I?

In her own quiet way, Pon let me know who it really was.

NEW HOME HAZARDS

20

Because our house was newly built, we inherited all the problems that come with new buildings in Thailand: leaky plumbing, stubborn water pump, sluggish electrical system and leaking gas pipes. New house problems in Thailand were handled a shade differently in the 90s than most expats were prepared for. Our water pump balked at pumping all night and as a matter of course we were out of water at least four days out of seven. No shower? Run to the nearest hotel pool shower. No flushing toilets? Keep pots of water handy to do-it-yourself flush. No running water for dishes? Eat out.

One morning I noticed water pooling around Pon's flip-flops as she stood washing the dishes. We looked under the sink, and as expected, saw the broken water pipe. Most workmanship at that time was done with the S&P technique—spit and promise. I also noticed some suspicious looking pink stuff clinging to the pipes under the sink and had to assume that what I'd heard about plumbers using Silly Putty to seal a break might be true. It's really not such a bad idea if you think about it. Have you ever noticed how hard that stuff gets when the kids leave it on your favorite sofa for a couple hours? Truth is I was surprised my pipes hadn't burst before this, as we'd already been in our house for three weeks. At last count, out of ten homes in our complex, seven had already burst their pipes.

I called for the maintenance man, accomplished by standing on the upstairs balcony, yelling and waving my arms at the guard posted in the six-foot tower. This was the guard's signal to yell at the guys loitering nearby, aka the maintenance men, who were hired by the builder to hang about the perimeter of the housing tract waiting to "fic somsing for Madame."

Into my kitchen walked a little moth of a man, rusty pipe wrench dangling precariously from a ragged back pocket, *waiing* and grinning, a soggy cigarette stub hanging from his drooping lower lip. Our helper's trade was that of plumber, and he went straight to the task at hand. He squatted down and looked under the sink for a couple of minutes, then stood up, gave me a gummy smile and walked out the back door. He was gone for two hours—siesta time I assumed—and returned with some sort of black, gooey stuff oozing from a small can, which he proceeded to pour on my highly polished marble kitchen floor.

Now, maids tend to take on the family they work for as *their* family and the house as *their* house. Pon was no exception. This was her floor and she was mad as hell and let him know it by yapping at his heels. Ignoring her lecture, our little plumber set to work, squatting on his haunches as he surveyed his kingdom of pipes and hoses under the sink. I was amazed he could squat like that and then stand up straight again. I do believe Asians could go through life without ever requiring a chair. They seemed to need only a two by two area in which to squat. Our plumber then disappeared into the little crawl space and occasionally stuck out an emaciated arm to grab dollops of the goop from the floor and transfer it to the errant pipes. All this he did in a space only large enough to hold a mishmash of pipes, a bar of soap and a bottle of bleach. While he did his Harry Houdini act, Pon continued to fume and fuss at him through the drain above his head, about the gooey mess he had left on her floor—while he fussed back at her from inside the pipes.

Fifteen minutes later he finished his work and began gathering his tools to leave. Much to my horror he produced a bottle from his tool box and proceeded to pour forth a stream of smelly green frothy stuff— some sort of acid I later realized—onto my highly polished marble floor to remove the gooey stuff he'd plopped there. I gasped. Pon gasped. He smiled a toothless smile as he looked up at us to see why we were gasping. Realizing he had poured out too much of the frothy stuff, he reached around and yanked one of my decorator towels from my cutesy little decorator towel rack and began wiping up the sticky black stuff, as well as the green disgusting frothy stuff, along with the long stem of ashes that had fallen from his cigarette into the oozing sticky mess that was now smoking and sizzling on my beautiful marble floor. When he'd finished his half-assed clean-up job, he dropped the towel in a corner, smiled at me, said "Finit Madame," *waiied* and backed out my kitchen door.

As I saw the hole eating its way through the marble floor *and* my decorator towel, I recalled something my late husband liked to quote: "As they say in the trades, a plumber needs to know only two things, shit runs downhill and payday's every Friday."

A week later Pon stood at the sink with water swishing around her flip-flops. I gave her 100 *baht* for the plumber, hid my decorator towels and left for the day.

The complex was plopped down right in the middle of a jungle. Our Thai neighbors on the perimeter of our block-wall lived in tin-roofed shacks. Discarded appliances, like decrepit bodies, were scattered throughout their yards, and all were normally window-deep in weeds. I wondered if the word "lawnmower" was even in the Thai vocabulary. I don't remember seeing one while I lived in the country.

Getting rid of unwanted grass was quite a spectacle. Most Thais were quite cavalier about high grass and weeds. If they got too high for their liking along the street, highway, or the front of their home, they had a solution: torch the weeds and get on with life. Living next to these fire-starters, even though we were behind a six foot block-wall, caused me much anxiety. Fire having no prejudice was just as apt to burn our house as theirs.

On windy days Pon and I were on constant alert, fearful that the wind would send embers flying onto their roofs as well as ours. Our houses were brick and plaster, with clay tile roofs, but the fear was still there. Our Thai neighbors' houses seemed to be built of tin and straw, and looked as if they might explode if set on fire. Pon and I watched in horror on "lawn-mowing" days as the palm trees exploded and sent flaming fronds skyward. Terrified by this sight, Pon would stand on our balcony crying and waving her arms. *"Mai dii, mai dii!"* she'd scream at our Thai neighbors as the wind carried the embers floating on humid air drafts—right toward our house.

During one such windy fire day, Pon put her life in the hands of Buddha as she tore down the stairs yelling something I couldn't understand. Flying by me she grabbed my arm and dragged me along with her. She ran outside where Dick's driving net sat helplessly in harm's way and began pulling it to the back of the house, imploring my help. By the time we safely removed the net and returned to the front patio we found that some of the embers had landed on top of the lawn furniture. Pon began hollering to our guards to get someone to put out the fire. There was a scramble of activity outside the gate as people seemed to be running in circles. Then I watched open-mouthed as five men ran into our yard carrying buckets, which they began filling from the swimming pool, handing them off to one-another, from the pool to the patio, until the lawn furniture sat smoking, melting and sizzling.

The bucket brigade had saved the day.

RULES, RULES AND MORE RULES

21

We had no more visits from *The Bosses* after the hotel visit. On the jobsite *Mr. JB* seemed pleasant enough. The rumors I'd heard about them would occasionally flit around my consciousness, like a moth's repeated passes at a lamp, but I mentally swatted them away as being pesky and unbelievable. I regretted that I'd ever heard them. I felt that they might have prejudiced my thinking; however, I still couldn't seem to shake them entirely.

The Bosses were now a constant presence on the periphery of our lives after the move into our new house. While we lived in the hotel, we were at least separated by a few safe miles. In our new home, however, their house sat only a hundred or so yards from ours. We put our uneasy feelings to rest by going out every night, checking out the touristy sites in our new surroundings, and finding interesting places to eat and meet with friends.

Mrs. A, as quickly as possible, sent bulletins home with our husbands, listing her *rules* for the wives. The schedule included what days and times the vans would take us to Best Supermarket, the Royal Garden Plaza complex, Foodland, or wherever she might want us to go, as well as when the vans would pick us up from shopping and bring us home. We'd also get notes about the time and date of her weekly meetings—which she declared essential. I had attended a couple of those meetings and found them to be profoundly nonessential; more drivel than importance, and mainly about her rules. Dick taped the flyers to the refrigerator and I recoiled every time I looked at them. Yes, I would like a ride to town to do my shopping, but at my convenience, not hers. Most of the wives I talked to felt the same way. At first we were happy there was a way into town every now and then, but it wasn't always convenient for everyone to go at her specified times. Some of us got together and shared rides, other times women I'd met from other companies would offer me lifts to town. I had no idea this would cause a problem, but soon learned that I was not to deviate from *Mrs. A's* schedule.

Gossip was something that fluttered in the air like sheets on a clothesline and could not be avoided whenever a group of expat wives got together. The rumor mill was always churning. The latest talk was that after *Mr. JB's* driver—we dubbed him *Mr. Spy*—dropped him at the jobsite, he was immediately dispatched to cruise around town looking for any rules being broken by the wives. Several of the wives had seen him parked around town, just sitting in his car. We all thought it odd that he was in town and not on the jobsite. Now we knew.

Another scary rumor was unveiled—and this time I listened intently. It seemed that *Mrs. A* now had her female spies in place, I'll call them *Frick and Frack* (names changed again to protect the guilty). The story was that these two were given houses strategically placed in the circle of our complex, allowing a full view of what was going on in our homes. When I heard this I had a sinking feeling remembering a visit I'd had from them. These two emissaries of *Mrs. A* had paid me a visit two days after we'd moved into our new house.

Frick: "Well, hi y'all. We thought we'd come by and see if there's anything we could do for you, being as you just moved in and all."

Frack: "And we know what a mess moving can be. Anything we can do to help?"

Me: "Oh! Glad to meet you. Come in."

They followed me into the living room making clucking sounds as they admired my teak knick-knacks.

Frick: "Our husbands have been with the company on overseas assignments for years, so if there's anything y'all need to know about this sort of thing, just ask us. That's what we're here for."

Frack: "Oh, for sure. We go way back with the company."

Me: "That's good, because I do have some questions." I led them to the kitchen where I poured glasses of iced tea for us. They fussed over all my Thai trinkets on the walls and counters, sounding as though we were old pals who'd shared a long friendship.

Frick: Well, now, do you have any questions we can answer for you?" They sipped their tea as they looked at me expectantly.

I put Pon's freshly baked Thai delicacies on the table in front of them. They politely declined, as if wanting to get right down to the business at hand. I dove right in making contented noises that I knew Pon expected. After I'd polished off three of them, and noticed Pon's look of approval, I took my time wiping my mouth.

Me: "Yes, I do have some concerns."

F&F: "Oh?" Four eyebrows shot skyward.

Me: "About her constant rules."

F&F: "Oh?" Four eyes oozing compassion.

Me: "The biggest concern is that I don't get what's going on here. I've been on overseas assignments before but honestly, I don't ever remember having any kind of rules that the wives had to follow. And I certainly don't remember the boss's wife having anything to do with the women, other than an occasional dinner party she'd host for the supers and their wives. Maybe you can tell me why it's so important that we don't do anything on our own and why we have to attend those meetings once a week?"

They looked at each other as if waiting for the other to begin. The silence was deafening.

Frick: "Oh. Okay, I'll start. Not to worry. This sort of thing is done all the time on these kinds of jobs. Just follow orders and you'll get along fine."

Me: "Orders?"

Frick: "Well, I mean...rules. I mean do you have a problem with some of her rules?"

Me: "Yeah. We're all adults here. Why she has to have us at compulsory meetings every week is beyond me. And why she sends home more rules with the husbands, I just don't get. Call me crazy, but it seems to me she has a real control issue going on. I've never had any wives rules sent home from other jobsites."

Frack: "Oh. Those meetings won't go on forever, but it is important that you attend so you know what's going on and all, you know, like the time schedules for the shopping vans and such."

Me: "Why? Why can't I just go when and where I want? If I feel like taking her van, then fine. But if I feel like meeting someone for lunch, or do some shopping, why can't I? It really feels like she doesn't want us to stray from her pack. Some of us would like to do things on our own, go where we want, you know? With her flyers, we're forced to plan our day by her schedule, not ours. I just don't get it."

Frick: "Well, gee, you do have a point."

Me: "Good. That makes one more who thinks she's a control freak."

Those words echoed in my ears throughout that day. When Dick got home I told him about their visit, and how I'd vented and how they'd agreed with me.

"Christ, Dodie. Don't you know when you're being set up?"

"Set up?"

"Sure. They probably were sent here by the old lady to get some shit from you and you sure didn't disappoint 'em."

"Oh, give me a ..."

"I know what I'm sayin'. Some of the guys on the jobsite were even talkin' about this today. Their wives also had visits from *Frick and Frack.*"

"Oh! And I thought they were so nice.*" So much for female intuition!*

It wasn't long before *Mrs. A* appeared at my door offering her brilliant talents for decorating. She told me where I should go to choose my furnishings, as well as the fabric for my drapes and sofas, and whatever else I did or did not need. "Don't forget dahlin, the company's givin' you a furniture allowance so they want to know how you spend their money."

This was too much like *The Stepford Wives* for me. I checked with the other newbies and found that she'd visited their homes as well with the same directives. How had they taken it? They groveled. Well fine, let them, but I wasn't about to. We'd all been to her lavish home for her "compulsory" meetings and were well aware of the luxurious furnishings she surrounded herself with. Even though the company paid for them, some of us felt that we'd like our own style, thank you very much, and would like to pick and choose for ourselves. These women talked a big tale to me, but when it came time to do their own thinking, they backed down. I was obviously going to be an early entry into *Mrs. A's* black book of Disobedient Wives.

Rules, rules and more rules came floating home, all of them ridiculous. I did try to fit into the meetings. I listened intently like a good girl; I nodded where appropriate and frowned in all the right places, but I watched her with a therapist's eye. I counted dozens of her rules as being nothing more than her needing control. But why? Why did we all need to go shopping on the same day? Why not carpool with each other when we did need to go? Why was she trying to keep us from spreading our wings and doing our own thing? If some of the ladies wanted to take the van, then fine. But why all of us?

I happen to be an organizer by birth. It's my Virgo persona—I have no control over it. I see a possibility, run with it, and try to find an expedient way to go about doing it. I soon learned that an organized woman was *verboten* in *Mrs. A's* group. Any suggestion I'd come up with during our meetings was poo-poohed by her as "Not appropriate, dahlin."

The wives had moaned and bitched so much about the van pool's schedule that I thought it should be put to a vote. I innocently suggested a solution at the next weekly meeting, thinking it might save some grumbling. I raised my hand like a good little controllee. "I was just thinking that maybe we should have an idea box and a complaint box at these meetings. It might be good to kind of get a feel for what works and what doesn't, you know?" I looked around the room at the very ladies who'd agreed with this idea, but suddenly their gaze seemed riveted to their laps. Not one of them seconded it. "Well?" I asked, as I stared expectantly at each one. Silence. The turncoats! They had whined about wanting those boxes, knowing I'd take it upon myself to try to get them, and now they were deaf, dumb and blind.

Most of these gals were new to the expat life, on their first tour, and were still wet behind the ears. Many were a couple decades younger than I, with names such as Debbie and Tammy and Kimmie. They hadn't been around the expat block, so to speak. I'd felt a responsibility to help them, like a surrogate mother. But not anymore.

"What's the problem?" I asked the group. "We all have ideas or complaints, don't we?"

Silence.

Squirming.

"Is that so?" came a voice I would swear was Cruella DeVille's. "They ah no complaints allowed heah, my deahs."

I gave the evil eye to all the gals who'd gone deaf and mute. Ten pairs of eyes were glued to the hand-made silk Persian carpet as if they were searching for lost contact lenses. *Mrs. A* quickly changed the subject. With a benign smile she told us she was going to start organizing some card parties for us at her home: Bridge, Canasta, and Hearts. There would even be some golf days. She would put out a schedule the following week. We were all surprised by this last proclamation, as if we couldn't plan these on our own. Some of us had already started getting together at each other's homes a couple times a week for cards and meeting at the golf course. Now she was telling us we should "all be together" at her house for these games. She even wanted to control our entertainment.

Jenny, a thirty-something innocent newbie asked if we could use our husbands' cars to go shopping—after, of course they were dropped off at work. That way, she offered, the ladies were free to run their own errands when it might be more convenient for them.

"What?" croaked *Mrs. A.* "Do you mean *drive* the cah yoah-self?"

"Ah, well…" Jenny looked around the room for some affirmation, but found none. She turned to look at me and I mentally flipped her bird. *Don't look at me, sister, after the way you people dropped your heads on my suggestion.* She swallowed hard, then continued. "…I've seen expat ladies from other companies driving around town alone, and just wondered if we could too."

"Heavens no!" *Mrs. A* bellowed in her best Tallulah Bankhead impersonation, a voice that struck fear into the women's hearts. "That is strictly against owh insurance rules."

The room was silent as the ladies digested this last bit of painful news. Another brave soul raised her hand. "Ah, well, can we then use our husbands' drivers for our errands?"

"What foah?" *Mrs. A* croaked, tired of this whole Q & A thing. "Ah have arranged company vans to make rounds to yoah houses for shopping and ah have sent those schedules home with yoah husbands. Don't you read them?"

Silence again—back to searching the carpet. *So much for freedom.* We all got the message. *Mrs. A* wanted to control every aspect of our lives—from decorating to shopping to entertainment. Later that week we found she also wanted to control the children's activities. She began patrolling the pool deck when the children were swimming. At the next meeting we had to listen to new rules on when the children could use the pool and what they could and could not do while in it. "The screamin' an hollerin' must stop," she declared, "along with the runnin' and hoase play."

My God, can you imagine? What kind of children would do such things?

When her rules weren't adhered to, as reported to her by *Frick and Frack,* always on watch, she would march outside, stiletto heels scraping against cement, and pull up a lawn chair next to the edge of the pool. There she'd sit, glowering at the children until they were called out by their apprehensive mothers. If that didn't intimidate anyone, then they were goners.

THE SILENT GOLF PARTNER

22

When Dick signed on for the Thailand project, *Mr. JB* instructed him to "keep quiet" about his background as a golf instructor. Dick felt uneasy about this request and wondered what it was all about. Later it became quite clear. It would be difficult for *Mr. JB* to explain why Dick was always his partner in golf tournaments.

For *Mr. JB*, having a man on his project with Dick's construction background *and* golfing expertise, was providential. Now it seemed obvious to us why he'd offered Dick every carrot in the garden to take this job. He needed him. And, *Mr. JB*—not one to overlook details— saw himself becoming a very low handicapper with his own private golf instructor sitting next to him in the cart.

Mrs. A planned the golf outings for the ladies, and put together a few competitive games, but nothing was taken too seriously. However, when the couples' tournaments were put together, *Mr. JB* took care of the pairings—with Dick as his partner. Dick soon realized that *Mr. JB's* sole intent was to be first, even if he had to cheat to make that happen; like dropping a new ball when his ball flew out of bounds, or indiscreetly kicking his ball out of the rough for a better lie. And, wonder of wonders, *Mr. JB* always seemed to take first place, with the little wifey taking second place. *Greater love hath no man.*

I had this brought home to me at one of our company tournaments.

Friends from the States, Les and Patty, had come for a visit and were invited to join in. For some reason, maybe because Les was Dick's guest, *Mr. JB* put him in their foursome. His wife, Patty, was assigned to *Mrs. A's* foursome. I was in another foursome and the cart with *Mr.-Second-in-Command* (name changed to protect the innocent). Our foursome had played exceptionally well and we were very smug as we completed the 17th hole, sure that we'd be close to first place with our great game. On the 18th tee, waiting for his boss, stood *Mr. JB's* driver. We shared with him our enthusiasm on our scores, to which he replied: "No good Suh. My boss he no lose."

"What do you mean?" my partner asked. "We saw him duff and go out of bounds. We know his score is higher than ours."

To which he replied: "Sokay, sokay. He haf me pick up his tofey for him.*"*

And, sure enough, *The Bosses* took first and second that day. *So much for honest, organized fun.* My friend, Les was amazed. As we drove back to our house, he said: "Does the old man always cheat like that?"

Money was not the issue here. *Mr. JB* had more money than he could ever spend, but losing face on the golf course was out of the question. The rich Thai golfers were notorious for heavy gambling and *Mr. JB* saw it as his duty to relieve them of some of that wealth. I wonder to this day if they ever knew he had his own private PGA teaching pro sitting next to him in the golf cart.

Dick fretted over this constant cheating. He complained to *Mr. JB* about it several times and was told "Take care of your own score card. I'll take care of mine."

On one of *Mrs. A's* "scheduled" ladies golf outings, I ran into the pro shop to pick up a sleeve of balls. I waited in line behind some friendly women and we began to gab. The first question most expats ask on meeting new expats is, "What company are you with?" These ladies, all from various companies, belonged to the Pattaya International Ladies Club (PILC), which was open to all wives of expats, as well as any women living in Pattaya. When they heard what company my husband worked for, a look of pity crossed their collective faces.

"What?"

"Bloody 'ell," said one of the Liverpool ladies. "Ow owful! Do they know you're in here chatting us oop?"

"Oh, come on," I ventured. "It's not that bad. Is it?" I could feel my large intestine readying for its usual spastic attack on hearing bad news.

One of the long-timers, a lady from Chile, chimed in, "Jou is heestory now, Amiga! We loose two esweet ladies from your company. They doan come back after the Madonna cut out de tongues and esent them packing."

They all hooted and high-fived each other.

"Eees eso! Jou axe eeenyone. Jou not be here long, gringa, if she esee jou yawing wit us."

They had a good laugh at that one, too. I attempted to laugh but it caught in my throat. Deep in my gut I knew she was right. They said they'd heard about our company's female boss. It's pretty hard to keep secrets in the expat community, especially from women. For it to have gotten to other companies I realized that it was more fact than rumor. These women told me they were all completely free to do their own thing. They could drive their husbands' cars or use their drivers for errands. They went to the PILC meetings once a week because they *wanted* to. The meetings weren't about how the club would keep them entertained, but rather what the women could do to help the community. The social calendar was just the frosting on the cake, filled with all sorts of entertainment. How I envied their freedom. I told them that my husband's company was a bit more totalitarian. We couldn't use our husbands' car during the day because we weren't insured to drive it and we certainly were *never* told about women who could.

They all laughed. "Think about it, girl," one of the ladies spoke up. "Most insurance companies insure whoever drives the car, as long as they're old enough and live in the same household."

"Oh!" I did think the insurance rule a bit strange when I heard *Mrs. A's* version, especially since I'd seen other expat wives tooling around town in cars during the day. These free women inspired me to get out of the herd mentality that *Mrs. A* demanded. We quickly exchanged phone numbers and I hurried out a side door of the clubhouse. I was now determined to live my own life in this country.

I began to join their ladies for tennis and golf once a week. The PILC ladies were women from all over the world. I learned something about their individual cultures and loved listening to stories about their homelands. They invited me to the PILC meetings as their guest, which was one of the most gratifying experiences I had while in Thailand. They had so much going on they had to give me a calendar of the club's activities so I wouldn't miss out on anything. Wow, there definitely was life outside our fortress. I wasn't a company employee, right? I could come and go as I pleased, right? I fought this inner turmoil on a daily basis.

I made a few "inquiring-mind" phone calls the next day. I took it upon myself, the born-again detective, to investigate the insurance phenomenon. I phoned the jobsite office and asked for the name of the insurance company. I said I'd like to keep it handy by the phone—just in case. I couldn't believe it when the clerk gave me the number. I sincerely hoped she wouldn't lose her job over it, but all's fair in love and detective work.

Well shut my mouth and call me Dick Tracy! The insurance did cover us; in fact it covered *anyone* from the same family who drove said vehicle. It was just another control issue thing. *The Bosses* were using the old mushroom trick on us—keep 'em in the dark and cover 'em with shit.

After one enjoyable day spent with some of the PILC ladies on the golf course, I came home glowing with excitement. "This could be so great," I exclaimed to Dick, "I've got to tell our ladies about this club."

Dick had some misgivings about me attending those meetings and getting in thick with women from other companies. "I don't know," he said gravely. "Are you sure you're doin' the right thing? You know, I've still not heard anything from the old man about your son, Dale, coming over. Do you want to piss her off to the point where she tells him to forget it?"

"Oh, come on! Don't tell me you're going along with her control crap? How can she control what happens on the jobsite?"

"Don't ever underestimate her. You've seen everyone cow-tow to her, even the old man. You hangin' with those other ladies might put her over the edge, for us and Dale. I don't go along with her bullshit but I just think you'd better watch your butt. She wants everyone to attend her damn meetin's and activities, and if you're not there you'll be on her shit list. Besides," he added, "if she bitches enough to the old man, it could jeopardize *my* job."

"Oh right! How can your job have anything to do with what I do? I can still go to her meetings. They're on a different day than the PILC's. And," I added knowingly, "you can't be fired because of me. How would that hold up with the Labor Board?"

"Labor Board?" he spit out. "Are you nuts? We're in a foreign country. They can do any damn thing they want. You know she wields a lot of control over the old man, that's a damn fact."

"Okay, but listen. I think I've got it all figured out," my organizer-self said. "How about I bring it up at the next meeting? I'll tell *Mrs. A* that it might be fun to get together with women from other companies, even have a few golf and tennis tournaments with them, you know, like our-company-against-theirs type of thing."

Dick frowned. "I don't know, but whatever you do let her think it's her idea or she won't go for it."

I truly felt that our ladies would benefit from meeting some of the other women and learning something about other countries. So far the wives might as well have been in Bumpook, Egypt for all they ever saw or heard about Thailand, or other countries. The PILC's gatherings were motivating and informative about the country that hosted us and offered useful information that every tourist or expat should and would want to know. I enjoyed them immensely. Every week they had a different speaker and the topic was always about Thailand and its social problems, and what we could do to help. Also, they had speakers from various charities that the PILC helped with in fund-raising. In contrast, *Mrs. A's* meetings were geared around her rules we had to obey.

I truly believed our ladies might enjoy volunteering for some of the PILC's charities, as help was always needed in the hospitals and in fund-raising. But I also thought it might give them a feeling of giving something back to the country they were occupying. There was no talk about Thailand or helping anyone at *Mrs. A's* meetings; they were totally ego-based.

The PILC also had a travel club. I thought it might be exciting for some of our families to join and have a guided trip outside of Pattaya— places they might have heard about but hadn't had a chance to visit because of the restrictions heaped on us by *Mrs. A.* I could already hear the ladies applauding my innovative ideas.

But, before I had a chance to talk to her about it, we took a little trip.

THE WAYWARD HONEYMOON

23

Our bedtime problems were status quo. Dick still had a problem with the three-night-a-week sex routine the therapist had advised. I could see him fighting the urge to control himself as he got into bed. But his childish sullenness gave him away. He just couldn't seem to shake it. I suggested we call the therapist to see if she had some other trick up her sleeve that might relieve both of us. I wanted to blame it on the pressure from the control freaks running our lives and worries at work, but I knew it went deeper than that.

A friend gave me a brochure about a great little hideaway a few miles up the coast, and I thought it might just be what he needed to bring an end to the funk he'd wrapped himself in. Maybe a quick getaway from the gossip and control might soothe our frayed relationship. And so we left Pattaya. I craved some much-needed privacy. *The Bosses* had left town and we were free as birds.

Sunset Beach was the name on the brochure and it certainly was all it claimed to be. The rooms were called "Honeymoon Bungalows" and rented for 2,400 *baht* ($100 US) for the weekend. Hours from the noisy city and hidden from the road by long, lazy paths, we found a strip of sand and ocean with unrivaled beauty. The water was an iridescent bluish green with astonishing color movement as the tides changed. The shores were pristine with sand so white you needed sunglasses to shield your eyes from the glare. If you've seen the beautiful, unspoiled outer islands of Tahiti or the Caribbean, then you can visualize this beach. It was spectacular. Dick felt very satisfied with himself as he carried me over the threshold and whispered in my ear, "Who else do you know who's honeymooned in Thailand?"

The quaint little thatched bungalow sat a few feet from the water's edge and resembled the hut in the movie, *South Pacific*. The windows had no glass, just four framed openings on either side of the room. Wide-slatted bamboo shutters gave a sense of privacy without a closed-in feeling. The bungalow was suspended on four wooden pilings, just high enough to thwart a high tide and rough seas, or possibly a Peeping Tom. It smelled of sea, salt, sand and coconut oil. I loved it. A mini refrigerator sat on the kitchen counter, along with a bottle of wine, a microwave, and a four-cup coffee pot with paper cups. What else could honeymooners want? In the rear of the cottage was a small room just large enough to squeeze in a double bed with the infamous concrete Thai mattress.

Lying in bed at night I felt one with nature. Small slits in the thatched roof allowed the moonlight to filter through, spreading Rorschach shadows along the walls. The primordial smells of fish, seaweed and the eternally deep ocean filled the air. I was lulled to sleep with the surf crashing on the shoreline just a few feet from our bed, with palm fronds swaying listlessly while the trade winds hummed a mystical rhythm. I had a complete sense of relaxation.

Our bathroom contained a small shower, western toilet and sink. Tacked onto the outside rear of the bungalow was a small shower enclosure without a roof. What a way to bathe. It was exhilarating. The soft caressing light of the moon reflected off the palm trees and allowed just a promise of light into our enclosure—always preferred by women my age. The stars, never so brilliant, made it seem as though I was showering in the stratosphere. I preferred this outdoor shower to the one inside; it was much larger, much cooler and I felt decadent. Dick dragged me out there every night—such a romantic.

Down a rambling path from our bungalow, parallel to the shore, was a surprisingly intimate restaurant with sumptuous Thai and Chinese food. Headlining every night was a three-piece band playing our favorites: *Countee Loads* by John Denver, and Stevie Wonder's classic: *I Jut Cawed t'sa I Love You.* We ate, danced, swam and overall enjoyed ourselves.

By day, tropical cumulus clouds topped with crowns of red, purple and gold sailed sleepily by. Looking out at the great expanse of the ocean, I thought nothing seemed as peaceful to me or quite as awesome and soothing as watching the swell and decline of the tides. By night the moon glistened on the phosphorus waves, illuminating the world as I breathed in the earthy smells. No lamp was needed to walk the many tree-lined paths. I felt insignificant against such an immense presence. Its scope and depth seemed unfathomable. Maybe it's the amount of salt in our veins that calls to us. Didn't we all crawl out of this vast ocean? With seventy-one percent of our planet covered with water, looking at the ocean makes one realize how small our lives are in the minuscule area we occupy on this planet.

The weekend turned out to be a three-day special. Instead of sex every other night it was three days in a row. I was optimistic that we might somehow find a middle ground to meet, but was afraid to hope for too much. Because we didn't want to spoil the weekend, we left our bedtime problems behind in Pattaya. Maybe things would seem better after a stress-free weekend.

Hating to leave but refreshed by our short get-away, we reluctantly said goodbye to our little honeymoon bungalow and set off for our return to Pattaya. On the drive back Dick said that he'd really put things into perspective over the weekend and wanted to get our relationship back on track. I wanted to believe him, but as he'd just had three days of sex in a row, that might have had something to do with his profound statement. I chose to wait and watch. Not once during our weekend did we think or talk about *The Bosses*. We were not going to let them ruin a good time.

As we pulled into our complex we saw the note taped to our door, silently fluttering in the breeze. We stood dead still as we read the message: we were to come at once to *The Bosses'* house. We walked to their house with apprehension. The maid opened the door and we solemnly followed her to where *Mrs. I-Am-A-Direct-Descendent-Of-Moses* would receive us and lay down her commandments. No one offered us a chair as we entered the parlor so I assumed this would be a short meeting.

From where we stood we could see *Mr. JB* eating at the dining room table. He gave no indication that we were there—or that he cared. *Mrs. Moses* appeared in the hallway, dressed in a flowing blue silk robe with matching high-heeled ostrich-feathered slippers. The look on her face smacked of disgust, with an "I'm at the end of my rope" expression on her face—one I'd used many times on my kids when they'd disobeyed me.

"Well, did you two enjoy yoah trip?" she purred, with just a hint of a smile now curving her taut lips.

"Yeah, thanks," Dick innocently replied. "How'd you know we went out of town?"

"We have owah ways, my deah. Don't evah think you can get away with anna-thing when yoah workin' foh us."

"Huh?" We said in unison. I was shocked by the venom dripping from her lips—molten lava from *Mrs. Vesuvius*. "Get away with?" Dick croaked. "We just went for a weekend trip, a belated honeymoon. The one we didn't get before the job started, and…"

"You broke one of owah commandments, my deahs," she interrupted. "You took a company cah without askin' owah pah-mission." She smiled, knowing she'd found our fingerprints at the scene of the crime.

"Excuse me," I interrupted, with just a trace of subservience. "We did get permission."

She ignored me as if I were a dust mote floating by, never taking her eyes off Dick. "You obviously don't remembah owah wahnin'…ah…owah rules." She smiled again. "No one is allowed to use the company cah out of town without…," she paused, obviously enjoying our helpless looks, "…owah *personal* pah-mission."

"Wait," Dick said, regrouping after the shock of this attack. "It was a spur of the moment thing. We called your house first and the maid said you wouldn't be home until Sunday night."

Silence as she fixed us with a steely eye.

Dick forged on: "We thought the protocol was to ask *Mr.-Second-In-Command* if you weren't around, so we did and he said fine. Wasn't that what we were supposed to do?"

Dick looked toward his boss, *Mr. Don't-Look-At-Me for Help,* who sat staring into his plate as if it might contain the formula for unraveling the mysteries of DNA.

"Well, now you know!" she growled, completely ignoring Dick's question. A few seconds of well-placed glaring at both of us brought us back to the problem at hand. "You will get pah-mission *only* from us."

My chest tightened when I thought about the trip that a few of us gals had taken to Bangkok a week earlier, along with one of her precious vans and driver, after first getting permission from *Mr. Second-In-Command.* God! I waited for her to pounce on me about that. I decided not to bring it up, but was also a little surprised that she hadn't heard about it yet from her spies. I wondered when the shit would hit the fan on that one, and we'd have to sit through another of her sermons on the mount. She dismissed us with a wave of her well-manicured fingers and left the room, her stiletto heels clicking a cadence on her imported Italian floor tiles. The maid held the door for us and we took that as an invitation to leave.

We walked home in shocked silence. I felt like my guts were being lipo-sucked out of me. She was now *looking* for ways to put us down, keeping track of our indiscretions, our wanderings. Our willfulness! What if she talked the old man into sending us home? We would be in a financial abyss. Everything I owned was in company storage. I'd leased out my condo for twenty-four months and given my car to my sister, with visions of a new Cadillac dancing in my head, and ca-ching, ca-ching ringing in my ears. Something else hit me as I thought of the ramifications of her wrath; my son might also lose out on this job.

But, hey, wait a minute. She can't do that. Can she? Dick was doing a good job at work, or so he told me, and he said that the client "loved" him. There was no one on the job site who could replace him. We were just being paranoid. We vowed we wouldn't use the car or driver again, leaving her one less broken commandment with which to confront us.

We discussed it late into the night: Who did she think she was? How could she tell us where we could and couldn't go? I guess she knew who she was but she didn't know who I was, and I wasn't going to let her run my life.

Dick wasn't quite behind me on this. His final succinct words that night were: "Let's don't fuck up anymore!"

MAIDS AND HIRED DRIVERS

24

Thai maids often assume that their employers are swimming in money, so I was told, and I suppose that's a good assumption when you compare the two incomes. The stories floating around were endless and amusing when it came to this subject, and one happened to come from a close friend. She had hired a very young, inexperienced maid. After a few months of employment the young maid asked Madame if she could borrow one million *baht*.

Madame gasped, "What? Certainly not! I don't have that kind of money. Why on earth do you need that much?"

"Need home," said the wistful maid.

"Why would you need one million *baht* for a home?" Madame insisted. "You can live here for free."

"You haf mut *baht*, big cah and big hout."

"I'm sorry dear, but I don't have one million *baht*. Even if I did, how could you ever pay me back?"

"Scu-me, Madame, no pay back, *mai pen lai*." Smiles.

However, at one of our weekly PILC meetings, we heard a not so funny story. A well-known Thai author was the guest speaker. He told us of the Thai's natural curiosity and candidness, and cautioned us to be considerate in our treatment of the maids. The story he related—admitting he'd only *heard* this but had no proof—was of a disgruntled maid who'd been treated badly by her employer. The story goes that the maid left the premises in a huff after her boss had screamed at her for some minor mistake, and the employer was found the next day with her throat slit. I had no such worries with my wonderful maid, Pon. She was about twenty years older than most maids and a lot wiser—although, she did ask me my age once. I sputtered and stammered and then just spit it out: "Thirty-nine," I said with fingers crossed behind my back. "Why do you ask?"

She giggled, "I sink you oder."

Okay. Not wanting to get my throat slit, I told her that I was actually forty-five. She accepted my answer—but then again she was a bit presbyopic.

Maids also take great pride in saving their employers money. Kimmie, a friend who lived nearby, called me the day after Easter to tell me of her experience. She had two small children; one still young enough to believe in the Easter Bunny, the other on the cusp. Family tradition called for special trails left by Mr. Bunny on Easter Eve, consisting of bits and pieces of green plastic grass and carrots strategically placed from the children's bedroom, down the stairs, through the halls and out the front door. From there the colored eggs were placed in the deep grass, as tradition dictated. They prided themselves on this completed bit of family legend as they retired for the night. Early the next morning they awoke to a teary-eyed five-year-old wailing that no bunny had come, there was no trail and, furthermore, he demanded to know why. The hapless couple looked at each other in surprise, jumped out of bed and tore down the stairs, only to find the path spotless. Nonplussed, they rushed outside and made a quick inventory of the planters and shrubbery that should have housed the bunny stash. Empty!

Upon hearing the commotion, their young maid joined them outside ready to receive her accolades. She informed her bewildered employers that she had single-handedly cleaned up the big mess the naughty children had left in the hall and down the stairs—not to mention the money she had saved Madame by rescuing the perfectly good eggs and carrots the children had hidden in the planters. But, *mai pen lai, s*he had made a huge deviled egg and carrot salad for Madame's lunch.

Many of the Thai maids gladly offered up their philosophies on men to their female employers. Pon was no different. She furnished me with all of society's woes and never missed a chance to malign the absent Thai husband. When I asked her why she'd never re-remarried, she said "Men! No wok, lazy, go away and haf many woman after baby come. Men, *mai dii.*" She'd throw this out at me whether we were talking about men or not. I assumed Pon had had it pretty rough with her father and her ex, as she portrayed all Thai men as being lower than dogs. That, coming from a Thai, who believe that dogs were once people who had lived evil lives, was quite a put-down. Her opinion of Thai marriages was not the "Till death do us part," type, but rather just a stopping-off period until the baby arrived, after which many husbands moved on. She explained that the uneducated Thai women were then forced to take jobs as maids or factory workers, and accept living alone. For the Thai men who did stay, she said, they were apt to retire early while the wife continued working to support them. She said her mother supported her father—until he left and took a young *"Wirgin."* She said when the women were too old to work as maids they moved back to their home villages and moved in with their sons, or their "second or third mother" (the name for the current woman living with their father), as tradition dictated. Their lot seemed hopeless to me.

I made a mental note: Never marry a Thai.

Then there were the stories of the drivers and their so-called narcolepsy. Our hired driver was prone to cat-napping during the day. I never quite understood if it was due to low blood sugar, a slow metabolism or just a laid-back persona. If we left the car for just a few minutes we'd find him in a deep sleep, head back, slack jawed, windows down and flies invading every orifice in sight.

Driving around town, Thai men could be seen lying on porches or the ground—anytime, not just during siesta time—fast asleep and oblivious to the flies buzzing around, insects taking bites, horns honking and kids playing noisily nearby. They were what you might call real power nappers. The minute Madame would leave the car, the hired driver would nod off, checking his eyelids for leaks as his chin descended into his collar. Five minutes, ten minutes, it made no difference. According to his peers in other types of employment, the hired driver had the best job in Thailand. He got to sleep most of the day in his car, ride around in an air-conditioned environment and was paid much higher than others who had to labor in the hot sun for twelve hours a day.

The hired driver would never admit he hadn't a clue where he was going or that he might be confused. This would be a sign of losing face—a big no-no for the Thai male. Now that I think of it, it sounds like a no-no for most men—Eastern or Western. The driver would drive aimlessly, miles off course, too proud to ask Madame where in the hell he was supposed to be going.

On a ride to a nearby golf course, a normal fifteen minute ride, my friend and I chatted away in the back seat while her driver drove on without a care in the world. After about thirty minutes we stopped talking and looked expectantly out the window for the clubhouse. What we saw were jungles and a yellow brick road that led to Oz.

"Sombat? Where in the world are we?"

"*Mai pen lai*, Madame, we go to gof cos."

"But, *where* are we?" she demanded.

"Go to gof cos, Madame."

When she pointed out that he'd been driving for almost thirty minutes and that the golf course was only fifteen minutes from her home, he smiled confidently. "M*ai pen lai,* Madame," and made a rapid U-turn, throwing us on top of each other with shrieks of helplessness. He then drove another thirty minutes, arriving for our 11:30 a.m. starting time at 12:30 p.m. No apologies from our happy driver, just a smile and a bow as he held the car door for us. He had found the gof cos, he did not *admit* he was lost, and Madame could now pray gof.

And, the biggie here was... he didn't lose face.

BUDDHA, MONKS
AND THAI CUSTOMS

25

The longer I lived in this crowded, noisy city, the more I became aware of the people and their relaxed manner. I noticed many saffron-robed monks on my excursions around town, coming and going through the city and country roads with an unhurried serenity. Why did everyone seem so calm? Other than driving like Indianapolis race car drivers, they seemed to be stress-free and tranquil. What made them so amiable? I needed to discover their secret. Did it have something to do with their Buddhist beliefs as I'd heard? What exactly was Buddhism and why hadn't it spread worldwide? What a treat it would be to have the whole world in such a peaceful state.

Needing answers, I decided to go right to the source. To learn about their ideology I signed up to attend a Buddhist cultural lecture for tourists. I'd heard that Buddhists were peace-loving, but now I could see firsthand how it worked in their lives and I was intrigued. The lecture was given by a Caucasian male who'd been teaching Buddhism for thirty years. He had come to visit the country, fell in love with its people and their spirituality, and decided to stay and spend the rest of his life as a monk. His talk was very inspiring and gave me insight into the Thai personality and their total *mai pen rai* way of life.

The phrase *mai pen rai* is rooted in the Buddhist beliefs and is used in nearly all encounters with each other, as well as *farangs*. It is pronounced "my-ben-rye," and is the quintessence of the Thai word for acceptance. It literally means "Never mind, no problem, or don't worry about it." One of the precepts that Lord Buddha taught was "acceptance." His message was to accept the lot you had been given in this life and you would be rewarded in a later. If you were tolerant, non-combative, did not kill and helped those in need, Buddhists could hope to be reborn to a higher station in life. Finally, when they had attained just the right plateau of spirituality in their life, they would reach Nirvana—a spiritual Godliness.

The Buddhists do not bemoan their fate; they go about the task of daily living with smiles and friendliness, sharing with the less fortunate—even though they have very little. Maid, street sweeper or janitor; these titles are only names in *this* life. Lord Buddha had a remarkable impact on the people of Thailand and one only need visit for a short time to realize that here is a civilization exuding happiness and kindness.

Adding to the peaceful spirituality, and an integral part of the *mai pen rai* lifestyle, are the Buddhist monks. Over seventy percent of Thailand's population is Buddhist, and every village has at least one *Wat,* the living quarters for the monks.

Saffron-robed monks are a common sight in the early morning hours in most Thai cities as they walk single file through the village chanting, heads shaved bare, eyes downcast, shoeless, holding their bowls and begging for alms. The Buddhist creed states that each monk must carry out this ritual for his spiritual well-being by showing acceptance of his abject poverty without shame, thus setting an example for the village laymen.

Alms-giving is also a way for Buddhist villagers to gain spiritual merit. It is believed that by housing or feeding the monks, a layman gains merit that will elevate his spiritual standing and enhance his progress toward final reincarnation

In the lecture I also learned that Buddhists have no deity. They answer only to themselves in the final analysis. This alone seems incentive enough to live a good life since Lord Buddha said that if you've been mean or vengeful to your fellow man, you are sure to return as a dog. I thought of the hundreds of stray dogs running around in neglect and the Thai's tolerance of them, which now made sense: one of those dogs could very well be a long lost relative living out their bad karma in the dumps—ergo the tolerance.

Buddhists find it odd that *farangs* seem so tied to time, always checking their watches and consumed with worry about *what's next* on their list instead of enjoying the *here and now*. I have to say that most Americans are guilty of time-watching. In the big cities of America, where life moves like a roadrunner on crack, most of us find ourselves being pushed along with it. We were raised by the clock and will probably die by the clock—right on time for our funeral. I'm sure one of the benefits of the relaxed Buddhist pace of life is that there's no dire need for acid reflux medication; upper or lower GI problems are rare. The only GI docs you might find in Thailand are called upon to treat the stressed-out *farangs*.

As expats, we often make many a *faux pas* while living in different cultures, and I was no exception. I made an honest but unforgivable mistake during the happiest of Thai holidays—*Songkran*—the Thai New Year. This is the cleansing time for the soul and the time Thais celebrate their Buddhist heritage. Water, being a cleansing metaphor, is sprayed, poured, and splashed on everyone within reach—a general time of merriment for all. I didn't know this bit of legend at the time. Ignorance is no excuse, I know, but I have to clear my name here. During some expat chatter when I first arrived, I remembered hearing that on certain Thai holidays we were expected to give our Thai staff the extra time off. No one seemed to know all the dates of these holidays, but we were told not to worry, our employees would let us know. That's one thing they were not shy about, so I was informed, so assuming incorrectly that my maid would inform me when such days were approaching, I promptly forgot about it.

The flyer from Dick's work told us that the jobsite would be closed for four days for *Songkran*. A group of employees had planned a few days' outing in Bangkok to get away from problems at the workplace, and we would be among the merrymakers. I told Pon that we'd be going to Bangkok for four days, and, because I was so thoughtful, I told her not to do any work while we were gone. She could just sit and put her legs up. I also asked her to make sure she locked up the house if she needed to leave for an errand. Unblinkingly, she answered, "Yeth Suh." What a nice employer I was. I mentally patted myself on the back for such generosity.

A few weeks later I had a wake-up call from a house-guest visiting us from Bangkok. Sharon, the daughter of a friend of mine from the States, had been a missionary in Thailand for over three years. One of the prerequisites for working as a missionary in a foreign country is to learn the people's culture, their language, and above all their customs. Sharon served as our interpreter when she dropped by to visit, and was the last word on Thai ethics and tradition. While we chatted over tea, I told Sharon about the great time I'd had in Bangkok over *Songkran*. I told her how I had generously told Pon she didn't have to do any housecleaning for those four days.

"You did WHAT?" she croaked incredulously.

"Ah… should I have just given her the weekend off?"

She immediately set about chastising me for this terrible *faux pas*. She marched into Pon's room, where they communicated in Thai for over an hour while I fretted and felt somewhat paranoid. I sat by helplessly, counting the tiles along the baseboard waiting for the reprimand that was sure to come.

Sharon called me outside and said she had a list of Pon's grievances.

"What grievances could Pon possibly have?" I asked, astonished. "I love her. I try to treat her as a member of the family."

"Well for starters," Sharon began, "Pon should have had the four days off, *with pay*, to go anywhere she chose during *Songkran*, the greatest holiday in her country."

"Oh. But…"

"In other words she shouldn't have been expected to house-sit for you. She should've been free to leave for the four days. To go up-country to visit her son, or anywhere she chose to go."

"Oh, dear," I sighed. "How stupid of me, but I didn't know…"

"It's your responsibility to know these things. When you live in a foreign country and hire locals, you are supposed to know the rules."

"But, why didn't she tell us?"

"It's not the Thai way."

"Oh."

"…and you also owe her 150 *baht* that you borrowed from her some time ago."

"Oh right, but I totally …"

"And," she continued, knowing she had me over the maid-etiquette ropes, "she paid a water bill of 200 *baht* for you when you were gone."

"Hold it, right there," I said, finding a way to save face here. "I knew nothing about a water bill. How could I know any of this? She didn't mention it to me."

Again with "It's not the Thai way."

Oh Buddha. Now I find out that I'm not the legend in her mind that I am in mine.

Sharon explained the Thai personality and beliefs. The most obvious one was the *mai pen rai* attitude. Pon had not complained to me about not getting the days off, she simply accepted it. Pon might have visited her son for the four-day holiday. She also had a friend who lived nearby who *did* get the four days off and they might have gone on the trip together. But, *mai pen lai.* I was heartsick.

I was terribly embarrassed about the 150 *baht,* too. I thought back to that day. I had summoned the local masseuse to our home one afternoon for a relaxing massage, but when it came time to pay her I couldn't seem to find any money around the house. Pon stood in the kitchen watching me search every cubbyhole, and sweetly offered her little pittance to help me solve my problem. I thanked her profusely and promptly made a mental note to pay her back as soon as Dick returned from work—which I promptly forgot.

"Why didn't she remind me?" I queried Sharon.

"Because it's not the Thai way," she answered—again. "And, *If* you had paid her back, fine. If not…" the "A" word again.

Well, to my way of thinking, the "A" word took a flying leap when Pon found a way to get recompense through Sharon. So you see, maybe there is hope for the Thai philosophy after all.

I made everything right by giving Pon the following three days off, and made it clear she was free to leave the area. I paid back the 150 *baht* that I owed her, plus the 200 *baht* for the water bill. When I apologized to her she *waied*, smiled, and said "*Mai pen lai*, Madame."

To solve any future *baht* problems, I put a small bowl on a shelf in the kitchen and made sure that it held at least 300 *baht* at all times. From this bowl Pon could buy any groceries she needed, or I could hit it if I caught myself short-*baht*ed.

THE BEAUTIFUL ORPHANS

26

I was having too much fun in this beautiful country and felt it was high time I gave something back. I signed up on the volunteers list for charity work. At the next PILC meeting I settled on one cause that opened me to much reflection and pain, but also to joy as I became part of something worthwhile.

I was introduced to the beautiful orphans.

The orphanage was in the capable hands of a Catholic priest, Fr. Ray Brennan, who had come to this position by chance and fate. No one knows for sure how it all started, but the accepted story was that in the 60s a young Thai girl brought her newborn to Fr. Ray for his help. The father of the child was a GI and had left for the States. Fr. Ray took the baby and then found someone to care for it and began looking for baby supplies. In the intervening years, Fr. Ray has taken in abandoned children, handicapped children with birth defects and/or missing limbs from an accident, as well as blind children and even some older folks that needed a helping hand. He also was worried about the street kids, some as young as three years old, who'd run away, or were kicked out, and were left to beg and steal to live on the streets. He opened a shelter for them as well.

In the 90s, while I was there, the orphanage held 143 children; about 45 to 50 were infants under five, and about 90 were over five years old. Since that time, the enterprise has swelled to 600 children who look upon Fr. Ray as their "father."

In the 90s, there was a full staff of office help and enough volunteers to make the load a little easier. Young girls, who once lived there as orphans, were going off to university, while some stayed on and participated in the children's care. They were free to leave the orphanage when they turned fifteen on the proviso that they had a job waiting for them on the outside. If they weren't viable for a job they could stay on and work at the orphanage looking after the younger ones, and many did just that. A part of the PILC donations went toward computer training for these young adults to provide them with job skills for the outside world.

The saddest of the adoption rule was the "No Papers" edict. Many of the children that were left at the orphanage were from a Thai mother and a non-Thai father, or there was no birth certificate given when the child was dropped at the doorstep, so the children were deemed unadoptable. The Thai Government stipulated that every child had to have papers showing their lineage in order to be adopted.

This caused me much pain. These poor children, through no fault of their own, were forced to live in an orphanage, never to be adopted. These children had no chance of ever living in a home with loving parents. The Thais did not want them and they were un-adoptable by foreigners because they had no papers. It was a no-win situation. Another problem was the Thai's belief that having twins or a handicapped child was bad luck. Thai superstition ran wild; the handicapped child might be living out some karma from his last life, thus the parents were afraid to keep the child.

No lack of helping hands was ever the problem. Volunteers came and went as expats came and left. Of the people who stopped by to visit the orphanage, many went home, packed their bags, sold their homes, and returned to be full-time volunteers with the children, while some took on administrative duties. As his aspirations grew, Fr. Ray's biggest problem seemed to be a cash flow. And just when he thought there was no more money forthcoming, someone would turn up with a large donation, causing him to again thank "The Boss Upstairs."

The children adored Fr. Ray and he was truly their father. Blind, handicapped, some missing limbs; they were treated as "beloved children" by Fr. Ray and happily climbed on him with hugs and embraces when he appeared.

The babies seemed to present the heaviest load. Sometimes there were so many that they had to put two to a crib. They were given the necessary creature comforts such as changing their nappies and propping bottles at feeding time, but often times there was no time for holding or rocking. The older girls did the best they could with the number of children they were responsible for. Often some of the older children were taken from their cribs, as time permitted, and placed on blankets on the floor. The children all seemed to be well cared for. Their clothes were clean if well-used. Hair combing and teeth brushing were chores not high on the priority list.

The first day I stepped into the Pattaya Orphanage, fingers reached in and squeezed my heart. I still cannot get that picture out of my mind—I doubt I ever will. This was the saddest place for me to visit as I still carry some profound memories of my own childhood in such a place, from age three to six, and even now I can remember smells, sounds and the insufferable, mean-spirited nuns.

The orphanage was decorated in all the regalia of the Thai culture, with Thai murals and bright colors. The nursery cribs were lined up side-by-side, old and battered, and were coated with layers of curdled milk and years of baby-teeth marks. The place echoed with tiny whines, laughing and crying. Some children played quietly in their beds, while others napped. Still others were busy playing or crawling on the cold floor.

I felt such heaviness in my heart for these homeless little angels. I couldn't help revisiting memories of when my children were born. The excitement of holding them was indescribable; to feel their sweet-smelling breath on my face and their warm skin against mine. And here were these tiny angels, never to know the feel of a mother's softness or her loving heart beating against their little bodies; never to experience someone who loved them unconditionally—be they twins, handicapped or mixed breed.

As I picked up one of these little treasures, I thought of what I'd been told during orientation: "Don't hold the babies too long, don't pick up the same baby more than once during a visit, always rotate the children you work with, don't let them become attached to you." *Sure! Right! Who's gonna' stop me.* The expat ladies who volunteered their time at the orphanage tried to abide by these rules, but most could not help becoming attached to one or more of the children.

During my first day as a volunteer, I spotted a little boy about five years old playing alone quietly on the floor. My heart did a flip-flop when he looked up at me. The look I saw in those soft brown eyes was all too familiar. He looked so much like my firstborn son when he was that age. The boy's hair was black, his skin olive, but the shape of his face and the expression in his eyes were the same.

I walked over to him, squatted down to his level and extended my hand. "*Sawatdee kha,*" I said. And he gave me the most incredible smile. His baby-white teeth gleamed as his eyes disappeared in a grin. He reached up and took my hand. *Okay—(gulp)—I was warned about this. I can't smear my mascara by getting teary-eyed. I'd better look for another child. I can't let them see me doing this on my first visit.*

My little friend's name was Zac. After I'd exhausted my short list of Thai words, I sat on the floor with him and we put a puzzle together. We didn't need words to feel the closeness. With each trip to the orphanage I was emotionally pulled back to Zac. I was reprimanded but couldn't pull myself away from this precious child. I'd amble around the room, holding different babies and he'd watch me, willing me to come to him. After a few visits like this, I noticed that Zac was being held by one of the older helpers when I'd arrive, or would be picked up by another person as soon as I walked in. *Okay, okay! I'll leave him alone, but just give him a kiss for me.*

I cried at night thinking about him. I consoled myself remembering Lord Buddha's promise: Zac would find a warm, loving family to call his own the next time around. Of that I was sure.

The PILC had a group of ladies who donated three days a week to these children organizing a playgroup. The women would take the children for an outing. The expression on those precious little faces was payment enough for these caring women. The shrieks of delight upon seeing an elephant, or splashing helter-skelter in a swimming pool was thrilling to see. Each week the director chose twenty children, ages five to ten, to go on the PILC playgroup field trip. To look at them you'd never dream they had a care in the world as they raced outside, skipping across the playground, dancing, or just swinging idly by themselves.

Although it was emotionally painful, I felt fortunate to be a small part of such great teamwork and to help the beautiful orphans.

NUUNG
SONG
SAAM

LANGUAGE BARRIERS

27

ost expats find it difficult to get their point across when they first arrive in a foreign country and are unable to communicate. The surest way to integrate then is to learn the language. When our company offered to pay for its employees to attend Thai language lessons, a few of the ladies were a little apprehensive, but for me it couldn't come soon enough. I wanted to converse in Thai instead of pantomiming myself into the ground. I admired these people and wanted to converse in their tongue. I also wanted to fit in, to no longer be a visitor but to be accepted. I knew I could never hope to think like a Thai, anymore than they could learn to think like a *farang,* but being able to converse with them was a giant step forward.

The women hailed from all over the world: Holland, Germany, Great Britain, South America, South Africa, Australia, Scotland, Mexico, Korea, Turkey, and America, and every lady had a different accent. The women's lessons were painful. If you've ever played the game "Gossip," you can appreciate how it went. The instructor would give us a Thai word to pronounce, which would start at one end of the table and continue around to the last woman. Problem was, it would return completely annihilated at the other end, while each woman was sure that hers was the proper pronunciation. We all tried our best to sound native, slaughtering the Thai language. The instructors would shake their heads in exasperation.

The Thai language has different meanings for the same word; voice inflections or tones used can change the meaning. Five tones are used in the Thai language; for example the word *"maa"* can mean "horse" and also "dog," depending on how you raise or lower the tone. I did quite well, I thought, and prided myself on an ear for dialects and inflections. I had transcribed medical reports for foreign doctors from upper Uganda to lower Slabovia for over twenty years, which I felt gave me a huge head start. The instructors informed us that when pronouncing the letter "R," we should roll it off our tongues. But, she added, we would most likely hear the "R" pronounced as an "L" since many Thais felt it was easier than rolling the "R." Hence: *mai pen lai, falang and lice.*

Most of us learned just enough to get around town; to tell the drivers which way to turn, the name of our destination, and the normal greetings. We learned to count to ten, which seemed to be the easiest part of the language, but none of us learned to write in Thai; it was as foreign as hieroglyphics. Some did better than others but all in all it was an ear-splitting experience.

The men were expected to take these language classes on the jobsite for at least two hours a week. Dick had a huge problem. Besides not being able to understand someone with an accent, he said he might have some type of inner ear problem that precluded him from hearing certain sounds. I called it deafness. When the phone would ring and I happened to be busy, I'd call to him, "Can you get that?"

"Get what?" was his usual answer.

When the cicadas were in a frenzy, rubbing their legs together, and you couldn't hear yourself think for the noise, he'd say, "Sure is quiet tonight."

I took pride in my own small victories of at least trying to understand the language as well as the culture. The problem was when

I'd greet a Thai in their own language using all the right tones, they'd answer in staccato, going on for five minutes with their response. I'd look sort of helpless then embarrassed and respond with "*Mai kao jai kha*" admitting I didn't know shit, that I was still a visitor and gooney bird for wasting their time. But none ever turned their back on me. In fact, they chattered on even more, probably telling me they were okay with me being a *farang* and an idiot. But I did think that they appreciated I was at least trying to learn their language.

In a country so different from home, with so many diverse nationalities, it's easy to lose your identity. I have a way of picking up accents without realizing it and then wonder why I'm constantly asked where I'm from. How I sound depends on whom I'm with at the time. While playing golf with my Scottish friend, Beth, I mentioned that her dialect was the hardest of all for me to pick up.

"Oh, aye," she said, "e koon oon-da-stan. E foun mee-sef t'kin Ameer-e-koon ta-oo-ter dy."

"Really?" I said, clueless as to what she'd just said.

"Weeeel, t'was e-see. E said 'cookie' steda 'biscuit' n 'Z' steda 'zed'."

Some of the ladies got together to play golf and tennis when weather permitted. Since we hailed from so many different countries, attempts to converse and understand each other at times could be quite entertaining. Our Brit friends put up with our pronunciation but you could see eyes rolling when we'd finish our conversations. They confronted us one day and told us they'd discussed it among themselves and with matters being as serious as they were, they'd decided to start giving us English lessons—the sooner the better. They couldn't abide us murdering the Queen's English any longer.

They never missed a chance to correct us: "Ah?" one of the Brits asked when our Texas gal commented to a friend "Ah love y'alls new hayado."

"Don't say 'ah' luvy, say I, as in the eye of a needle."

"Huh? That's what ah just said, 'ah.' Ah ya haad a hearin?"

Or, when our Salvadorian gal said, "What time do jou want to play golf Tursdee?"

"Jou?" said a Brit standing nearby. "Did you just say 'jou' instead of 'you?' My luv," she said with perfect elocution, "how can you butcher the English language so casually?" She looked skyward for patience.

"Que?"

"Listen, luvy, this will help you pronounce it right. Start by putting your teeth together and spread your lips like an EEE sound, then push them out as if you were puckering up to kiss me. Watch me: EEE-UUUUUU—You! Got it? Go ahead, try it. I'll bet you can do it. Let's give it a try, shall we?"

"Jou better not be kissing me or I kick jour butt."

Laughs and guffaws swept the seriousness by the wayside and that was the end of the lesson for that day. These corrections went on until the Brits waved the Union Jack in total surrender. Soon enough I found myself speaking with a vedy British awkcent and thought I sounded raw-tha sophisticated.

SEX AND THE CITY

28

In the 50s, the urban influx to Bangkok surged, as the surrounding villagers moved there seeking jobs. But as the population grew, the infrastructure did not. The population in Bangkok soared from two million in the 50s to the present eight and a half million, causing the five-hour gridlock. As people from the cold climes of England, Australia, Germany and the Scandinavian countries came looking for the warmth and an inviting place to spend their holidays, the sex trade boomed and the population soared. Then, in the 60s, GIs from Vietnam took their R&R in this pristine country and the sex-for-hire trade, already firmly established, grew exponentially. Like ants to a sugar spill, they came upon hearing of the sensual beauty, the warmth of the country—and the sex for hire.

The sex trade is alive and well in many other countries, but the Thais seem to be more open about it; not hiding it in dark alleys or snarky motels. It's out there in your face and you can deal with it as you wish.

However, with all this, Thailand was irrevocably changed from what was known as a quiet and peaceful land to the immense tourist attraction that it is today. Bangkok and Pattaya are now sexual moveable feasts, with discos, go-go bars, VD clinics, German beer halls, Japanese night clubs, as well as massage parlors and sex-act floor shows. As stated in an article in *Travelers' Tales* by Ian Buruma,

"Bangkok is the playground for the world's frustrated males."

Sex in Thailand is looked at quite differently than in most western countries; man-man, man-adolescent boy, man-adolescent girl—all quietly accepted. As the bars were opened, girls from poor villages flocked to Bangkok and Pattaya for fast, easy money. Commercial sex in Thailand is something you can join in and accept—or simply ignore. Signs that read "Physical" or "Traditional" Thai massage are just that; signs that read "Body" massage are for the senses that accompany the male visitor with *more* on his mind than muscle aches.

In one of the hotels we visited, massage parlors were strung along the perimeter of the pool. Beautiful, young girls would stroll in front of their cabanas looking like manna for a starving man and catching the ever-watchful tourist's eye. You could hear the melodious chants echoing off the hot pavement: "Massage foh you, Suh, make you feel goot."

An incident that conveyed the Thai proclivity for guilelessness occurred one evening while dining at an elegant French Bistro tucked into a small shopping center. While there we had an eye-opening experience that summed up Thailand's *mai pen rai* attitude toward sex. We noticed several tour buses passing our window and parking next to the restaurant. I was curious and called our young waiter over. "Why are all these buses stopping here?"

He answered with the largest smile and loudest voice he could muster, "Foh fuckee-fuckee show."

I had just taken a sip of wine and immediately choked. "What kind of show?" I whispered, hoping he'd whisper back.

He repeated it even louder this time, as though I was hard of hearing. Again with a huge grin he announced, as if he owned this production, "Foh fuckee show, Madame."

Trying to look blasé, I wiped the wine from my chin and blouse and continued to eat without looking up. When I didn't hear any gasps or see anyone fall into a faint I assumed the other diners had heard this before.

We left the restaurant and casually walked toward the buses. I needed to have a closer look at the type of people going into this show. There were three Greyhound-sized buses parked at the curb and several giggling girls in the doorway of the club. As we approached, one of them grabbed Dick's arm. "Come insigh Suh, good fuckeen show foh you."

Dick took a step forward. I grabbed his arm and took one step backwards. "I don't think so." I smiled as I pried her dainty hands from Dick's arm. She giggled and waved as I hooked my arm through Dick's and tugged him down the street. One of the more brazen girls caught up with us as we walked away and grabbed Dick's other arm. He looked guilty as hell, almost like he felt he should apologize to her for *me* being there. *Men are so easy!* I tightened the grip on his arm.

"You come back latah, yeth?" she called, giggling as she ran back to her friends. *In your dreams, lady. What nerve!*

A couple weeks after settling into our new home in Pattaya we were treated to a most amazing floor show at the Tiffany. The performers were transvestites (or *katoeys* as they are referred to by the Thais). This looked to me as the Thai equivalent of a show called *Boylesque,* which has appeared to rave reviews in Las Vegas for about ten years. Having seen the Vegas version, I couldn't imagine how the Thais could pull this off. But considering their lack of money for lavish stage productions and costumes, they did an excellent job and it was fabulous. The female impersonators were breathtaking in their beauty, as well as talented. Because the Thai people are delicate in stature, a male can easily pass for a female when adorned with costumes and makeup. With their small shoulders and waists, small hands and feet, you can imagine what a little makeup, stage gowns, wigs and jewelry can achieve. An old-timer told me later that one reason the transsexuals appear so feminine is that they are able to purchase hormone drugs over the counter at an early age—before they become fully adult males—which renders them virtually hairless on their arms and legs. They truly were stunning, and the talent was natural. They sang American songs—with a slight accent—but their voices truly sounded like the star they were imitating; Cher, Barbra Streisand, Carol Channing to name a few. It was a great show and we saw it several times.

Many more "floor shows" flourished in Pattaya and Bangkok, mainly on Patpong Road for the more adventurous. We did see one while there, and it's something I'd like to forget. I believe the same kind of floor show can be seen in Tijuana, Mexico, the Philippines, and many other countries that offer tourists this type of entertainment. However, there was much more to see in this Land of Smiles and I wanted to take in all its beauty. Somehow, naked people groping each other in a sex-dance frenzy just didn't do it for me.

The common thread here, I felt, was that the tourists expected this sex trade and the Thais delivered. Which brings me back to something I read: "If there were no market for this type of activity, there would be no Beach Road or Patpong Road sex trade." I believe it is called supply and demand.

THE COMPUTER GEEK

29

I was a guest at a PILC meeting one day and casually mentioned to my tablemates that I was a wannabe author and computer nut. I told them I'd even included my computer in our shipment to Thailand. They were amazed that I'd want to do work while I was in this land of milk and honey. *Work?* My computer's my best friend. I can't even write a simple note anymore. When I started the job of packing it was the first thing I put on my "to ship" list. No, it wasn't work to me. I told them about the frustrating days when I'd first arrived in Thailand. I knew my computer was out there somewhere; either in some port or on the high seas. I worried about it like a mother for a lost child.

"You wouldn't believe the trouble I went through. I thought for sure the Thai Evil Spirits were after me."

They wanted to hear all about it, so I launched into my sad little diatribe. How each night, before I fell asleep, I'd faithfully write the day's adventures into my journal. The good, bad and the ugly. The physical presence of the journal by my bedside gave me comfort that soon my shipment would arrive and I could begin transcribing my journal. I had no doubt that my computer and I could write the Great American Memoir. But I had only pencil and paper to work with, which seemed to thwart my ability to be creative. My fingers fly on a keyboard, but slow down resentfully when I pick up a pencil. I wanted to capture the sounds, smells, people and illogicality of this country, and I had to write it down so I'd not forget any of it. Every evening when Dick would walk in the door, I'd ask the same questions: "Did you hear anything about our shipment? Did anyone say they'd received theirs?"

"No and no," was his normal reply.

I continued to write in my journal throughout our hotel stay. My worry was that our room attendant would toss the dog-eared pages into the trash, as she did with everything else that wasn't held down with airplane glue. I zealously tucked the pages into my suitcase whenever I left the hotel room. Then came the move into our new home—joy of joys! To be out of that small hotel room was like peeling off a pair of extra-hold pantyhose. But alas, Suzy Homemaker began to rear her long-forgotten head. Our shipment had yet to arrive so I was still without a computer. What else could I do but shop? I decorated my new home. I had to buy, buy and buy, as if all the shops in Pattaya were dependent on my *baht* to keep their doors open. I got all the cutesy Thai knickknacks that every tourist must have; beautifully carved wooden Thai figurines, wildly colored fish, Thai angels and gargoyles, delicately etched celadon bowls and vases. Whatever they had on the shelf was exactly what I needed. And just when I felt I had everything I wanted, darned if I didn't see something else that I couldn't live without.

Dick's mantra was always the same: "Is this something you need?"

"Need? What has need to do with it? I want it."

The shipping company called regularly to inform us that our shipment was pushed forward a few more days. Their version of a few more days varied extremely from mine. The date of arrival, originally planned for sometime in October 1990, was now inching toward sometime in January of 91. The holdup, the U.S. shippers assured us, was naturally on the Thai-end of the voyage.

I fretted and whined on a daily basis. I could live without everything else, but please, Buddha, I needed my computer. Dick couldn't bear to hear it any longer and promised to bring home a computer from the office. He knew if my little fingers were flying on the keyboard he wouldn't have to listen to my misery. He didn't fool me for a minute. I knew he thought it might be much easier to spend a few days in jail for pilfering a computer than losing the money I spent on my shopping sprees. When he brought home the company computer I swooned with joy. Out came the dog-eared journal and I began to transcribe from morning till night—with maybe a few golf games, tennis matches and sightseeing in between.

We—the computer and I—started on the wrong foot. The word processing program on the company computer was WordPerfect 5.0. I'd never used this version before and hated it the moment I laid fingers to keyboard. The memory was substandard and anything I typed took up volumes of space on my RAM. Any teensy-weensy little extra effort I asked it to make, it reneged, stuck out its tongue and spit back a prompt that said: *In your dreams, lady!* I tried very hard not to let it hear me swear and moan. I'd turn my head away from the damn thing and curse out the window. I even tried not to complain and whine to Dick. Eventually I was swearing and whining to both Dick and the computer—and the plants outside the window.

Dick took the diseased computer back to his office and a techie sent it off to Bangkok to check it out. Two weeks later a repairman came to my door with the healed computer. It was all I could do to keep my hands off of him—while he held my computer. "Thank you, thank you," I whispered. I don't think he understood my excitement but I did see a small grin when he saw me stroke the hard drive. I immediately set upon transcribing from my journal. Four days in, the program seized again. I tried everything short of using the fire axe on it. I gave up, cursed out the window and unplugged it. One of the old-timer expats had warned me to unplug everything electrical when not in use, sharing stories of bucket brigades instead of fire departments. She needn't have gone any further. I didn't want a fire ravishing my beautiful Thai furniture.

Most of the company's office equipment was purchased in the States and this 110-volt turkey had to be hooked up through a converter, which sat on the back of my desk. I unplugged it from the converter and promptly called Tan, a Thai neighbor, who claimed to be the computer guru in the area, and requested his help. When he arrived I yelled for him to go into my office saying I'd be up shortly.

The story I got when all the smoke and ash had cleared was that he'd noticed the computer was unplugged and thought he'd found my problem. He then plugged the 110 volt power cord into the wall socket's 220 volt outlet—then pushed the On switch. I heard an unearthly sound, a couple of animal-like groans, and as the miasmic fumes wafted down the hall to me I knew I no longer had a computer. I smelled the acrid odor of burning electrical wire. I screamed as I came running, "Oh no, Tan. Please tell me you didn't plug my computer into the wall."

A soft male voice floated up to me on gossamer wings from under my desk, "Yeth."

Now I knew for sure. Those Thai evil spirits I'd heard about were definitely plotting my demise as a writer. It took another four weeks to repair the computer, mainly due to Bangkok's *mai pen rai* Repair Service. A month without a computer is a lifetime for a writer, so I reverted to Suzy Homemaker—shopping and playing daily—although I diligently wrote in my journal every night, which began to weigh-in like an Internal Revenue manual.

When the repairman returned my computer—for the second time—I was a bit nervous. After he left I walked up to the desk and slowly extended both hands. *It's okay, it's me. Remember me? Lick my hands and let's be friends.* Then I began to transcribe from my journal in earnest. After three arduous days and dozens of typed pages, as well as screaming, ranting and raving at the dinosaur word processing program, I erroneously hit a key that the crotchety machine didn't like and out jumped the little computer-demons to gobble up my words. "No!" I screamed, but alas, all was gone. My computer had had a miscarriage. Dick found me in a pool of tears when he got home, little salt rivulets running down my cheeks, my life ruined, and all my creative juices floating around in cyberspace. A few glasses of wine, more tears, and I decided that tomorrow was another day. I'd worry about it then.

The next day I began to search for all my hand-written pages to start anew. Where was the box? I'd placed a box on the floor by my desk, dropping my journal as I transcribed them. When I walked into my office I felt a cold sweat beneath my under-wire. *Where in the hell was that box?* I ran downstairs to ask Pon if she'd moved it in her frantic quest for cleaning. She was nowhere in the house. When I ran into the yard I saw that her motorcycle was gone. Store! She's gone to the store. I'll have her bring it to my office when she returns. I poured myself an iced tea and sat out by the pool. When I heard her motorcycle I ran to the driveway. "Pon, hi, thank Buddha you're back. What did you do with the box of papers on my office floor? I need to retype them."

Her face went white. She shook her head but said nothing.

"Pon! Please tell me you didn't throw them in the trash?"

Her silence spoke volumes. Before she had a chance to answer I raced to the back of the house where we kept the large trash bins. Empty. I then remembered hearing the truck lumbering down the alley early that morning. I sat down on the grass and cried.

At the end of this cataclysmic day, I found the last ten pages of my journal—only ten of about ninety-five.

At this new turn of events I *knew* the evil spirits were against me. They are very real in this superstitious land of Buddha, you see, and you'd better respect that fact. Maybe it was the cursing. They must have taken umbrage at my ranting and raving and punished me. At that point I gave up. I refused to type another syllable until my shipment arrived from the U.S. and I could work again on my friendly computer from home. When it finally arrived I was in heaven.

The girls were clucking in sympathy as I finished my story. While I sat there reminiscing I felt someone tugging on my arm...

THE NEW EDITOR

30

One minute I was daydreaming about my computer problems and the next thing I knew my arm was in the air being waved about by the girl sitting next to me. "Wait!" I said, laughing. "What's going on?"

"You're volunteering," she said with a chuckle.

"For what?"

From the podium came the sweet voice of the PILC's lovely Dutch president, Marion. "Duuty has yust wulunteered fer de newsletter editor's yob. Let's give her a hand."

"Yeaaah!" CLAP, CLAP, CLAP!—from the audience.

"Huh?" SKIP, SKIP, SKIP!—from my right ventricle. I tried to suck in some air but my throat had blocked off air to my lungs. *I'm the new editor?*

My thoughts morphed into a soggy bog. There was no way I could get away with this. *Mrs. A* would demand some sort of torture for me. "Tear out her fallopian tubes and bring them to me," she would cry in her imperious voice. But how could I back out now? They were all looking at me with such admiration. I love admiration.

Okay, I can do this. I stood, gave a hands-over-head double-handed shake and sat back down. Yes, this was nice. To be admired and looked-up to, that's the good life.

Friends came up and shook my hand, saying how glad they were to have me do the newsletter. How selfless of me to volunteer. They said I'd make it more interesting and funny—all the things that made it easy for me to blush and grin. I puffed up like a pool raft and then deflated just as fast when it dawned on me: *Wait! What have you done, you idiot?*

"But then, again, why not?" my Self-Destructive Angel whispered in my ear from my left shoulder. *"It's your life! You aren't the employee here. Go ahead and do anything your little heart desires."*

My Self-Preservation Angel chimed in sweetly from my right shoulder, *"Okay, she's right, but who's to stop* Mrs. You-Will-Not-Stray From-My-Pack *from ruining your life? You know she'd never approve of any of her women joining in another company's activities, especially volunteering for a position."*

Oh God! I'd really screwed up.

"Oh, pah-leeze," chimed in Lefty," *we've got every right to do as we choose."*

"Yes," said Righty, *"but I hope this doesn't push her over the edge."*

I decided to tell *Mrs. A* my little secret at our company meeting the following week. I'd lie on my back with my belly exposed—like a dog expecting a beating but hoping for a belly rub. I'd tell her, naturally, that I'd continue to attend all her meetings. And that doing the newsletter for the PILC wouldn't interfere with any of her activities. In fact, I cleverly thought, I might tell her I'd do a newsletter for her group. Yep, that'd do it. She'd be ecstatic at the thought of someone actually chronicling her incredible words of wisdom in a newsletter.

Then I got the bad news. At *Mrs. A's* next meeting, before I had a chance to tell her about my plans, I listened in disbelief as she announced her calendar. I felt weak in the knees when I heard her read her "new" schedule. She had planned every function for our group to coincide with those of the PILCs. She'd even changed our weekly meetings to the same day, same time as theirs. That way her controlees would never have time to venture out of her pack. I knew then that she'd done some scouting. She felt that the PILC might be a threat to all her well-formed plans of keeping the wives under her thumb. That would not do.

I sat in shocked silence.

The compulsory weekly meetings—which she claimed were not compulsory—were held at her home where she presided over them like *Leona Helmsley*. These meetings had commenced with twelve women at the start of the project, and had mushroomed to over fifty as more employees came aboard, causing mass confusion with overcrowding as female chatter rose along the walls and climbed to the ceiling.

To *Mrs. A's* horror, she overheard several of the new ladies complaining of the noise and confusion at the meetings. She nearly fainted when one of the new wives waved her hand and asked: "Why aren't these meetings held in a hotel meeting room or somewhere bigger, like maybe where the PILC holds their meetings. Wouldn't that be better than this crowded place?"

"Oh my God! Did you hear what I just heard?" said one of the old-timers. "She's not going to be here long. Someone should warn her that you never suggest or think at these meetings."

CLANG, CLANG, CLANG went the cow bell *Leona* used to call her meetings to order. "Ladies, Ladies, Ladies! Pah-leeze!" she'd bellow in her Cajun voice, then a little softer, "We must continue with owah meetin'. Ah have so many moah rules and regulations."

I made a self-preservation decision that I'd hold up on my confession. Maybe it would be best if I just phoned her with the news of my editorship. I didn't want to cause any blips on her radar screen, but I was determined that I would not give up the editor's job. I sincerely felt that it was an important part of my giving back to the community and to the many women in the club who depended on it.

Within three days of that meeting I noticed construction workers on *Mrs. A's* property. The word spread that she'd commissioned a contractor to add a 1,000 square foot addition to her already oversized home. She also commissioned them to close in an outdoor patio in order to contain all her ungrateful attendees during the meetings. Nobody was going to escape her—or her rules.

Three days later I received a phone call from a friend chiding me for missing an important meeting. "You should have been there. It was life-shattering news."

"I didn't know about a meeting," I sighed. "Let me guess, could it have been something to do with *rules?*"

"Sheesh, don't yell. I'm just passing on the news."

"You mean the *Good News* from *Mrs. Moses.*"

"Yeah."

"Go ahead."

"She called a special meeting. Her panties were really in a wad. She told us that her so-called 'sow-ses' had seen one of the wives riding in the front seat with a hired driver."

"Heaven forbid. Could her 'sow-ses' by chance be *Mr. Spy?*"

"No one knows. But that's not all. You're not going to believe this one. This newbie speaks up and asks what's wrong with that and the old lady nearly lost her uppers."

"They have so much to learn, these young girls. So, what'd she say? Was she pissed?" I asked, knowing full well it must have sent her to the drugstore for dental cement.

"Well, yeah, but I can't say it like she did. Something to the effect that: 'Don't you evah let that happen. They ah *draw-vahs!*' She said the word 'drivers' like they were some sort of terminal-stage lepers."

"What happened? Did everyone snicker?" I knew that would never happen, but God, how I wished these ladies would get some ovaries and stand up for themselves. I really felt that *Mrs. A* was a coward. She could spew her rules with an iron mouth as long as no one balked. Perhaps if the ladies banned together against her she might back down. I seemed to be the only one asking questions at the meetings. Questions that most of the ladies wanted answered but didn't have the nerve to ask. I was appointed as their mouthpiece. It did not gain favor with *Leona*.

"Snicker? Are you crazy? Everyone just looked around kinda digesting this new rule, wondering who was in the hot seat now."

"So, how'd it end?" I knew full well that no one would challenge her.

"Like always. She just went from one rule to another."

The rules were never-ending. We checked them off on the lists sent home from the jobsite. New rules daily: time schedule changes for shopping vans (never mind that we might have had other plans for that time); new areas where we were to meet up with the van and areas to meet for rides home, new game times and pool times. Times and places changed weekly.

Knowing her control issues I anticipated that the editor's job would cause major problems with Mrs. *You-Don't-Scratch-Your-Butt-Without-My-Permission*. However, try as I might, I just couldn't understand why she gave a hang. I wasn't interfering with any of her activities. I attended all of her meetings. I was being a good little employee's wife, but it pissed me off. As far as any of us knew she wasn't employed by the company, she just slept with the boss—an awesome position (pun intended). I now thought it prudent to keep the editor's position to myself a little longer.

Mrs. A phoned later that night, all syrupy and schmoozy. "Ah just wanted to varafy a rumah ah heard today."

"Oh. Hi." My throat and anal sphincter constricted at the sound of her voice. "What would that be?"

"Well, now," she drawled, "correct me if ahm wrong,"—yeah

right—"but my sow-ses tell me you were seen goin into a PILC meetin'."

"Who are your sow-ses?"

"Yes or no!" she hissed.

"Yes," I answered, jerking my backbone up a little straighter. "I've been to several of them. Why would that be classified as a rumor?"

Silence. Heavy breathing.

I launched into the questions I'd asked myself many times. "Why is it a problem if I attend their meetings once in a while? In fact, why would there be a problem if any of our ladies attended them?" Oh shit, now I'd done it. Why is my mouth running before my brains in gear?

Silence again. I took that as an opportunity to forge ahead. "You know, it might be educational for our ladies to attend some of the PILC meetings. Learn what's going on in Pattaya, learn about Thailand, meet new friends and volunteer and such."

I waited for another silence, which came, followed by, "Well mah deah, of co-ass you ah free to go whea-evah you like,"—yeah, right again—"but you do know that you missed a compulsory meetin' today, don't you?"

"No, I didn't know anything about a meeting. It wasn't on the last *rules* sheet Dick brought home." I'd hoped she got my meaning.

She ignored the innuendo. "The men were told at work to make sure theyah wives attended this meetin' today."

"I'm sorry, but Dick obviously forgot to tell me." Now I worried that Dick would be in the doghouse. "But I thought you said your meetings weren't compulsory?"

Silence—again. "Maybe we'll just have to come on down to those PILC meetins' and see what all this fluff is about?"

"Great," I lied, "I was going to talk to you about that." Crap! Here I go. I couldn't stop now. "I think the ladies would benefit from attending those meetings, and…" I was getting nervous at this point and could hear myself talking way too fast, but I couldn't stop, "...I thought you might like to check it out for them."

Silence.

"Hello?"

"We'll see about that."

"Excuse me?"

Click!

Gulp!

Dick thought I should give up the editor's job rather than cause more problems for us. I held on fast to my independence. I felt she'd have nothing to reprimand me for if I was careful and attended her damn meetings. Now I understood why she'd changed the company meeting days. She couldn't take the fact that I was still striking out on my own. Well, she'd just have to handle it. I'd go to her meeting one week, then to the PILCs the next. I'd call the PILC secretary and get the scoop from her for the meeting I missed. I didn't like being told what to do with my private life, but I certainly didn't want to cause a problem for Dick. I felt my idea would work for everyone, without having to be blatant about it.

Balance was the key here, I felt. But I was constantly trying to balance myself right in the middle of the tightrope that *Mrs. A* held—and slowly shortened. It was like having a ball and chain around my ankle. I took one step forward and she'd pull me back two. I couldn't get past the frustration. I saw only the edge of my problems and not the whole. I fixated on what was going on at the moment and wasn't looking ahead at what could be. I would find out in time but for right now I would make my own decisions.

Dick felt he was doing a good job at work, but lately he'd been coming home with stories about things going wrong in his area. He didn't go into much detail, just said that he disagreed with the boss about something to do with his end of the job. Then after that, he said, the old man totally looked the other way when they passed in the hall and just basically being an asshole. Strangely, this had coincided with my phone call from M*rs. A.* We both knew what the immediate concern was for *Mr. JB.* He seemed to be more worried about his wife's hold on the ladies than he was about his million-dollar project.

I would not give up the editor's job—yet.

We took the *baht* bus to Beach Road, restaurants and shops so as not to use our driver too much. I didn't want to give them a chance to confront us with any wrong-doing. We did our own thing, went out with friends and tried to keep a low profile. We tried to follow most of the rules, without giving up our personal lives. But without admitting it to each other, I think we both knew our life in Pattaya was on very shaky ground.

BAHT BUSES AND HAPPY DRIVERS

31

Picture a small pick-up truck with rock-hard bench seats placed on either side of the bed, a piece of tin thrown over the top to ward off the sun (Thais are not given to tanning), and a floor-to-ceiling metal pole stuck in the middle of the bed to hold on to—for dear life. You've just met the ignoble *baht* bus—or *songtow.*

Beach Road and Pattaya City were teeming with them. All of them honking as the drivers careened around town, never seeming to watch the road in front of them. Picture Disney's Mad Hatter ride with a New York City cab driver. The bumpy road, coupled with the truck's poor springs, was tooth-jarring. The price for these rides was whatever the driver thought he could get. If you looked like a *farang* and asked, "How much?" you'd probably pay top *baht.* If you jumped in the back and acted like you did this every day, you'd pay slightly more than the Thais.

A Thai friend instructed me on the correct way to disembark from the bus. "When the driver stops for you, climb out, then casually walk up to his window and hand him five *baht.*" She assured me that this was a fair rate. "Then immediately walk away," she added, as if that would end the encounter. Fat chance! It might have worked for her but most times the driver would cruise along beside me, hollering that I owed him more money. But I played it like she said, hoping they'd give up and drive away, all the while the beating in my chest tapped out Morse code.

"Don't worry about it. It's easy," she said when I complained about being chased by irate men in pick-up trucks. "Just keep walking, they'll give up." Easy for her to say, she wasn't the one the driver tried to run down. I have to admit I did enjoy yelling out where I wanted to go and then jumping off when I got there. I think it was the pioneer spirit in me. It was great not having to endure any stateside driving aggravations such as spotting an available parking space and nobody ticking me off by taking the spot I'd just made two laps around the mall to grab.

I was one of the few company ladies who rode the *baht* buses around town. Most were terrified by *Mrs. A's* stories of "Don't trust those buses or drivers." I think they feared they'd go the way of the *Man on the MTA.*

I also loved exploring the city, not having to watch where I was driving; however, I did spend a lot of time watching where the driver was driving. I'd ride them to the tennis courts, then jump on another bus later in the day to go to the market or drug store, and then hop on another one and head home. I never had a problem, and in fact, I found them all to be polite and thoughtful—aside from the drivers that tried to run me down. But to listen to some of the company ladies, I took my life in my hands: It isn't safe for a woman to run around by herself in this country, yada, yada, yada.

"What?" I said incredulously. "Where in the name of Buddha did you hear that?"

"From *Mrs. A.* Where else?"

"Why would you believe her? It's just her way of keeping you from living your own lives here," I proselytized. "Get a grip. Go for it. Have a ball! Look around and see how many *farangs* are riding those buses." My words usually fell on deaf—or terrified—ears. People would hum and sing, but the song never changed: "If ya want yer husband ta keep his job, ya better not stray."

Expat ladies from other companies used the *baht* buses or used their drivers to get about town. The more daring of the ladies even drove the car themselves. But we *baht* bus gals thought we were elitists. I know the Thais liked that we made ourselves at home.

I did a lot of people-watching. Traveling the incredibly perilous roads with speeds up to 150 kph, passing on the right or left, and going into and out of the wrong lanes, I realized that no one seemed to be stressed—except the *farangs*. The horn was the weapon of choice and used to its fullest potential. In the States a horn normally signifies "Look out jerk" or "Get your effen car out of the way," and could be accompanied by the one finger salute or, in extreme cases, a 38-caliber slug honing in on your cranium. But in Thailand it was quite different. Here the horn meant "Scuz please, coming by," or "passing on left or light." They seemed to have some sort of built-in sonar system. Even though they drove like Demolition Derby drivers on the city streets, they managed to miss each other by millimeters while weaving in and out of traffic with smiles. When they'd hear a horn behind them they'd politely move over and make way for the horn-honky. It was amazing. But on the Sukhumvit Highway it was another story, and they seemed to abandon any sense of safety. Too many lives were cut short due to the insane speed and indiscriminate lane changes of the drivers.

Many of the roads in town resembled ox cart trails. Some were mainly dirt and crumbled asphalt with potholes eight inches on-center, as the asphalt, unprotected from the awesome sun and monsoon damage, gave up the ghost. I'd not seen a smooth road since my arrival and I had traveled quite a few miles—or so it seemed.

The highways were crawling with monster trucks, hauling, milk, gas, cement and water—each driver with his own time-warp schedule. I saw no roadside scales for the huge trucks to thwart overloading and adding to the highway damage. I assumed that this was a big part of the road devastation. The car-to-motorcycle ratio was about ten to twenty. Huge buses were about one in every four cars. The buses were always packed to overflowing—literally—with excess passengers hanging out the doors and swinging wildly out into traffic yelling greetings as they roared past other vehicles.

The buses and trucks were far and away the leaders for speed and life-threatening lane changes and the cause of most fatalities. It reminded me of my horseback riding days in my youth. Ever notice how stable horses always strive to get to the head of the pack? With ears back, they bite and snip at the closest horses' flanks to attain their goal, taking the hapless rider on a perilous trip. Although there seemed to be no animosity, it did appear that these drivers always vied for the lead.

We had a driver assigned to us when we first arrived in Thailand. By Thai standards, he drove safely; by American standards he could have been a card-carrying member of NASCAR. As drivers swerved in and out, skimming our car with their side-view mirror—or in the case of motorcycles, brushing our side-view mirror with their shoulders— Dick would moan and groan, his favorite expression being "Dumb shit." Our driver soon adopted this as gospel. While driving with him one day, a motorcycle swerved by and barely missed our car. My driver turned around, gave me a knowing smile and asked: "Dump chit, Madame?"

I hoped this didn't mean we'd brought the white man's ugly ways to these lovely people.

I had yet to develop the *mai pen rai* attitude as we traveled at breakneck speed toward St. Peter and his Golden Gate, but I did learn to just close my eyes and dream of shopping. That is until the day I nearly met St. Peter.

CHEATING THE GRIM REAPER

32

Our husbands had to travel the deadly Sukhumvit Highway to work each day. This highway spans the route from Pattaya to Bangkok and has been credited with hundreds of fatalities. I know of five people who were nearly added to those statistics.

One of my tennis pals was involved in a terrifying collision on the Sukhumvit. While driving her Jeep wagon she was hit by a tanker truck that pulled out in front of her. Unable to swerve in time to avoid the collision she took the full force of a head-on and was thrown from the jeep, unconscious. Two unidentified men in a pick-up truck stopped at the scene of the accident. They hefted her inert body into the bed of the truck and drove her to a hospital. She was found to have a broken pelvis, ribs and femur, along with multiple other injuries. When I consider the precautions US paramedics take to prevent any movement to the spine or neck after a collision, it's a miracle that she wasn't crippled for life after her transportation in the rickety truck bed and over the tortuous roads. The reinforced chassis on the Jeep was credited with saving her life. She was in the hospital for three weeks and it was three months before she was stable enough to walk. She never found the two Good Samaritans to thank them for their life-saving ride to the hospital.

My near-death experience was also on the Sukhumvit Highway.

How I'm still alive to tell about it is one of life's many mysteries. Could be my karma hadn't been fulfilled yet. But, I did live to walk another day. Well, maybe not exactly walk. I did a lot of limping and foot-dragging. We were hit by the same type of monstrous truck speeding toward our car, but our driver was able to swerve in time to take the brunt of it on the rear passenger side of the car—my side.

That cataclysmic day I'd been with some of my PILC buddies. We'd just finished our tennis match and were heading for our cars. The lady who was to take me home was still playing so I grabbed a lift with Noni, a friend who lived nearby. I rued that decision for many months. Make that years.

As we piled into Noni's car, we began jabbering about our tennis games while her driver headed for the Sukhumvit. Noni and her driver, Dow, were in the front and had fastened their seat belts. Marlene and I were in the back discussing a bad line call as Dow turned onto the Sukhumvit. After maybe thirty seconds, I happened to look up in time to see a mammoth tanker truck crossing the median and coming right at us. I screamed. Dow braked and swerved to the left, but too late to avoid the collision.

The truck bearing down on me seemed as immense as a freight train. I can't remember if I actually watched it hit us, but I think a knee-jerk reaction would have been to throw myself to the other side of the car out of harm's way. I remember hearing the sickening sound of screeching metal against metal. At the same time it felt a like a giant hand had picked me up by the scruff of the neck and violently slammed me back and forth. Witnesses told us later that when the truck slammed into the car, it sent us skyward, flipped us at least three times before landing on its roof, then slid across all four lanes, wrapping around a tree on the side of the road. I can attest to at least three of those flips. I distinctly recall being thrown around and ramming my head into three immovable objects. I still can't believe we weren't hit by oncoming traffic as we slid across that busy highway, with it moving well over 120 kilometers per hour.

I remember vividly that it was totally black—from the initial collision to the dead stop—as if I were wrapped inside a velvet cocoon. It was deathly quiet. The first sound I heard after the initial crash was the eerie whining of tires as they lazily spun on their axles. I had no idea the car was on its roof, until all of a sudden everything came into focus and it was daylight again. I was disoriented; the inside of a car looks completely different when you're sitting on the headliner. I assume that the darkness I encountered was my subconscious turning off. Maybe I blacked out, as they say, or perhaps my mind went into hibernation until the potential for pain had ended.

Noni and Dow must have escaped the car while I was still in my dark little world. Now I could hear them talking outside the car and felt relieved that they were safe. I heard Noni yelling our names: "Marlene, are you okay? Dodie? Come on, get out." She didn't have to coax me. I wanted out before the car exploded. Okay, maybe I'd watched too many Hollywood car crash scenes, but you never know. I didn't want to be a crispy-critter inside a burning coffin. And I don't look good with singed hair.

I looked around. The rear window on the driver's side was the only means of escape for us. The area between the front and rear seats was impassable. We would have to use the back window, but it was shattered, with only a small opening of about sixteen inches with glass protruding inward. I cringed as I realized we'd have to crawl out on our bellies and push ourselves along with our elbows and knees to clear the skin-shredding orifice.

Marlene offered to go first. She yelped as bits of glass invaded her arms and legs and I grimaced as I saw spurts of blood flowing from her skin. I glanced around my area and tried to get oriented. My purse was compressed between the front seats. I had to make a quick decision: my purse or my life. I knew it wouldn't fit through the small opening at the same time as my body; it was the size of a small Volkswagen. And even if I could get it through, I worried that someone might walk away with it. As with most traffic accidents in Thailand, people came out of the woodwork, standing around and giving their two-*bahts* worth and generally causing more confusion.

I peered out of the hole in the glass and found I was eyeball to ankle with someone. I couldn't tell a friend's ankle from a foe's. Then I spotted some bloody tennis socks. "Hey, who's there? Identify yourself."

Marlene groaned, "It's me, Dodie, hurry up. Get out of there."

"Okay, hold on a second." I reached forward and grabbed the leather strap on my purse and gave it a mighty tug. The purse resisted, then released and flew toward me like a SCUD missile, hitting me in the chest with a great whump. I let out a yelp.

"Dodie, are you okay? What was that noise?"

"I'm okay, just trying to get my purse. Here, I'll push it through."

"Forget your damn purse!"

Forget my purse? That was my life's blood. It was a traveling bureau drawer; money for emergencies, tissue for the Eastern Toilet, a banana for potassium, a change of tennis outfits, shoes in case I got a blister and, of course, pictures of my precious grand kiddies. Oh, and my tennis racquet.

"Please take it. I don't want it to burn up in here." I shoved it through to her while chunks of glass gave way, slicing into my hand and arm. After I'd cleared away as much glass as possible I began to inch forward on my hands and knees. Someone grabbed my hand and helped me stand upright on my shaky legs. I took inventory of all my body parts and they seemed to be present and accounted for. Other than bleeding from my scalp, forehead, elbows, palms, arms, knees and ankles, I thought I was in pretty good condition. We'd certainly fooled the Grim Reaper. The car was a goner, but the four of us were conscious without any broken bones—that we knew of—and all heads seemed to be on the appropriate necks.

Our tennis buddies, who'd left the courts after us, came upon the scene of the accident a few minutes later—before we'd extricated ourselves from the car. They saw the crowds, the car upside down and wrapped around a tree, and of course they thought the worst. They told us later that they knew we were all dead by the looks of the car. "No one could live through a crash like that." They were all too terrified to even walk up and look in. They stood across the street, held each other and cried.

Several people gave us a lift to the hospital in their pick-up trucks—love those good Samaritans. We waited over three hours for a doctor to check us out and take x-rays, and were relieved to hear there was not a broken bone in the bunch. However, we all had glass embedded in our scalps and every appendage we owned. The emergency room had no magnifying glass to check for possible shards of glass in our bodies, leaving the nurses to handpick what pieces they could see—without washing their hands or putting on gloves. *Yuk!* I could just imagine all the mighty bacteria licking their chops. Please Buddha, don't let me need a blood transfusion or brain surgery while in Thailand.

At home, Dick reminded me of a mother monkey, picking glass from my ankles, knees, elbows, scalp and shoulders whenever I yelped and found a new shard. Little pieces continued to make their way through my pores for another couple of weeks. Just when I thought I was glass-free, another sliver would show its face and here would come Mother Monkey to pick me clean.

I'd never been involved in a car accident and I was quite amazed by it all. I remember thinking as I sailed around the car, slamming my head on the first of the three obstacles: *Okay, that wasn't so bad.* Then the second slam: *Okay, that was a little harder, but I'm still okay.* Then the third: *Okay, already. Enough! I'm alive, let's knock this crap off.* Amazingly, I didn't feel any pain or fear. I did think my neck might be three inches shorter but I never did like my long neck. Now I could toss all my turtleneck sweaters.

It's amazing what goes through your mind at a time like that. Marlene said she thought about her kids. Noni thought about her car and what her husband would say. I was a tad irritated that it was so dark and wondered when the damn thrashing would end.

That near-fatal experience also left me with some very profound thoughts about pain and death and dying. Several days after the accident, when I felt well enough to really dwell on the whole episode, I realized something very profound. I remembered that throughout the whole incident I was never afraid—ticked off maybe—but not afraid. It never once occurred to me that we might be flattened under an oncoming truck or that we might burst into flames as we slammed into an immovable object. Nothing! It just pissed me off because it seemed to take forever for the flipping to come to an end.

Why wasn't I terrified out of my wits? Why didn't I scream or cry? Could it be that my subconscious took the reins and put my consciousness into some sort of holding-pattern until it was all over? The experience was a huge awakening for me and caused me to have a new sense of peace about death and dying. For example: when we hear horrifying details about a gruesome death or watch some appalling events on TV, we sometimes try to imagine how it must have felt to be the person in that airplane, train or car wreck. I don't do that anymore. I have to believe when that car crashes or that plane slams into the mountain or that person gets gunned down, that they're not thinking about the end of their life, as much as they might be ticked off that there's now a glitch in their plans for the moment as they sail through this subconscious state. Maybe the last thing they worry about is pain. I now feel a sense of peace realizing that everything goes black and then you wake up. Or…you don't. Either way, there's no pain. I hope! Maybe that's all any of us can hope for when we leave our mortal bodies. No pain. No fear. I like that concept.

I stayed in bed for a few days after the accident trying to let my body heal before I marched out to conquer the country again. It was miserable lying in bed, agony to sit up and excruciatingly painful to walk. My head felt like a piece of overripe melon. Several of my PILC friends came by bearing gifts of candy, wine and sympathy. I was surprised that I'd heard nothing from any of the company ladies.

But I did get a call from *The Boss Lady* two days later. "Ah just heard about yoah accident." she said. "It's too bad, but you must admit, my deah, if you'd been where you should have been, this would not have happened."

"What?" I yelped. Oh damn, that hurt my head. Not now, please. I need to heal. Why now with the lectures. Will she never give up? "'Where I should have been?'" I was sore and aching and didn't want to listen to her crap. "I was playing tennis with some friends. Did I miss a compulsory meeting or something? Where else *should* I have been?"

"Why, with yoah *own* ladies, honey. You know that. That's why I have so many rules for you ladies. Ah am tryin' to protect you."

'My own ladies?' Barf! "Don't worry about me. I'm doing fine," I lied. "Thanks for calling. I can't talk now, time for a pain pill. Bye." I hung up before she had a chance—a first.

How did she know I was playing tennis with the PILC ladies? I could see the Cruella DeVille smile as she pictured me laid up in bed, hurting and wishing I'd followed her rules. *Barf* again.

Noni and Marlene had some rough days, but not as many as I did. They were more or less removed from the initial blow that I took, but all in all they survived. I had a few return trips to the hospital for more x-rays of my back because the first x-rays were fuzzy. They said the second set of x-rays came back negative, but I wonder. To this day, years later, I still suffer from bouts of exquisite back pain that comes and goes with activity. When it hits, I'm down for a few days. While I'm incapacitated, my mind goes back to Thailand and the scary events of that day.

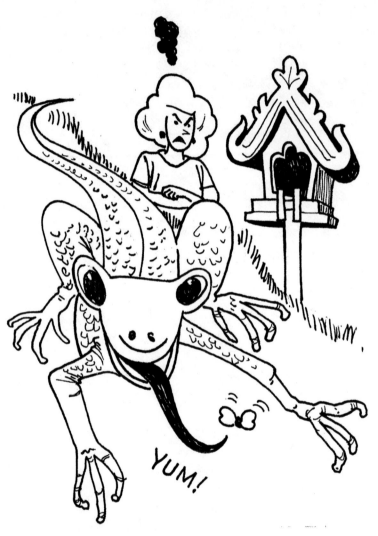

HOME SECURITY 101

33

I'd heard that bad luck is better than no luck, but enough is enough.

I was slowly healing, and even though my aches, pains and bruises seemed to be declining, I was still walking with a limp. The headaches continued for several weeks, however my memory of the crash lingered long after. I was so paranoid I didn't want to step outside. I was terrified to even get near a car. Dreams were constant and always the same: my car's brakes touched the floorboards as I sailed ever nearer to the abyss. I awoke struggling, half off the bed with the sheets so tight around my legs I couldn't move.

My PILC pals continued to drop around during my recuperation, along with a couple of my Thai neighbors. We discussed my nightmares and fears, my bad luck and my proclivity for getting my butt into hot water. The Thai ladies had the perfect solution for my problems: I needed a few geckos running loose in my house. They said geckos were good luck and I should try to keep them inside my house. In addition to bringing me good luck, they said, the geckos kept your house free of insects and other varieties of creepy-crawlies.

I liked the thought of some good luck for a change and began looking for the little critters, hoping to find dozens of them hanging out in my house. I'd never really seen one up close, but when I'd asked Pon what those clicking noises were I'd heard from time to time, she said it came from geckos. I guess I wrinkled my nose at the thought and asked her to sweep them out. But now I'd changed my thinking. I wanted them to hang around. "No more," I told her. "Let them stay." I was in desperate need of some good luck. Pon looked at me again with her "crazy *farang*" look.

I started searching in earnest then and found I was host to quite a few geckos. These little guys were about the size of your ordinary garden-variety lizard, but swift as lightning. I found they loved to hide behind drapery pulls, doorjambs, closet doors and computer keys. When I began to really search for them I found I could get a good look if I was very quiet. But as soon as they felt me near they'd go zipping by so fast my stomach would drop like an express elevator to the basement. Geckos might be invisible most of the time but you know they're around by their odd sounds. After swallowing an insect they make a strange clicking sound—as if putting tongue against teeth and sucking in—like tsk-tsking someone. Every time I heard that sound I had a visual image of an unsuspecting insect sliding down the esophagus of one of these little guys. No matter how much I told myself that they were ever present, I still jumped sky high and shrieked whenever one whizzed by me.

I talked to them too. You know how you're encouraged to talk to houseplants to make them happy and grow? Well I began to talk to my geckos. *"Sawatdee kha,"* (I assumed they were Thai). I'm happy you're here. Please make yourself comfortable. This is your home and I'm just a visitor here." I even quit swatting the pesky flies, knowing the geckos would appreciate the extra morsels. I just let them fly around me and hoped Mr. Gecko had room for one more bite. Every home could do with a fat, healthy gecko. I wondered if it was possible to take a few back to the States with me.

After the move into our new house, a Thai friend suggested we purchase a Spirit House for our yard. The idea was to protect the family and home from evil spirits. This little number was usually placed on a pedestal and resembled a high-class birdhouse. She said according to Thai spirit protocol it should be placed in your front yard for all to see and you could then sleep in peace. The logic behind this was very simple; if a thief were to come through the back window of your home and didn't notice the spirit house in the front yard, he soon would be made aware of his error as the spirits also preside *in* the house and attack from behind—spiritually, that is. The intruder would then be rendered harmless and would run from the house with his tail between his cowardly legs.

Okay, I thought, I definitely need a spirit house. Her husband purchased one for me and hauled it home in his truck, along with a four-foot pedestal. I have to say it looked quite impressive. He helped us with the digging, told us where it should be placed in our yard, and told us what direction it should face. But what he didn't tell us, and we learned much later, was that you *must* have the spirit house dedicated by a monk. You *must* put offerings in it daily. You *must* pray to the spirits daily, and you must offer your thanks for its protection. Reflecting back on all my bad luck, I had to blame it on that "undedicated" spirit house. No food. No offerings. No flowers. No prayers. No monk. No wonder I had so many problems.

When we'd first moved into our new home, during some of my shopping frenzies, I'd purchased several Thai artifacts. I had no idea what they represented other than I thought they were quaint and cutesy, and very Thai-ish. Some were small Thai angels, some were Thai gargoyles, and some were large ornate bowls with pictures of gargoyles and angels frolicking together. I thought the gargoyles looked rather spooky but I never considered that they might be evil. Sharon, my all-knowing missionary and expert in all things Thai, visited us again a few weeks after my car accident. I told her about *The Bosses,* my car accident, and briefly told her of my nighttime problems with Dick. She strolled around my house taking inventory of all my souvenirs and then said casually, "I'm sure the reason you're having all this bad luck is because your house is filled with Thai evil spirits. "

"Huh?"

"Look around," she said. "Everywhere I look you have them." Here she pointed to all the adorable statues of gargoyles and cranky-looking faces carved out of teak wood. "These are all products of the devil and can do you nothing but harm. The sooner you get rid of them, the sooner your problems will end."

I scoffed at this ridiculous idea—for a second—then reflected on the events that had been screwing up my life. I decided that she might just have a point. Those gargoyles did look rather evil.

A few weeks after Sharon's visit, I decided to scale down some of my Thai purchases as my house now resembled a Thai furniture showroom. I began boxing things to ship home to our storage. The first order of business was to pack my Thai gargoyles; I just couldn't bring myself to toss them. They were really quite cute in a ghoulish sort of way.

Sharon called me a few weeks later. "Well?"

"Well what?"

"Have you disposed of the evil spirits?"

"Oh, they're gone," I sighed. "I shipped them home to storage."

A long silence followed. "Shipped them home? Why didn't you just toss them?"

"Huh? Oh, well, I did think about it, but they were made from teak wood and smelled so good I just couldn't bring myself to throw them away."

"Well my friend," she sighed, "I hope your storage company doesn't go up in flames."

I called my storage company post haste and asked if it were

possible to remove a few things from my packing crates. Sure, gladly, but it would cost me $50 to open my crates and another $50 an hour to search out my evil spirits. Why hadn't I thought to pack a dedicated spirit house and a gecko or two to protect my storage?

There are people who've never lived in foreign countries but will tell you that thieves, burglars, cutthroats and murderers abound. Scores of horror stories were always tumbling around the expat community like leaves on a windy day. People were being robbed right in their bedrooms as they slept, the stories went, while the villain helped himself to their treasures. But it was always what someone had heard, never knew for a fact. Several burglaries were documented but they were in very remote areas with no security guards and very few expats.

We, on the other hand, had incredible security. Our guard sang loudly most of the night to keep from falling asleep. So even if a burglar wanted to burgle, he'd be put off by the singing guard. We did have one guard who took little catnaps on his shift. Our neighbor told us he had returned home late one evening, quite tipsy, and couldn't find his gate key. He climbed over the six foot fence right under the snoring nose of the snoozing guard. That was a tad worrisome.

Taking all the scuttlebutt into consideration, I felt that the *mai pen rai* attitude should be applied here. To solve the problem of night-time intruders, I suggested we leave the bottom floor of our house for the bad guys to pillage, if they were so inclined, and lock our upstairs bedroom door at night. That should do it.

Our maintenance man, Sampon, told me that a picture of King Rama the 9th would surely keep away all prowlers and thieves. King Rama was worshiped by the Thais as being responsible for much of the freedom they have today. That sounded good enough for me and I immediately purchased a large picture of the King. I propped the picture against a wall in the dining room. I asked our maintenance man,

Sampon, if he would please hang a picture for me. I made a pencil mark on the wall where I wanted him to hang it. Sampon looked at the wall then lowered his head.

"What? If you're too busy you can do it some other time."

"Scume, Madame, *mai dii,* no hang on dit wall."

"Why?" I was forever trying to figure out what was *mai dii* and what was goot. Sampon pointed out that the other side of this wall was our bathroom. Oh Buddha. "*Têe kôr toht, King Rama*—Sorry." We then moved the King's picture to another wall, which pleased Sampon—and I even got a goot out of him.

I liked that the King was downstairs watching over our house during the day and hoped at night he was doing the same as we slept peacefully upstairs. If the snoozing guard was inept at his duties, and if the King wasn't as powerful as our Sampon thought he was, and if the spirit in the spirit house was napping, then the bad guys were welcome to anything they wanted—downstairs. Upstairs, I closed my ears to any strange sounding noises, secure in the fact that my bedroom door was locked—and a few geckos were running amok behind my curtains.

LEAKY PLUMBING

34

I was still plagued with nightmares of cars versus trucks and nurses sans gloves, and most mornings as I climbed out of bed in a semi-comatose manner, I felt like a water truck had slammed into me. Oh! Then I remembered. It wasn't a dream.

Slowly, but painstakingly I'd make my way to the floor and try to stretch my pain away. Exercises did help, along with some wonderful pain meds from my friend the pharmacist. Eventually my aches and pains receded and I began to venture out again. First walking to town and Beach Road then eventually stepping back into a friend's car. "You need some fresh air," my neighbor said. "You can't stay in this house all day. You've got to get back on the horse, as they say. I'm tired of hearing your excuses. Get your shit together and let's go." She was right. I'd had a major case of malaise long enough. It was time to move on. I got back to the business of enjoying my life.

Then another truck hit me, this time below the belt. I didn't make it to the ladies room in time. I'd been playing golf with some friends and had just unloaded on a monstrous drive—well, monstrous for me—when my pipes sprung a leak. I needed to find a restroom. Fast! My friends watched with astonishment as I dropped my driver and commandeered the golf cart, yelling over my shoulder that I'd meet them at the next tee-box.

"You're going to need a bladder repair," my stateside doc had informed me six months earlier. "And I wouldn't wait *too long* if I were you. Your cystitis attacks are coming too often, which is one of the symptoms." I'd neglected to heed his advice and suddenly realized I had waited *too long*. I'd had a few warning signs: pain during intercourse, along with some embarrassing signs—damp knickers— and had to admit that I'd better get my bladder hiked up a tad.

I was apprehensive about having bladder surgery, or any kind of surgery, in Thailand, but after interviewing a highly respected Thai GYN, I felt relatively safe with the idea. She spoke passable English, that is I could understand her. She'd received her medical training in England, which cinched the deal for me. During our interview she assured me that the surgery would take no more than two hours. "I do bladah repah many time. Doan worry." She ended the visit with exactly what I wanted to hear: "In sree day you casseta come out, you pee-pee, then go home."

It sounded relatively simple. How could anything go wrong? Three days at most and my catheter would be removed. I would be discharged and my bladder and spirits would both be uplifted. I was to find out just how wrong her prediction was as the days passed.

I now had a decision to make. My cautious side played with my mind. Stateside would be the safest way to go in case of any unforeseen complications. However, my reckless side opted to have the surgery here and save a ton of money and time.

Another factor that contributed to my decision to have the surgery in Thailand was the Christmas Eve potluck that some of us had put together. How I got railroaded into most of the work I'll never know. Perhaps I offered to get the menu together and make up the invitations, but somehow it became "Dodie's Potluck." We also were expecting some outside guests. The Chaplain of the 7th Fleet had called one of the ladies in our group to see if we'd be kind enough to host a few of his boys during the holiday weekend. He said their ship would dock in the Gulf of Siam on Christmas Eve after being at sea for six months, and the boys were hungry for some Americana and good home cooking. We all agreed: "Bring 'em on."

Now, considering my surgery, reason dictated that if I were to fly back to the States for the procedure I'd miss the party. I'd also most likely have to spend Christmas in the hospital. No way was I going for that. I rationalized that it was now mid-December and if I were to have the surgery here, I'd be up and running in a few days. I wouldn't have to miss the party and, best of all, I wouldn't have to spend Christmas in a stateside hospital. Okay, sign me up.

But before that, I had the January newsletter to finish. It was due out the last week in December, which was fast approaching. All that was needed was a few finishing touches and some quick proofreading. If I could find someone to get it to the printer and distribute it, my path would be clear. The editor's position I'd so stupidly signed on for was now more than a job, it was my nemesis. I called in some favors from friends. They would take care of getting it to the printer and take care of the distribution for me. With that responsibility laid to rest, I made plans to check into the hospital a week later.

Dick wasn't too happy about the whole idea. He'd been sure that my complaints of pain during sex were just excuses. He was mad because he'd had to forfeit his three-nights-a-week routine and his pouting had returned like an unwanted guest. I was furious with him. Where was the caring? Was his whole life centered below his belt?

I dragged him to the doctor's office with me. She explained the whole procedure, and why I needed the surgery now. He finally accepted the idea but could not shake the woe-is-me look.

Things were quiet on the jobsite, with no new rumors. I could now get some long overdue surgery and get back on my feet in time for the Christmas party, then life would be good.

Two days later I was admitted to the hospital without incident, and that was the last thing that happened without incident.

MS. INTOLERANCE

35

When the paperwork was completed I was shown to my room. I plunked down on the familiar concrete mattress and surveyed the meager surroundings. My hospital room was clean but sparse. I had a lovely view of the jungles and a few dumps from my small window. A peculiar odor permeated the place, somewhere between mildewed mops and Thai chili. The room, billed as "Private" was more like a broom closet in drag. Picture the offspring of an outhouse and a phone booth. It barely had enough room for one cot-sized bed and a very small chair for a very small person. The western water closet, way beyond being too small, looked as if it might pose a problem for me. It was roughly the size of a Pullman car bathroom. After a few tries I got the procedure down pat. I would back into the little cubicle, align my butt to just the right position and flop onto the toilet seat. The sink was conveniently close by and I found I could wash and dry my hands and/or brush my teeth while still sitting on the commode.

The next insult greeted me soon after admission. Here, in this land of tolerance and acceptance, in this very hospital of all places, I encountered probably the only Thai who was not tolerant, and who most assuredly lacked the *mai pen rai* outlook on life. She was a "uniwersity graduate," she haughtily informed me, and would be my nurse pre-and post-operatively. She had no idea about my pain tolerance of course, way down there on the Richter scale.

The morning of my surgery, in walked my little uniwersity graduate wheeling the prep cart. I smiled and said my usual *Sawatdee kha* greeting and tried my best to look like a dignified and proper patient. She obviously was on her own timetable and had no intention to be waylaid by *farang* chatter. I grew a bit apprehensive as she silently pushed her cart next to my bed with a business-as-usual look. My heart quickened as she removed a razor from a plastic bag—unsealed—and walked toward me as if I were a cadaver she was about to dissect. In her other hand she held a bottle of yellow liquid that I prayed was antibacterial soap. In one fell swoop she threw back my sheet and began to drizzle the yellow stuff between my legs.

"Please! No shave," I whined, looking fearfully at the used razor now lying on my bed. "How about just a Betadine scrub and a poodle cut?" She continued to drizzle then grabbed for the razor. "No lather? Aw, c'mon. Surely you…" She wasn't listening. She began to rake the used razor across my pubic area from top to bottom—and from bottom to top—while I yelped, "Stop, stop, damn it, you're hurting me."

She *spoke* little English—and *heard* none.

Okay then how about "*Yoot, yoot,* damnit; *jep, jep,"* I squealed as I tried to pull out of her vice-like grip. She continued to ignore me, trying for a better hold by wedging her tiny body between my legs, spreading them apart as if I were a turkey she was about to stuff. She continued to rake the antiquated backhoe into all my tender little crevices and folds. "Oww! *Cha cha*—slowly," I yelped, tears streaking my freshly applied foundation and mascara. She tsk-tsked me—the height of admonition from a Thai. I scanned the room for a means of escape. My eyes stopped on a familiar-looking water bag hanging from her cart. All of a sudden it hit me. "Oh no! You're not giving me an enema." Without even a blink from her almond-shaped eyes, she dropped the razor and grabbed the insertion tube, and with malice aforethought, rolled me onto my side and with one well-placed aim, plugged me in. "Ahhiii!"

As sometimes happens to middle aged women, certain muscles are unwilling to cooperate—like sphincters that sometimes lose their will to thrive. "Oh-oh," I whimpered, grimacing as water from the enema bag back-flowed onto the bed, pooling up on the nice clean white sheets she had so meticulously placed that very morning.

That did it. I had her attention now. Her curved eyes narrowed into straight, tight lines. Her tiny rosebud lips went flat. She was pissed. *Did she think I did this on purpose?*

"No, no, Madame!" she admonished me in perfect English, "you mut hold watah. No caca, no caca."

Well, excuse me, Ms. Land of Smiling Faces! There will be no enema for this kid. I tore loose from her Terminator grip, jumped out of bed with water streaming down my legs and ran limping for the bathroom with her in hot pursuit—brandishing the enema tube. I did my rendition of Simon and Garfunkel's *Slip-Sliding Away* into the bathroom and slammed the door against her tiny size three nursey shoe. As you might have already guessed, I did not endear myself to *Ms. V.R. Siamese-If-You-Preeze* and from that point on she was after me with a vengeance.

I was feeling no pain, thanks to the anesthetic, and was sooo happy with the world as they wheeled me to my room from Recovery. Then she walked in. As my drug-induced fog began to clear I saw a slightly fragmented, thin-lipped mouth. I know I saw a little balloon above her head that read: "You're all mine now, Round Eyes." *I must be dreaming. Not her again!* She stood staring down at me while another balloon popped up that said: "I bet you thought you were rid of me. You lived through surgery, but now…"

Post surgery *Ms. Intolerance* evened the score as she methodically *ripped* off the tape from my surgical site—way up there—and smiled gleefully as she gave the blood pressure cuff a few extra pumps until I had Marty Feldman eyes. The next morning I was moved to another floor and happily waved goodbye to *Ms. Intolerance.*

My stitches pulled and burned, pushing my pain tolerance to the limit. I longed for a sitz-bath. I wondered if this hospital offered such a treat. I had to find out. I grabbed the English-to-Thai dictionary from my bedside drawer and looked up the word "bath"—*aang-aap-nám.* Okay, I knew *nam* was water, so obviously I needed to find the Thai word for "sitz." My dictionary had seen better days. It had been given to me by a departing expat who'd received it from another departing expat. Some of the pages were unreadable and others were missing. No "sitz" revealed itself.

I thought back to my childbirth years, when sitz-baths were a part of your healing process and also a reward for the pain of childbirth. Women would wait eagerly for the nurse to accompany them to this amazing treat; this wonderful phenomenon that has passed from woman to woman as the single most wondrous experience of their hospital stay, second only to seeing their newborn child.

Now I wondered. Could I be so lucky? I looked around for the call button…

THE HOT POT SITZ-BATH

36

The call button was not on my bed, or the wall behind my bed. I found it strategically placed just out of arm's reach and anchored to the wall. I had a sneaky feeling that *Ms. Intolerance* had ordered the placement. Okay, I was being way too paranoid. Since I was snuggly catheterized, precautions had to be taken. I had to ease my sore bottom off the bed to reach the bag, which was hooked below my reach on the mattress, unhook the bag and tubes, then gimp gingerly to the wall and push the call button. And wait for the nurse to answer. I would then try to make myself understood— *dream on*—then limp back to my bed, re-hook my catheter bag and tubes, and *wait.* This procedure was repeated a few times with the same beginning, middle and end. Finally two smiling nurses appeared in my doorway. I thought I'd probably have a better chance to get the sitz-bath if I used a few simple Thai phrases I'd learned in Thai 101. I knew that "water" in Thai was *nam* and "hot" was rón, so it figured that *nam ron* would produce hot water. What it did produce was several giggling nurses peeking in my door watching the crazy *farang* talking funny.

Exasperated, I decided to try pantomiming. Pointing to my butt, then to the toilet, followed by the water faucet and then to my butt again, they decided I needed a bedpan, laxative and a drink of water. While I had them in my room I thought I'd better ask for more pain medicine. My stomach began to cramp and my sutures burned. In my handy-dandy dictionary I found that "stomach" was *tong* and already knew that "pain" was *jep*—so wouldn't it be plausible that *tong jep* would mean stomach pain? Wrong again. Look, I know I said it right. I have a good ear for dialects. I have transcribed foreign doctors' medical tapes from lower Slobovia to upper Uganda but it just didn't work here. I thought back to something a Thai friend had told me: When *farangs* open their mouths to speak—before the Thai waits to hear what's coming out—they automatically assume it's going to be English. So before your sentence is finished they're interrupting with: "*Mai kâo jai kha.*" Help! Or should I say: *chûay!*

I grabbed my head, pointed to my butt, and writhed in agony, looking up to see if anyone was getting this. It finally produced some results. A few nods of understanding and off they rushed down the hall, returning with Lomotil, a bedpan and pain pills.

I had to refer to my dictionary constantly. I knew the Thai words and felt I pronounced them correctly. After all I *did* take two months of Thai language intonation. The nurses just turned a deaf ear. They were totally agreeable to *anything* I wanted—they just didn't know *what* I wanted.

I found a scratch pad in my purse. Maybe a picture might be worth a thousand pantomimes. I sketched what I thought was a Van Gogh-like drawing of a sitz-bath. The nurses smiled and nodded, giggling as they watched me sketch, as if I were a child who wanted approval for my artistic drawing. "Sitz bath?" I asked, trying to look intelligent.

"*Mai kâo jai kha.*" She didn't understand me.

I put my sketch pad away.

While I was in the midst of all this, my doctor dropped by to check on me. All I had to do was say the magic words: "Sitz-Bath." She knew exactly what I wanted and gave the order. Thank you, Buddha.

A sitz-bath in American hospitals resembles a miniature bathtub and is plumbed with hot and cold water. The nurse comes for you a couple times a day—post-partum, post-hemorrhoidectomy or post-anything to do with your fanny—and helps you ease your bottom into the warm sudsy water. It's sort of like giving your fanny its own private bath. The warm water and medicinal soap reduce inflammation and promote expeditious healing.

This hospital had a totally different procedure for their sitz-bath. The nurse walked in holding a cute little pink plastic dishpan, about sixteen inches in circumference, and placed it on top of the toilet seat. Into this dishpan she poured a drop of antibacterial solution—hopefully. I watched from the bathroom door as she went about her preparations. *Surely this little pink thing wasn't for me?* She glanced back at me from time to time and I'd give her a huge smile without knowing what the hell she was up to. She left the room and returned carrying what looked like a large coffee carafe, then poured the contents into the dishpan and motioned for me to come to her. She turned me around, backed my butt up to the pink dishpan, and gently pushed me down. As I slowly lowered my bottom into the snug plastic contraption, out poured water from an overflow hole and I ended up with my rump sitting on the bottom of a moist pan with water oozing around my thighs and down my legs. Not a pretty picture. It wouldn't have been so bad had I been blessed with the standard Thai-sized bottom. I'm sure it worked brilliantly for them. This was not the wonderful, soothing experience I'd looked forward to.

A couple days later, as I pattered down the halls for exercise, I spotted the infamous carafe sitting on the nurse's station. A clerk stood filling a coffee cup from the carafe and smiled at me as I walked by. *Hey, that's my sitz-bath pot. What's going on here?* The next day my doctor solved the puzzle. With no running hot water in the hospital, the ubiquitous Hot Pot—used for instant coffee, tea or—sitz-baths—sat on the nurse's station awaiting its next intended use.

Pantomiming became a means to an end as the days wore on.

Picture this crazed redhead, catheter tube swinging between her legs like the Pink Panther's tail, gesturing up and down the halls with the back of her gown flapping open like a tent in a monsoon, begging for some pain pills, hot water and toilet paper.

Ah, yes—the infamous toilet paper. Have I mentioned it yet? It's like requesting caviar in Bangladesh. I'm convinced Thais have a secret look reserved just for those of us who go through that disgusting procedure on our behinds. Remember, the Eastern squat toilet is the toilet of choice—with water to splash daintily over everything—from stem to stern. It was hard to find toilet paper in the Land of Smiles while I was there, except in hotels or markets catering to the wasteful *farangs.*

The next day my doctor brought in a heat lamp that she vowed would ease my pain. She placed the lamp at the bottom of the bed and aimed it at my sutures. The idea of the heat shrinking the sutures held promise, but with legs askance and a short drooping sheet barely covering my lower half, I'm sure I provided various janitors and anyone else who cared to take a peek with a view they'd like to forget.

After three days all the aggravations of my situation had me so depressed that I felt a shower and some makeup might lift my spirits. A cold shower was the next insult of the day. I'd hang my catheter bag on the neck of the showerhead while holding the tubing in my left hand so I wouldn't trip on it. In my right hand I held the shower hose with the on-off valve. I would take a deep breath, turn on the valve, scream and jump as the cold water hit my tepid body, all the while trying to keep from slipping on the slimy tile as I stooped to pick up the infinitesimally small bar of soap the hospital provided—that I kept dropping. But as I carefully bent down to pick up the soap, I had to keep a watchful eye on the catheter bag, still hanging precariously from the shower head, to make sure I didn't pull the plug.

As time progressed, the futility of what I was going through had me so agitated I looked as though I'd never seen the inside of a shower or the outside of a Lancôme counter. And, I was not sleeping well. Insulation, a prerequisite in U.S. construction, was nonexistent in this hospital. The corridors and my room sounded like the inside of a snare drum. The hospital rooms were not segregated, more like co-edish. In the room adjoining mine was a very elderly Thai lady on her way to meet Buddha, a two-year-old with croup and amoebic dysentery, and a morbidly obese European recovering from a hemorrhoidectomy. The child's crying and coughing, the old lady's moaning and hacking, and the obese European's belching and thunderous flatulence continued most of the day and night, wafting into my room.

The doors to the patients' rooms were permanently propped open; an invitation to the curious. With the doors open, why not look in as you pass by, right? So visitors to the obese, gaseous European would look in on me regularly, as did the family of the croupy child and any janitors who happened to be sweeping by.

During my hospital stay I came to realize something quite profound. We Americans are a different breed when it comes to hygienic measures and warding off bacteria and their accompanying maladies. Living in other third-world countries I found that "sterile" is pretty much an industrialized nation's fixation.

Sterile precautions were nonexistent in my room. I'd had this brought home to me several times, but this one incident was the worst: a friend came to visit me one evening and witnessed an act by my doctor that still makes her laugh years later. I'd asked her to set up my heat lamp before she left for the evening, thus saving me hours of pantomiming. As she draped the sheet over me my doctor entered the room. She said "Goosevenin," and without a stop at the sink to wash her hands, without pulling on sterile gloves, she pulled my sheet aside and began to probe—with her unwashed, ungloved fingers—my surgical site. God knows who or what she'd probed last. After scribbling some notations on my chart, she smiled and said, "Goosnite" and left the room—without so much as a *look* toward the washbowl. I don't know who should have been more grossed-out—me or the person she was about to probe next.

Looking back on that hospital stay, I must add that everyone else on the nursing staff was kind, caring and tolerant. I did complain to my doctor about *Ms. Intolerance* before I left the hospital. She assured me that I wasn't the only tortured soul who'd complained, and that the nurse would be transferred. Whatever that meant. I sincerely hoped the transfer would be to the surgical stockroom, where she could count enema bags and used razors until time for retirement.

HOSPITAL WHISPERS

37

I knew I was skating on a slippery-slope with *Mrs. A* before I entered the hospital, but being the optimist that I am I'd hoped it would all blow over by the time I was discharged. Maybe she just needed some time to forget all her petty grievances against me. Maybe we could start anew.

However, when she didn't show up at the hospital, or even call, I became a tad worried. It was odd, I thought. As the boss's wife shouldn't she at least visit one of her hospitalized ladies? I really didn't care to see her, but if she did drop by I'd be polite and try to work up some sympathy from her.

She did not come for a visit nor did she call to see if I'd lived through the surgery. As the hours ticked by she became an all pervasive presence in my mind. I made a vow that when I was discharged I'd try to mend some badly worn fences and be rid of this constant dread that hung on me like a sodden cloak.

My PILC buddies showed up every day and stayed for long visits, gleefully covering all the fun I'd missed while cooped up in my broom closet. A couple of brave friends from our company dropped by, staying maybe ten minutes, furtively checking their watches. I was shocked when they asked if there was a back exit from the hospital. How far had this thing gone? I watched them take peeks over their shoulders, expecting to see *Mrs. A*, who might have them shot for giving aid to the enemy. *Guilt by association.* They did have their husbands' jobs to consider, I rationalized, and I did appreciate their loyalty to me. They briefly filled me in on the latest from the meetings, and could hardly wait to lay it across my sick bed. "So, what's been going on?" I asked Sandy, giving her the green light for the excitement de jour.

"I've got some good news and some bad news. Which do you want first?"

"The good if it outweighs the bad."

"I don't think it does, but anyway, after the meeting yesterday Lydia was showing everyone your PILC newsletter. We all thought it was pretty cool."

"Where'd Lydia get the newsletter? She's not a PILC member."

"She said her neighbor delivered the newsletters for you and had a couple left over."

"Is that it for the good news?"

"Yeah. Sorta."

"What's the bad news?"

"Well, two things, really. One of the girls asked *Mrs. A* if she'd seen you, and were you gonna be out of the hospital in time for the Christmas potluck."

"Really? How'd she handle that one?"

"Pretty smooth, I thought. She just said she'd not had a chance to call you yet but that the potluck would "most certainly" go on with or without you."

"Okay, give me the rest of the bad stuff. I'm tired. I can't take much more of this."

"Okay, well, as I said, we were all looking at your newsletter and saying how cool it was and all, when *Mrs. A* walks up behind Lydia and looks over her shoulder."

"Oops."

"'Oops' is right. Lydia nearly jumped sky high when she looked up and saw the look on her face. I guess you hadn't told her about being the editor, huh?"

I sat up in bed and tried to catch my breath. I felt like I'd been hit from behind by another truck. "No. I didn't. I really didn't get a chance. But considering how many spies she has floating around town, I'm sure she had an idea what was going on. Besides, I really didn't feel I had to ask her permission, so I didn't." I said this with much more bravado than I actually felt. "Go on."

"Well, your picture was on the front page, so you had to know somebody would show it to her. You probably shoulda' told her, huh?"

Silence.

"Don't you think?"

"I made a choice."

Sandy checked her watch, the door, and then did a quick look-see out the window. "You're right. It isn't anybody's business what we do, but she isn't just 'anybody.'"

"Okay. Alright, so what happened then, I mean, when she saw the newsletter?"

"Well, what could Lydia do? She just stood here looking scared."

"Then what?" I really didn't want to hear this. My gut and sutures were beginning to tighten like piano wires.

"Well the old bat grabs it from Lydia and says in a real sugary voice, 'Let's have a look at this, shall we?' so Lydia just backed away." My friend waited respectfully while I digested this news. "God, what else could she do? She had to hand it over, didn't she?"

"Of course," I lied. "I'm not upset at Lydia. It just didn't work out the way I planned, is all. Before all this bladder stuff came up I was going to bring some extra copies to our next meeting to show everyone the great stuff that's going on with the PILC. I'd hoped to get some interest in the volunteer program, but then she up and changed all our meetings to the same day as theirs, so I just said screw it."

"God, you've got guts!" Trina laughed, breaking away from her lookout post at the window.

"What guts? I wanted to keep it above-board. I thought if she saw all the stuff the PILC had to offer she might get interested in the club."

"Dream on."

She was right. It was a 'dream-on' thought. "So go on, let's have the bottom line here."

"Well…" Sandy paused, knowing she was getting to the good part. "…then she takes a quick look at the front page, sees your picture as the new editor and gets a sour look on her puss like she was standing over a pile of manure. You know, like she gets when she's ticked at someone?"

"And?" *Oh be still my heart, gut and sutures.*

"Then she tosses it on the floor."

"You're kidding me, right? She did that in front of everyone?" *Now I was in scalding water.*

"No, I'm not kidding. Then she just looks off into space, like she wasn't talking to anyone in particular and says, 'That redhead is outta here!'"

Gulp! Thanks, ladies. On your way out could you ask the nurse to send in some cyanide capsules?

The next day two of *Mrs. A's* henchwomen, *Frick and Frack,* phoned to say they'd be up to see me. The word around our circle was you never told these two a thing that you didn't want repeated back to her.

I thought back to when they'd made their first visit to me after I'd moved into the new house. I remember thinking how nice they were, going out of their way to make me feel welcome. How I'd sung like a canary about my problems with *Mrs. A.* How they'd both frowned and shook their heads in tandem, agreeing with my every bitch. I had no idea I was digging my own grave—with my tongue as the shovel. Now, lying here in the hospital with time to reflect, I remembered how the Christmas Potluck idea had come about. It was *Frick and Frack* who'd first mentioned it. They were also the ones who'd first mentioned the phone call from the Chaplain to host his boys for the holiday. In fact, now remembering it very clearly, those two had spurred me on with the idea of putting it together. "Good idea. Why don't you head the committee, Dodie?" What the hell was going on here? Was I set up?

How had things deteriorated so fast? I started to put the pieces of the proverbial puzzle together. Things that should never have made their way to *Mrs. A's* tympanic membranes were well known to her. The only conclusion I could come up with was that it had to be *Frick and Frack* carrying my gripes back to her.

Dick had warned me, but I blew it off at the time because they'd seemed so nice—and I do like nice. Why hadn't I seen it before? I had noticed them going back and forth to each others' houses many times and had even seen *Mrs. A* walk into their homes without knocking—a sure sign of complicity. Back then I hadn't been thinking of spies so I guess I'd had diarrhea of the mouth when they dropped over to chat me up.

But for the last few weeks before my hospitalization I'd avoided them because something worried me about those two. I didn't know what it was but I decided it best to keep my motor mouth closed. The less they knew about my life the better, especially if they spent so much time with *her*. Now I knew why Mrs. *I-Have-My-Spies-Watching-You* was so shocked when she saw my newsletter at her meeting—I hadn't told *Frick and Frack* anything about being the editor.

But now, here they were, sitting on the edge of my bed, looking like they'd buy me the world if I'd just get better and come home. "Oh, guess what?" *Frick* said. "*Mrs. A* called the Chaplain and told him we couldn't host the sailors on Christmas Eve."

Beep! Please record your answer: "Oh?"

"Really!" chimed in *Frack*. "Can you believe it?"

"Yes."

"Well we think it stinks and told her so."

"Really?" No facial expression or vocal inflection.

"But she did say we could go ahead with our potluck Christmas party."

"Good." Slight smile.

"You will be home for the party, won't you?"

"Damn straight!" Big smile.

They gave up after a while, blew some air kisses my way and were gone.

C'est la vie! Who needs 'em?

Tears.

Dick came to the visit me bearing flowers and hang-dog looks. The house was too quiet. He missed me, he was sorry for all the pouting, he'd try harder. But did he mean it? His insistence for sex every night and the ensuing fights brought on chest pains and made me realize that it had to stop. He promised that things would change once I got home. *We'll see!*

After some small talk he gave me the scoop at work. He said he'd stopped *Mr. JB* on the jobsite and asked him again when he was going to send for Dale. This time, he said, *Mr. JB* looked pissed that he'd asked. "Not now," he said as he looked at his watch. "Got a meetin' to go to. It don't look good."

I could feel my gut reacting. What the hell did that mean? I couldn't bear the thought that my behavior might have caused Mrs. *Control Freak* to ruin my son's chances of getting on this job. Dick said that maybe the old man had meant "not right now" as in maybe after the first of the year or something. Lots of things change on the jobsite every month, he said. He wasn't going to jump to conclusions before he knew for sure. I shouldn't either.

I called my son that night. The minute he heard my voice he said, "Well?" I didn't have to ask him what he meant. "Honey, the thing is they aren't bringing anyone new on the job right now. Dick says maybe after the first of the year the client will okay another position. It's only December. The job will go on for two years. Just hang in there."

"Mom, I've been hanging for three months. It's driving me and my wife nuts. What kind of job are they running that they can't forecast their manpower ahead of time?"

He was right. But how could I even start telling him the crap that was going on here. They weren't the nice people I thought they were. And *why* did I even want my son to be employed by these two freakos? Why would I want to put him through this craziness? "Just be patient. We'll hear something soon."

I hung up the phone with a pain in my heart. I couldn't even imagine the regret I'd live with if I were the reason he didn't get the job. I had to be positive. Maybe things would change if *I* changed. As soon as I was out of this place I'd throw myself at her feet and kiss them or do whatever I had to do to make her think I was repentant. Maybe if I towed the line, fell in with the other women, dropped the editor's job, she'd tell the old man to hire my son…

I could do it. How hard would it be to just go with the flow? No matter that the flow was about to drown me. I knew I could do it. I would do it.

I needed to sleep. I'd worry about it tomorrow.

GOING A.M.A.

38

our long and uncomfortable days had passed since my surgery and my doctor now felt it was time to pull the plug—the catheter. Oh happy day! I was ecstatic. Before she would remove it, however, she had a job for me. She placed three huge glasses of water on my tray and smiled: "You mut finit sree glasses in one ow-wah, then you mut pee-pee sree glasses, then I take out casseta and you go home." Fine with me! I was happy to comply. She removed the catheter and I guzzled them down like a lumber jack in a beer drinking contest. An hour later my stomach was distended and I could feel a round balloon hanging somewhere below my navel. I waited.

Nothing happened.

Hour two brought more of the same. I walked the halls trying to get things moving. Nothing! I sat on the toilet and read, hummed, sang. Nothing! I began to feel the all-too familiar pains of a stricture. My singing turned into wailing. I sounded like a circus barker, begging anyone within earshot to put the catheter back in; *Ms. Intolerance*, the European, the janitor. Anyone. The nurses tsk-tsked me and called the doctor back to my room. "Wot wrong? You doan wan go home?" she asked with a hint of resignation in her voice.

"Of course I wan go home, but I can't pee. It hurts like hell and nothing happens. The pressure's killing me."

She stared at me for a few moments, trying, I'm sure, to

understand why *farangs* were so dense. "If you wan go home, you mut pee-pee."

"Please, doctor, it's just not going to happen and I'm dying here from the pain. Please put the catheter back in and I'll try again later… Soon. Tomorrow."

After a few minutes of chiding me for "holding back watah" she inserted a new catheter. This procedure took another twenty minutes with me moaning while interested nurses and visitors watched from the hall.

It was the same story that night. No luck. The doctor stressed the danger of infection of inserting multiple catheters, but I gave her no choice; either insert or I couldn't be held responsible for what I might do, such as jump to my death from the first floor window. My urethra was burning from all this in-and-out crap and I just wanted to go home. At this point I felt I'd probably go through life with this damn catheter dangling between my legs. No more of this kind of pain. I wanted out of here. *Help me someone, I'm being held captive by a Thai catheter.*

I then made two executive decisions. I was going home the next day with or without the damn catheter. If I hadn't peed by noon, I would leave the hospital AMA—Against Medical Advice—and would fly stateside to see a urologist as soon as I could get a reservation. The other decision came after a phone call from a friend. She told me that *Mrs. A* had announced that the Christmas potluck was going on with or without me. I decided it would be "with" me and hence decision number two.

It was Christmas Eve day, and I was champing at the bit to get going. By two in the afternoon, after giving it two more shots with the water—and no release—another catheter was inserted and I packed my bags. With the catheter tube wound once around my thigh, then tucked into my waistband, and the bag taped to my inner thigh, I jauntily exited the hospital AMA and headed for home and the Christmas potluck. Once home I rested until I knew the party was in full swing. I showered, dressed in a cute little outfit that would hide my new plastic hitch-hiker, and Dick and I headed outside to join in the fray. *Frick and Frack* were greeting the guests as we walked through the patio and there was no way around them. "So nice to see you're up and about. We were hoping you'd make it." *Barf!* They joyfully told us that the party was a huge success thanks to the excellent planning of *Mrs. A. Barf again.* Dick left to get us a drink and hopefully find someone to talk to. I looked around at the other couples, all animatedly bobbing heads and waving hands as they visited, and here I sat, alone on my sore tush, and watched.

"*Thanks to the excellent planning of Mrs. A?*" What was the deal here? Did she cancel the work I'd done and then redo everything. Was she that much of a control freak? I had typed up some flyers for the party, made some phone calls and was waiting for someone to assign the potluck dishes when I had to bow out in favor of the hospital. I called a couple of the ladies and asked them to distribute my flyers and take over the rest of the phone calls for me. They'd all agreed to help. Silly me—again. I thought it was a done deal. I'd assumed that others had their own jobs to make this come together, and happily went on my merry way. A friend told me later that at *Mrs. A* had asked a few of the ladies if they knew who'd organized the potluck. The women, not knowing why she asked, had told her that I'd called them to ask for help and that's all she had to hear. This would be her royal party and all present must defer to the Queen. Hubby's job was on the line and the ladies would sing like canaries. Long Live the Queen!

I was surprised to see *The JBs* walking around in their company smiles as they distributed Peace on Earth and Good Will to Man. I remembered the day I walked over to their house with my insincere invitation. Inviting them was not my first choice, but I knew there'd be hell to pay if I didn't. I'd told her that some of us in the complex had talked about having a Christmas potluck over the holiday and would they be able to attend? She looked at me with eyebrows arched, as if she were about to say, "Really?" then must have changed her mind as her face went from surprise to boredom. I waited for some sort of response. She seemed to think it over for a second then told me they'd be out of town with clients that weekend. Silly me, I took that as a no. Why did they show up? Was I totally dense or what? I still didn't get it. Now, neither one of them spoke to us, nor, for that matter, even bothered to look our way. I took it as a sure sign that we might indeed be in deep shit.

I was cold, both physically and emotionally, as Dick and I sat off by ourselves and watched the revelers. My peers were busy chatting-up *The Bosses* and found very little time for us—guilt by association again. I left with my private demons and went home to bed. Peace on Earth and Goodwill to Man. Bah! Humbug!

After crying myself into a stupor, my mind tried to make sense of all this. As I listened to the Christmas carols and happy chatter floating in from the patio, I got it. *Geez, Dodie, do you need a brick spy to fall on your head?* She couldn't let her ladies think that someone other than herself had deemed to give them a bash. All was well in Controlville. It also must have been the reason she cancelled the sailors' visit; she assumed it was my idea. Who gave a damn? She could take credit for the party. I should have known that nothing would happen unless *Mrs. A* ordained it.

I needed to sleep. I told myself that this whole mess would be cleared up by the time I returned from the States, especially since I planned to bow down and kiss her well-pedicured feet. I'd worry about it then.

I was miserable, beaten down from the infection, and did not want to face the exhausting flight to the States. Maybe I could do this on my own. I'd give it the old college try. Over the next three days I worked diligently at getting rid of my little plastic hanger-oner. I drank three glasses of water, waited two hours then hi-tailed it to the emergency room—in pain—but not yelling, to get un-cathed and hopefully fill three glasses for them. It didn't work. I was terrified that those sneaky little bacteria were galloping in with every catheter change.

After three days of this, it was now time to yell "Uncle." I knew I had to leave. On the last insertion by the ER doc, I had the distinct feeling that something was awry. It felt as if the tip was not anchored correctly, like I was sitting on a #9 knitting needle. When I complained to him he told me not to worry about it; I'd get used to it in time. Right! Easy for him to say. He'd been sitting on something since birth. This was a new feeling for me, and I didn't like it. I was curious now. Do men really feel their "boys" when they sit? When I got home I had to find out. I asked Dick. "What?" he said, as if he'd misunderstood me. "Feel what?"

"You know! Your stuff. Your things. The stuff between your legs. Where do they go when you sit down? Do you sit on them?"

"Christ! How the hell do I know! I guess. Well, maybe. Why?"

"Never mind. I have my answer."

On December 28th I left for the States to see a urologist and end this misery. I had to find out what was going on up there. Why couldn't I pee and get this interloper out once and for all? I thought about my hasty decision to stay in Thailand for the surgery. I thought about what my doctor told me during our interview: "At end of sree day, you casseta come out, you pee-pee, then go home." What the hell was happening to me? It had now been over nine days. My casseta was hanging on for dear life with no signs of pee-pee and I was flying stateside.

Talk about bad luck and bad decisions.

**FRIENDLY AIRPORTS
AND UNFRIENDLY SKIES**

39

If ever you take an international flight and want to get through airport glitches quickly, do it in a wheelchair. What speedy service I received in the Bangkok airport. I felt a tad guilty as we glided through never-ending lines of tired, disheveled travelers. The airline employee who pushed my wheelchair careened wildly around the lines of people while I hung on to the armrests. He zigzagged through security, ending with an abrupt stop and a wheelie. I pictured him in the Indy 500.

At the security gate they asked me to raise my right hand and swear I was not hiding any jewelry, guns, dynamite or drugs somewhere on my person. I think they would have been more horrified to see the little pee-pee bag under my clothes. The airline employees were most respectful to this poor *farang* cripple.

The flight from Bangkok to Tokyo would be eight hours. I was miserable when lying down, how was I going to sit for eight hours with this knitting needle invading my private places. The First Class section was full when I boarded at Bangkok. As I limped down the aisle I managed a disinterested look at the cozy First Class passengers, sipping their Perrier and Merlot as the rest of us poor steerage passengers filed by. *Shame on them!*

I had asked for a bulkhead row to have a little more room to spread out and I was ecstatic to see that the adjoining seat was vacant. *Finally,*

I thought, *things were going my way. Dare I hope I'd reached the end of my bad luck string?*

I continued to be miserable on the eight-hour flight, but I did manage to grab a few Zs, half sitting and half arching out of both seats. I'm sure I looked like I had a huge hemorrhoid problem to those passing by. I hiked my legs up and managed to doze off in this contorted body position while visions of Tony Roma's famous ribs invaded my dreams with heaping stacks of ribs and greasy onion rings piled high on my plate. I'd just put a shovel-full of the onion rings in my mouth when someone poked me mid-bite. The flight attendant placed a tray of soup and salad on my table and disappeared. *Hey wait. Where's my ribs?*

I did my best to ingest most of the strange looking things floating haphazardly in my soup. I knew some were eggs, but they were a kind of baby-doo-doo mustard color—a color one doesn't like to associate with eggs, and they were rather rubbery. When my fork touched them they recoiled. Scary! My salad gave me cause to worry as well. I definitely saw something move in there, half hidden between the arugula and the snow peas. I probed it with my fork and it scooted under a bamboo shoot. Calm down, I told my over-active imagination, everyone's eating it and no one has fallen face first into their plate—yet. After eating I slipped a Valium into my hot tea and woke up in Tokyo. I couldn't believe I'd slept for nearly four hours without the usual ten quarts of water I was supposed to drink and the thirty trips to the bathroom.

Customer service at the Narita Airport in Tokyo was courteous and efficient. A female airport employee greeted me as I limped onto the jet-way and helped me into the ever-faithful wheelchair. She was all smiles and bows as I said my *domo arigatos*. This girl was so tiny I felt I should be pushing her. I guessed her weight at about seventy pounds and just a tad over four and a half feet tall. At my best weight I had her doubled, but the smile never left her sweet, strained face. She helped me get comfortable and off we went to my next gate.

It had to be an Asian thing. They all seemed to drive the same—cars, shopping carts and wheelchairs. We zoomed in and out of queues of travelers where she found an elevator amid the crowd and down we went to a special exit. She pushed me through a tunnel that was so long I thought she might be wheeling me all the way to LAX. It finally ended in an underground parking structure. She rolled me up to a group of four Asian ladies, all in wheelchairs, seemingly on their last voyage, and looking like they might be pushing the backside of eighty. Two large vans with lift ramps were awaiting us. The attendants wheeled us aboard and we were off and running to our waiting jet.

Parked next to our plane was a monstrous truck with a ten-foot wide lift ramp. The ramp was lowered and two-by-two we were loaded like cargo onto the truck, then lifted up like freight being hoisted into a container and pushed onto the plane for the last leg of the journey. I felt like a malingerer sitting among these frail, sickly ladies. I smiled apologetically at the octogenarian beside me. In her best attempt at English she whispered: "It tellible to get ohd, neh?"

Maybe I was sicker than I thought.

The last leg of my trip was a close second in aggravation to my hospital stay. Sitting for a thirteen-hour flight from Tokyo to LAX with a needle tip poking my inflamed urethra made me very cranky. Each time I stood up, sat down, or walked, I could feel the needle inching around. And with each inch I'd have a little more pain, a little more burning, and a little more misery. Disappointingly, my seat wasn't bulkhead this time, and the window seat was occupied. Sleep was impossible. *I could see I was not quite at the end of my bad luck string.*

Needing to empty my catheter, I decided to use the First Class lavatory. I knew it was a no-no for us steerage passengers, but I didn't have the strength for the long walk to use the coach lavatory. When I passed through the curtained-off area of First Class I noticed an empty row, no newspapers or purses tucked into small places. I took a peek in the lavatories and they were both empty. I knew this was my lucky day. I could see myself stretched out on both seats, feet up and weight off my irritated lower half. I would ask the First Class attendant to admit me to her wonderful world of lean-back seats. I knew she'd seen me limping into her powder room when a slight frown marred her otherwise flawless face. I prayed she might be sympathetic. As I walked back toward my seat in coach I had to wait until she moved to get around the small vestibule. She seemed lost in the vagaries of adjusting magazines in the bulkhead rack.

It was now or never. "Ah, hi. I'm sitting in the second row in coach..." I waited for some sign of recognition—or pity.

She looked at me as though contemplating her next Botox treatment. "Yes?" She answered, bored beyond endurance.

"Well, ah, I'm really hurting and I've got this, ah..." She looked past me, scanning the aisle for someone more interesting to talk to. "Um, I know this sounds terrible but I've got this, uh, this catheter tip in and it's trying to, you know, ah, come out, and I'm..."

She snapped around to face me. Her eyebrows were now touching her hairline. "You've got what?"

Well! That's a little better, I thought, *let's show some sympathy here.* I knew I'd better lay it on fast or I'd lose her again. "Umm, a catheter tip that's half in and half out."

A distasteful look crossed her face. She immediately pulled herself together and served up a sympathetic smile. "Well now, we can't let that happen, can we?"

Oh, oh. Now what? She doesn't like me—or my catheter.

"Where did you say you were seated?"

"Right there," I pointed. "Coach. Second row. Aisle seat."

"Yes, and what can I do for you?"

"Well I noticed you had an empty row in First Class and wondered if I could move up here so I can stretch out and take some weight off my sore urethra."

Her face morphed into a scowl as she busied herself wiping imaginary dust specks from the magazines in the rack.

"Ma'am?" I said, trying to bring her back to my problem.

"Oh, yes. Well, um, how about an extra pillow to sit on? It would be impossible to move you to First Class, as, um, that's completely against company policy. Sorry." She turned and walked into First Class, lifting the curtain and letting it fall behind her like a black velvet door in my face.

I limped back to my seat with thoughts of placing that extra pillow over her uncaring face—the extra pillow she never returned with.

Health experts will tell you it's important to keep hydrated on long flights. However those same experts have probably never flown a thirteen-hour stint with a pint-sized catheter bag that needs empting every thirty minutes. I knew I should be drinking gallons of water, but the effort of getting up and down to empty the catheter was arduous and painful. It took me five minutes to produce the oomph needed to stand up, then another five minutes to do it without the catheter tip stabbing me. This entailed some butt wriggling. I noticed a few eyebrows heading scalp-ward as I struggled. I then had to gingerly walk down the mile-long aisle to the coach lavatory. Once inside the tiny lav, I had to undress, unhook, unwind and empty; then hook up, wind up and dress up. While going through this draining routine—both literally and figuratively—I pictured the pilot announcing, "Ladies and Gentamen, please take your seats immediately. We are going into a steep dive to get under this weather front..."

When I was at the point of pulling my own plug, the pilot

announced our descent into LAX. As the mass of travelers prepared to disembark I decided to let *Ms. I'd Rather Eat Dirt Than Help You* know she'd caused me a great deal of pain. Limping my way to the gangway, I followed closely behind the First Class passengers. When I got to her I stopped. "Thank you so much for all your help on this painful trip."

She was taken aback for just a flash then I saw the realization in her eyes. She knew I was being sarcastic but ignored the inference.

"Oh, well, yes, ah, you're welcome. Please fly with us again." She proceeded to address the next departing passenger over my shoulder.

I held my ground. No one was going around me just yet. "By the way," I added, "Flo? Or is it Ms. Nightingale? I wonder if you'd be so kind as to jot down your badge number on this cocktail napkin."

She faltered.

"I believe I need your badge number when I write to Customer Relations." People were stacked in the aisles behind me. I could hear the rumble of disgruntled passengers. I'm sure I heard chanting and tom-toms.

"I, ah, could you please step to the side, Ma'am, and let the other passengers disembark?"

"Well I suppose I could but there's really no place to stand up here. Could you ask them to back up for me?" Now the natives were really pressing in on me. I stared at her, all smiles and expectancy.

"It's 12530," she blurted out. "Now please disembark or I'll have to call the captain."

And, disembark I did, with a smart snap to my limp. Funny how pain abates when you feel good has triumphed over evil.

JOHN WAYNE
INTERNATIONAL (?) AIRPORT

40

I was helped off the plane at Los Angeles International Airport (LAX) and introduced to Dave, my antagonist for the next hour-and-a-half, and the proud bearer of the "priceless" wheelchair. Dave, a young, good-looking black man was not an airport employee, he proudly informed me, but was employed by a subcontractor who furnished wheelchairs and their attendants to the airport. Dave was a polite young man, doing what he was told to do. He had his act together and knew all the loopholes. I was a little more relaxed knowing I was with an American driver as he pushed me through the airport. As time went on I realized that he cared more for his damn chair than he did for my sore butt.

The first pang of angst came when my baggage took forever to appear on the carousel and Dave incessantly looked at his watch, fidgeting as if he should be somewhere else. By now I was beyond exhausted. My lower quadrant was inflamed and screaming to be free of my weight. My catheter, which needed to be emptied, began to peek its head out from under the hem of my slacks. I was afraid if I asked Dave to wheel me to the restroom he might go AWOL. Long after most of the passengers had claimed their luggage and what seemed like hours—for Dave, as well as for me—my luggage appeared. He piled what he could on my lap and positioned my carry-on alongside my wheelchair. He gave me the handle and assured me that the wheels would make it weightless. Ha! With my right arm flailing behind, growing longer with each revolution, I struggled to hold on as Dave headed for Customs. They glanced at my passport and waved us through without question, as they do most wheelchair sitters. I guess being in a wheelchair turns you into an honest, law-abiding soul.

Dave moved at warp speed now as he headed for the roped off area, alive with swarms of people waiting for their loved ones. "Do you see your ride, Ma'am?"

He's kidding me, right? The waiting area for international arrivals is normally teeming with people; a mass of bodies, indistinguishable, all clumped together in a gaggle of humanity. This place looked like Macy's the day after Thanksgiving. Some were holding signs aloft, jumping up and down, yelling, laughing, and waving, and in the midst of all this I was supposed to find a short stocky guy in a baseball cap? *Where in the hell was my ride?*

I'd been very clear about my arrival time when I'd called my friend, Gail, for a lift. Gail is the embodiment of the word "friend" and was ready and willing to help her buddy get back to the States and to a good doctor. She had appointed her husband, Joe, to pick me up at the airport and I was assured he'd be on time.

"Not yet, Dave, but I'm sure he's here. You can leave me here if you like." I reached for my purse to give him a tip.

"Sorry Ma'am, can't do it, company don't allow me t'leave the wheelchair. I have t'keep it in my sight at all times."

What does that mean? Surely he wouldn't dump me on my sore tail and take off? I looked at this broken-down wheelchair, amazed that it was still in use and that someone would actually worry about losing it.

"Can you see your party yet, Miss?" Dave asked for the umpteenth time—*and don't think I didn't notice the "Miss" bit—flatterer.*

I scanned the crowd looking for a familiar face, but everyone looked familiar with my poor eyesight. After more than twenty minutes of Dave looking like he might dump me any second, I thought I'd better move on to Plan B. "Dave, would you mind wheeling me over to the pay phone? I'll call his wife at work and find out what time he left home." The phone booths were filled to overflowing with people queuing up behind them. I had Dave push me to a wall phone. Have you ever tried to make a phone call from a public wall phone while sitting in a wheelchair? Today, years later, our conscientious country has placed public phones lower on the wall to assist the handicapped. But this was pre-A.D.A. and they were all at standing height. I thought Dave might offer to dial the number for me. I looked back to see if he might be waiting for me to ask him. His attention was on a cute little purple-haired twit with hip-huggers hugging so low they should have been called cheek huggers. I wanted to yell "Plumber Alert." He stared at her, grinning and tapping a foot to some silent rap tune playing between his ears.

I leaned forward. The wheelchair was either very narrow or I was very wide. It was way too difficult to reach the phone over my purse, my makeup kit, rubber donut and my pillow that had traveled with me around the world, all piled high on my lap. I tried to wriggle forward but that caused pain. I reached for the coin slot, which was two feet higher than my wheelchair. I felt the stricture welling up in my throat and knew it was just a matter of minutes before I started bawling. I gave up. I cleared my throat to bring Dave back to earth. He looked embarrassed when I asked him if he'd mind dialing the number for me. *Wouldn't you think he might have thought of that?* Both numbers I asked him to dial were busy. The final insult was when he replaced the receiver and the bloody phone company kept my money. *Doesn't the phone company have enough money?* I had no more change. I sniveled and asked Dave if he'd mind getting me some change for the phone. You guessed it! Dave couldn't leave the freakin' wheelchair. So off we went, pushing and pulling, all the while my catheter was slip-sliding with gravity, ever dangerously full and ready to overflow. With visions of leakage around my wheelchair, I thought it prudent to have Dave wheel me to the restroom first. He was not happy but he handled it well; he pushed me so fast I could hear sloshing coming from my catheter bag.

On the ride back to the phone I chattered nonstop trying to distract Dave from checking his watch every half second. I gave him Joe's description, told him he'd probably have on a baseball cap. Told him that baseball caps weren't designed for Joe's head, or maybe it was that Joe's head wasn't designed for baseball caps. Whatever! I said he was short, stocky—anything to keep his mind off his damn watch. It didn't work. I told Dave—again—that Joe was to pick me up at eight-ish and that I was really sorry about this. I said that Joe was very reliable and assured him that he must be on his way. In fact, he probably was parking the car that very minute. *Hurry up Joe, damnit!*

It was now 9:00 a.m. Dave and I were both checking our watches now. Still no Joe! I did see a fellow, baseball cap askew, mustache, stocky. I almost jumped out of the wheelchair. "It's him, it's him," I gleefully yelled to Dave. "I think." On closer inspection this guy didn't look quite as odd in his baseball cap. At the wall phone Dave offered to dial the number for me—*about time, I'd say.* I think he just wanted to get this over with and dump my butt. He handed me the receiver. When I heard Gail's familiar voice I started crying again. "Gail, oh my God, I'm so glad to hear your voice. I feel like a woman without a country. Where is Joe?"

Gail is my closest and most trusted friend, and has been for over forty years. And she knows my luck—and Joe's. "You're not going to believe this, Dodie," she sighed. "Joe went to John Wayne Airport, the dumb shit!*"*

Now, Gail doesn't normally swear so I knew she was upset. "He just called. He's on his way to LAX and should be there in about twenty minutes. Don't give up."

"Twenty minutes? My wheelchair guy's about to toss my butt. Why did Joe go to John Wayne Airport? Everyone knows that it's only for domestic flights."

"I don't know," she sighed, "I guess the old saying's true."

"What's that?" I sniffed.

"That anything with tires or testicles will always give you trouble!"

I had to laugh in spite of myself. "Don't worry," my thoughtful friend said. "I have everything ready for you at the house."

"Thank you," I sniffed. "I think I just need to lie down and get off my sore butt for a few days. I've been on it for over twenty-four hours and I'm cold and hurting."

"I've put some PJs and socks in the guest room. Just get between those flannel sheets and you'll be nice and warm. You need to sleep before you think about doing anything."

Bless her heart. It was so like Gail to take care of every detail. "But I do have to get in to see a urologist as soon as possible."

"It's a done deal," she said. "I made an appointment with a urologist for tomorrow. If you need anything from the drug store, just tell Joe and he can pick it up for you."

I handed the receiver back to Dave. "Another twenty minutes," I told him, then began sniveling again because of the hopelessness of it all. Dave did turn his back, respectfully, but I still saw him check his watch—*can you believe that, in my time of sorrow?* The rap music in his head must have started again, as he was bouncing around behind me, waving at his wheelchair homies as they passed by, "Hey, man, whashapinin?" he'd yell, or "Catchalater, man." Then to me, "Hope they don't let the boss know I'm just sittin' here doin nothin'."

That did it. "Dave! What do you want me to do, stand here and wait? It's going to be another twenty minutes before he's here."

"Ah, no Ma'am, but I could wheel ya outside and you could wait on the bench 'til your ride comes."

Seeing the look of resignation on my face, he must have taken that as a sign of defeat and headed for the exit. When the automatic doors opened the cold smacked me in the face with a punch. It was December in Los Angeles and mist was falling. I held out my hand, felt the moisture and felt a sudden urge to cry again. "Dave, could you possibly just leave me and the chair inside for another ten minutes and then come back for it? It's freezing out here."

After his litany of company rules, I told him to go. At least I wouldn't have to sit here and watch him suffer from spastic colitis. He wheeled me up to the concrete bench and began to unload. He tactfully looked away from my tears as he placed my rubber donut on the bench then reached for my hand to pull me up and out of the wheelchair. He piled the rest of my belongings on the bench next to me, turned his beloved wheelchair and started walking away. "Wait, what about your tip?" I called to his back as he vanished behind the automatic doors in three giant steps. I guess he was rushing to catch up with his wheelchair homeys, heading for his long-overdue coffee break. I could hear him now: "Y'all won't believe the ride I just had. Cryin' and axin' me to do all kinds of shit for her. Man, was I glad to dump her ass."

It was now 9:30 a.m. I'd been on the ground well over an hour. I'd been in transit for nearly a full day. I'd been acclimated to a country with a climate of 100 degrees Fahrenheit and 100 percent humidity. And there I sat; aching, shaking and freezing my buns off on a cold concrete bench in fifty-five degree, bone-numbing drizzly weather.

I pictured trying to empty my catheter bag of frozen urine.

I spotted Joe walking toward me from the parking garage. The look on his face said it all. "I'm sorry, I'm sorry," he grumbled as he reached for my carry-on. I felt it would be thoughtless of me to cry at this point, so I just said "Hi." He mumbled that he'd be right back with the car and pick me up at the curb. That was encouraging. *Please hurry, Joe!*

After Joe had packed me and my armada into his car and successfully merged onto the 105 Freeway, I felt it was safe to talk. "Joe?"

No answer. Eyes straight ahead. Shirt noticeably damp.

"Joe, I was just curious. Why *did* you go to John Wayne Airport instead of LAX?"

"HOW THE HELL DO I KNOW! I JUST DID!"

Geez, you don't have to yell.

A mile or so down the road, when I felt it was safe and Joe seemed a little less likely to yell at me, I decided to press for details. He told me how it all came about after my phone call to Gail:

"Joe," Gail called as she hung up the phone. "Dodie just phoned from Thailand."

"I hope it wasn't collect."

"Oh stop! She's not doing well after her surgery so she's flying home to see a specialist."

"Whadya want me to do?"

"Just pick her up at the airport. Her plane gets in at 8:15 Monday morning,"

"Righto!" Joe went back to the train pictures on his monitor and became lost in dreams of locomotives versus steam engines. It seemed like the logical thing for Gail to ask him, right? He's self-employed, works at home, and has nothing better to do than to drive to LAX in rush-hour traffic.

But Gail didn't say "LAX," she said "*the*" airport. Because they usually fly from John Wayne Airport when traveling, it seemed logical that it was the first airport he thought of. Right?

When Joe arrived at John Wayne Airport, a forty-five minute drive from his home, he felt smug and satisfied with himself. After all, it was just 8 o'clock and Dodie's flight wouldn't land for another fifteen minutes. Hey, no problem with parking either. Cool! He sauntered into the terminal, hands in pockets, whistling *The Orange Blossom Special*—he's a train nut—checking monitors for incoming flights. When he found nothing posted from Tokyo he began to get damp under the armpits. He approached a check-in counter. "Hi," he said. "I'm looking for flight number two from Tokyo. Where's it come in at?"

Three little agent heads snapped to attention from adjoining counters. "Sir," one of the agents offered, "no *international* flights land at this airport. I think you probably want Los Angeles International Airport."

"What?" Joe felt his heart skip a beat.

"Sir, this airport is for domestic flights only, no international flights come into this airport," she repeated, this time a bit impatient. "If you'll wait just a minute I'll phone LAX and find out the status of your flight."

Joe glanced around for an escape route—a hole of any type to fall in would be fine. He felt surrounded by agents. He took deep breaths while he tried to focus on something pleasant, such as moseying through train yards, taking slides of locomotives, anything besides standing and waiting for the obvious bad news—and the looks from the wiseass agents.

"Sir? Your flight at LAX was a little early. It's been on the ground since 8 a.m."

"Ohmigod!" Joe glanced at his watch: 8:15. He did the math. Driving time to LAX from John Wayne Airport at that time of day could be at least an hour. He felt the blood drain from his face and the unmistakable wetness of his shirt clinging to his back. With no escape hatch in sight, Joe had to walk as tall as he could—for what seemed like miles—to get the hell out of Dodge. He was sure he heard the sounds of young girls tittering as he half-walked, half-ran down the long concourse. Swearing and fuming he drove to the nearest phone booth and called Gail, who told him he was a dumb shit, then hightailed it to LAX; a mere twenty minutes from his house had he driven to the right airport.

Joe finally arrived at LAX an hour-and-a-half after my flight landed; thirty minutes after Dave had plopped my sore tush on a cold, concrete bench, and twenty-nine minutes after I started bawling—again.

THE MIDDLE-AGED WIRGIN

41

After some much-needed sleep and warm, comfy friends to whine to, I felt worlds better and my pain eased. I told them about the debacle on the plane with the uncaring flight attendant and they suggested I get it on paper immediately before time eroded the painful memories. I whisked off a terse note to the Customer Relations Department at the airlines, telling the whole gruesome story, sparing not a pain.

The airlines reply arrived some two months later, and Gail forwarded it to me after I'd returned to Thailand. I began to read it with great excitement, knowing that at the end of the letter a free round-trip ticket to some exotic far-off place would be forthcoming. But what the airlines offered was a reprimand for their over-worked employee and their "utmost" sincerest apology.

I couldn't believe it. All that suffering for naught! Oh, well, my hope was that *Ms. Nightingale* would be demoted to lavatory duty—in coach.

My second day at Gail's I was able to see a urologist. He walked into the examining room, lifted the sheet draped over my spread-eagled lower half and with speculum in hand whispered, "Geez, Louise!"

I froze. "What does that mean?"

He didn't answer, but he didn't look away either. "Barbara," he said to his nurse who was busy squeezing gooey clear stuff onto a gauze pad. "Get over here and look at this." Barbara dutifully walked over for a peek. "Geez, Louise!"

They stared between my legs much too long. I wanted to slap my knees together and put an end to the shocked look on their faces. I felt my body, along with the room, becoming tropical. The table had become a stage for my disfigured female parts, with the audience entranced. Staring down at me from the ceiling was a picture of a clown; he also looked shocked. The doctor's little hint at humor, I assumed, trying to loosen up his spread-eagled patients.

The doctor sucked in air between his teeth, "Ah, are you married?"

Flat on my back with legs in the air, it's a bit difficult to act indignant. "Yes, I'm married. Why would you ask?"

"This is just my opinion, mind you, but I'm pretty sure your husband will have a problem here with intercourse."

"Huh?"

"The doctor who did your bladder repair has you sewn up to the size of a ten-year-old old virgin."

"Huh?"

"Who in the hell stitched you up like this?"

Five days, five catheter changes and five substantial doctor bills later, I was able to urinate on my own. The diagnosis was pretty simple: he said that the Thai doctor had done the proper bladder repair, but maybe just a skosh *too* proper. The reason I wasn't able to urinate without the catheter was that she'd stitched the bladder too high and it wasn't able to release urine. Now that the bladder had had time to relax, things would work just spiffy. With the final removal of the catheter, the doctor said my life would return to normal—whatever that was.

The gynecologist I saw next for the "ten-year-old-virgin" problem was Asian. He felt he knew the culture well enough to say that it was not uncommon for Asian surgeons to give their female patients a little tuck after some GYN procedure. It was no different than a woman in the States who undergoes a minor abdominal surgery and the doctor sucks out a little unsightly blubber from her tummy while he's got her laid open. He added that the Thai doc did what she most likely does for all her postpartum patients—restores their virginity. I guess this was the Thai wife's answer to her husband's wandering after she's had a baby. And, to whom does he wander? *Wirgins.* That said, he did agree with my urologist that the Thai doctor was a bit overzealous with her stitching.

My final prognosis was that I'd need an episiotomy before having intercourse. Did I plan to have that done before I returned to Thailand, the good doctor asked? I don't think so. It was not something I was ready to think about. Before I even considered the episiotomy, he said, the infection caused by the multiple catheter changes would have to be cleared up. This would entail about ten days on antibiotics. He made a guesstimate based on his calculations and believed it would be at least two months before I should attempt intercourse. *It looked like my string of bad luck was coming to an end.*

BAD NEWS AND GOOD FRIENDS

42

I spent six weeks of R&R with Joe and Gail. When I thought I might live again and had sufficient rest and good friends to complain to, I was ready to take on the world. My friends had welcomed me into their homes, provided a sanctuary for me, and treated me like a queen. There were a few differences, though, that existed between Joe's internal thermometer and mine. Because I'd come from a warm climate, and not being at the top of my game, health-wise, I was always freezing. Joe liked to keep it cold enough to hang beef, while I wanted it warm enough to grow orchids. When he wasn't looking I'd push the thermostat up to eighty. He'd walk by and drop it to forty.

Gail was the intermediary; "Joe, she's been sick." At which time he'd throw me a hateful look behind her back.

But Joe and I did have something in common. Most days, as soon as Gail would leave for work, we'd high-tail it to the closest Winchell's for donuts and coffee. "Don't let on to Gail that we're doing this," Joe said. "We're both trying to diet and I'm sure *she* doesn't cheat."

"Why would I tell her? She'll figure it out on her own when she notices your waist expanding."

"Are you gaining weight?" Gail asked one morning eyeing Joe's waistline. She watched him for signs of sweating, a sure sign of guilt.

"No. Why would you ask that?"

"Because I noticed you're getting a little thick around the middle. You're not cheating on goodies while I'm at work, are you?"

"Hell no! Ask Dodie, she's here all day." He gave me the evil eye.

Now, where did my allegiance lie? With my kindest and best girlfriend? or with her stocky husband who had the same sugar addiction as me?

"Nope, he eats like a bird," I lied—without sweating.

During the time I was with them I was on the phone many times with my son, who had continual questions for me. "Mom, don't you think I should be listing my house just in case? What if they call me over and I don't have time to get it sold?" Then he hit me with the question that I didn't want to answer: "When're you going back?"

When? was not the question. *Why* was I going back? I wanted to stay here, to forget the nights and the days that Dick spent in his sullen funk. But I couldn't do that to my son. He'd put all his energy and hopes in this overseas job. I had to find something to tell him.

A few weeks before I entered the hospital, when things were at a very low point between *The Bosses* and us, I'd put out the word to some of the PILC ladies to be on a job-watch alert for my son. Some of their husbands worked at large companies in the area and he might have a chance for employment through them. I printed Dale's resume and handed them out to some of the women. If he didn't get a call from *Mr. JB,* he just might find a good fit with another construction company. That was my daily prayer. The chances seemed good that he might be hired as many companies were just starting up, but the salary would be much lower of course as he would be considered a local hire, which didn't pay the salary that a company would to their own internal people. I knew he was counting on the great salary that the foreman position would have offered, but that didn't look like it would ever happen. Especially now that I'd done the unforgivable—I'd become involved with the PILC.

Another problem that I had to consider was that our tax-deferred days were not up until September. If I were to leave the country ahead of that date, as his wife I'd be stuck with paying half of the deferred taxes. That I could not do. But, either way I knew I wouldn't be there past September. Dale was a big boy. If he was hired by another company, then I would leave. He'd do fine. But, I couldn't tell him any of this until I returned to get a feel of what was going on with *Mrs. A.* It was a secret that ate at my gut constantly and I knew this stress was taking a toll on me.

"Will Dick call you if they need me?"

I had no clue what was happening back there. The job had been in full swing since September and still no word about Dale's position was offered from *Mr. JB.* This did not bode well. "Of course. Dick says to just hang tight."

I had constant anxiety, a premonition of something terrible happening, but I couldn't relay this to Dale. I tried to sound optimistic, telling him to keep positive but to hold off on listing his house until he had the job offer in writing. He accepted this but I could hear the disappointment in his voice. I needed to get back to try to mend fences with *Mrs. A.* I'd hoped a miracle might occur and Dale would still have a chance for a good paying job.

The next time we talked Dick said things were ominously quiet and it worried him. *Mr. JB* had nothing to say to him at work, he said, sometimes walking right by him without even a nod. Before I became the PILC editor, *Mr. JB* would stop Dick on the jobsite to shoot the breeze and talk golf. Since my involvement with the PILC, the old man would ignore Dick as if he wasn't there. The boss's wife did indeed have a firm hold on the family jewels.

During every phone call Dick complained about things being screwed up at work. He'd had a few calls from friends on the jobsite, things they'd heard that worried him. The rumor mill was alive and well. No one knew what to take to the bank or what to flush.

The next time we talked there had been a new turn of events that Dick was concerned about. He said he'd first noticed it a couple days earlier when the guys in the office, who usually confided in him about *Mr. JB's* shenanigans, were now obviously pulling away and visibly shunning him. I asked him if he'd stepped on any toes while I was gone. His answer was an adamant "No," but added that he didn't take any crap from them either. Another rumor he'd heard was that the client was unhappy with him. No one seemed to know why, but it was another reason to be paranoid. He was obviously shaken by all this and started second-guessing himself. "Maybe I should've just looked the other way instead of tryin' to be honest."

"What do you mean?"

"Maybe it's nothin'. I don't know."

"What happened? Tell me, please!"

"Well I had a delivery that I'd been waitin' on all day and when the guy got here, it wasn't right. I mean I checked it and it just wasn't up to spec, so I rejected it. Then the driver goes roarin' off the jobsite all pissed off, so I called the old man."

"And? Did he stand by your decision?"

"Hell no! He had a shit fit right on the phone. He screamed at me, told me to accept what's delivered and to quit fuckin' around with their time and money."

"Oh my God! He yelled at you? What'd you say?"

"Nothin'. He slammed down the phone. I couldn't say much. I wonder what the hell's gonna happen next?"

And I wondered *when* it was going to happen.

SISTERS
AND SOUTHWEST MIRACLES

43

A week before I left Joe and Gail's to return to Thailand, I took a flight to San Francisco for a quick visit with my sister. I needed my Little Sissy Fix. Now that I was in the States for a few weeks, why not burden her with my problems.

Since I am the oldest, it does seem that I'd be the wise and all-knowing sister. However, it has never worked out that way. Whenever I'm in a pickle, need advice, or just plain feel like bawling on her shoulder—I call my sister. Whenever one of my children is in a crisis—I call my sister. Whenever I've perceived a hateful slight, been given some harsh criticism, or felt my world crumbling around my ankles—I call my sister. She has a way of bringing things into perspective for me by opening avenues of thought I'd not envisioned, separating the shit from the bullshit. So, of course I'd already told her the problems going on in my life with Dick, and the chest pains I'd been experiencing lately because of it.

She picked me up at the airport, and as always gave me her undivided attention. She listened raptly to my complaints. Then we headed downtown for some inward soothing from her favorite bakery. We downed cups of Chai tea along with blood-sugar-elevating sweet delights. When we'd both satisfied our emotional hunger with some physical happiness she asked me the prophetic question: "Why are you still with that schmuck?"

"I can't leave yet. I have to give my son the chance at his dream.

Also, there's the tax situation that more or less has me roped into staying."

"And?"

"And what?"

"And when all that happens and Dale gets the job, you just up and leave? Is that your plan?"

"Yeah, I guess. I have no idea what my plan is. All I know is that I have to hold on until something gives. I know he doesn't have a chance with our company anymore, and after all the crap we've been through, why would I want that for him. I do have some feelers out with other companies and my friends are all checking with their husbands about a local-hire job for Dale. If I don't go back, I don't know how I could handle the guilt if he missed out on a job. I have to keep trying. Maybe one of my friends will come through."

"Then it looks like you've got your answer. Put up with Dick's crap and pray that Dale gets called before you have a heart attack."

"That sounds scary."

"No, what's scary is that you *think* you have to stay. You don't owe anyone anything. Except yourself. Your health seems much more important at this point than any promise you made to your son. Believe me, taxes are the last thing you should be worrying about right now. You've told me you have chest pains. You also know that those pains are precursors to a heart attack, so what makes you think you'll dodge that bullet? And what good does that job mean to Dale if you have a massive heart attack and drop dead in Thailand? Think about it, is all I'm saying."

Four days later, without any resolution but lots of tea and sympathy and sweet rolls, my sister drove me to the airport to fly back to Joe and Gail's. I would spend two more days with them, see my doctor for one last check-up, and then head back to Thailand. She hugged me and said in my ear, "Leave the putz and come back to your family who loves you." Again, prophetic. I watched her walk away and was saddened. She was right, but for right now I had to put all this prophetic thinking on hold. I'd worry about it later.

Travelers who've flown the friendly skies of Southwest know they do not have assigned seats; it's first-come, first-served. I still had a low-grade infection and wasn't feeling too peppy. Even though the flight to John Wayne would only take forty-five minutes, I decided to ask for pre-boarding and maybe have the luxury of a bulkhead seat so I could stretch out. I sort of limped to the ticket counter and asked for a pre-board card. The agent looked at me rather dubiously. She handed me the pre-board pass with a zero on it, then added under her breath, "Yeah right, a pre-board."

"Excuse me?"

"I said," she answered, without looking up from her computer, "If you can get in line first, you'll get boarded first."

I made a note of her name.

I took my pre-board pass and held it covertly to my breast while I slowly limped toward the boarding gate—dragging my left foot just a tad. I placed myself in a strategic spot just to the left of the entrance to get a jump on the passengers holding cards 1 and 2. At the announcement for pre-boards I moved quickly, still dragging my left foot, but was nearly flattened by two pugnacious porcine types waving their 1 and 2 cards in my face.

I said, "Pardon me," and stepped in front of them. "I'm a pre-board."

"Sure you are," they chanted in unison.

What hateful people. The couple looked at me with disdain and tried to block my way with their girth. Putting one foot in front of them I started down the tunnel. As they picked up a little speed they managed to file in right behind me, wheezing and bitching. The more hateful they were toward me, the faster I limped. The tunnel looked ten miles long as I gimped along. I could hear their voices echoing off the walls, "Oh look, it's a miracle. She can walk again."

Now that was downright spiteful.

My face was beginning to tingle—a sure sign of hyperventilation. I slowed my pace a little and gave more drag to my heel. I stepped into the plane and was disappointed to see that it was a connecting flight and already over half full. I took the last bulkhead seat available—a much preferred seat for the more-than-pleasingly-plump. I made a huge production of taking my rubber donut out of my carry-on and plopping it on the seat, while the frumpy twosome squeezed into the two seats behind me. *Oh great. Of all the people who do this all the time, why do I have to be confronted by these two?* Throughout the forty-five minute flight I could hear such tidbits floating my way: "Isn't it marvelous what mind-over-matter can do?" and "We've been flying Southwest for years but this is the first miracle we've ever witnessed."

Oh, kiss my grits. I was now highly indignant. How would she feel if her tutu had been stitched up tighter than a mason jar—or her urethra inflamed?

The flight seemed to take two years. *Come on! Land and get me off this plane so I don't have to suffer their slings and arrows.*

When the plane finally taxied to a stop, they again began their chant in full force. "Oh, I hope someone is here to pick her up. She could collapse before she ever reaches baggage. Oh, no, wait! Maybe an ambulance attendant is waiting for her on the tarmac. Oh, my, what a horrible fate. But wait! We could witness another miracle, right here in front of us."

And on and on they went. I was doing a slow burn and my under-wire was dripping. I didn't move. I wasn't about to let them follow me down the jet-way again. I felt my seat being shoved forward as they heaved themselves up and out of their seats. I turned to watch something very important out my window but I could still hear them as they trudged by.

"Well, another miracle. She lived long enough to land."

Barf!

When everyone had disembarked I finally exited the plane. Just as an ounce of prevention I thought I'd better drag my foot, but couldn't remember which foot to drag. Then I heard my mother's voice in my ear: "It's easy to remember the truth, but hard to remember fibs." *Why are mothers always right?*

Thankfully, Gail was late picking me up at the airport or I'm sure they'd have followed me to the car singing their little miracle song. You'da thought I'd committed some gruesome crime. Jeffrey Dauhmer probably didn't get this much shit.

**THAILAND BOUND
IN A FIRST CLASS BED**

44

Even though Dick and I talked once a week, I hadn't been able to divulge the "wirgin" bit. I couldn't deal with his ranting just yet. I kept putting it off because I didn't know exactly how to tell him without a big argument over the phone. Maybe I'd call from the airport, like five minutes before I stepped in the plane: *Oh, by the way, I'm stitched up like a ten-year-old virgin. Oops, gotta go, they're closing the boarding gate.*

I had told him what the urologist said regarding the bladder being stitched up too high, and about the infection from the catheters, however, I held back on the waiting period for the infection to clear up. I knew when I returned I'd hear ranting and raving, and see pouting and tantrums, and I didn't want him to have too much time to dwell on it. If I'd told him too far in advance my doctor would've had a wild man waiting on her doorstep. I also didn't divulge that I'd most probably need an episiotomy, and that it couldn't be done until the infection from the catheter had cleared up, yada, yada, yada. I wanted to wait for the *opportune moment.*

On the last night stateside, Dick phoned to say he'd see me at the airport. We chatted about mundane things for a while, then the connection went bad. He said he was having trouble hearing me so he'd better sign off.

It was now the *opportune moment.* "Oh, okay, well, there's something I might have forgotten to mention."

"Forgotten? What'd you say?"

"Well, we had so much to talk about I guess..."

"Talk louder, I can barely hear you?"

In my best medical-slash-anatomical vocabulary I tried to describe the dozen or so extra catgut sutures that my doctor had seen fit to place in her quest to restore my virginity.

"What! Repeat that!" he yelled. "The connection keeps shorting out. Who's Doctor Virginia?"

This was not going well. "I said...The doctor took some extra stitches when she sewed me up." I held my breath.

What the hell does that mean?"

"She sewed me up too tight."

"Yeah, good, everything's alright?"

Okay, I'd done my part. He couldn't accuse me of holding back. Not my fault that he's half deaf and the Thailand phone system is screwed up. I felt I was off the hook.

"Well, just so you know," I rattled on, knowing he wouldn't get any of it, "the doctor said there'd be a problem with intercourse."

"With what?

"Intercourse."

"Why the hell would he say that?"

Oh, great. Now the line clears up. "Um, well, the urologist thought I was about the size of a ten-year-old." There, that should do it. No more beating around the static phone lines. I moved the phone away from my ear.

"What the shit..."

"Okay, let's not get into this now. I've got to get to bed. I have to be at the airport at 4 a.m. We'll talk about it when I get back."

"Wait..."

"Dick, I can't get into this right now, people are sitting here..."

Click.

Well, that was nice. Whatever!

My time away from all the rules and stresses had been the perfect medicine for me. I rested, read and visited my children. I loved Thailand and its people but I didn't know how long I could stay in the marriage. I would have to make a decision, and soon.

I was actually looking forward to the flight back to Thailand; a flight without needing to arch my back and slant my pelvis. With the catheter tip removed, I'd get to sit like all the big girls—flat on my butt. But I was still feeling puny. I'd gladly have taken Dave and my wheelchair right then.

Shortly after I'd found my seat, removed my shoes and situated my rubber donut just so, the captain's voice came on the intercom informing us that two passengers had checked their bags but failed to show for boarding. We would wait for another twenty minutes at which time their luggage would be unloaded, according to FAA rules. At the time, federal law prohibited baggage on an international flight if the owners were not on board. Fearing a possible bomb, I was most agreeable to await the passengers or dump their luggage. True to his word, after twenty minutes the captain ordered the unclaimed bags removed. This was no small job as it entailed emptying the baggage compartment of at least 500 pieces, sorting through them to find the abandoned luggage, and then reloading again. Two hours later we were airborne.

The thirteen-hour flight to Tokyo would be long, but I was comfortable and ready to get on with it. I'd stuffed my carry-on with books and magazines, and looked forward to reading and relaxing like a real traveler. I read for a while, munched on some cardboard-tasting chicken and guzzled mineral water. How freeing it was without worries of overloading a catheter bag, no knitting needle inching around under me. I watched a movie and then fell into a dead sleep. I awoke as they announced we were approaching Narita Airport in Tokyo.

Cat-napping en route helped restore some of my energy, which promptly deserted me when we disembarked in Tokyo. We were advised of a two-hour delay for our flight on to Bangkok. No reason was given. *Can't anyone run an airline on time?* The terminal was crowded to capacity with no extra seats to be found. I had one pull-cart and a huge over-the-shoulder bag loaded with books, magazines and my rubber donut. I laid claim to a four-inch concrete ledge in the waiting area, but my donut kept slipping off. It was too much work trying to adjust the slippery thing to the ledge so I offered my space to a frail little lady who thanked me profusely in Japanese—at least I thought she was thanking me. One never knows. With nowhere to sit, I stood off to the side and read. My back, legs and parts south ached.

I'd traded in some miles to treat myself to Business Class and knew I'd be boarded right after First Class. Even though we had assigned seats, I was surprised how much pushing and shoving went on to be first in the boarding line. Haughtily, I stepped in front of the two Japanese gentlemen who'd nearly run me down trying to get in line. "*Gomenasai*,"—excuse me—I said, remembering a little Japanese from a sailor I'd dated in my youth. *That's scary.* They say as you get older your recent memory fades but your long-term memory gets stronger. *What was his name?*

As I found my seat and tried to get my donut and rump to co-exist, I prayed the adjacent seat would remain empty on this eight-hour flight. No such luck! I smelled him before I saw him. *Mothballs!* I immediately detected the odor of mothballs. I detest that smell. Somewhere in my distant past—I should be able to remember it now—I must have been subjected to this odor and it must have been a bad experience, because whenever I smell mothballs, I don't think of moths or balls, I think of something old, deteriorating and decaying. *Oh, God. No. Please.* With my over-active sense of smell I felt I might need the barf bag before we were even airborne. A very large Japanese gentleman *fell* into the seat next to me. An ex-sumo wrestler, I guessed, definitely one sushi roll away from morbid obesity.

Ten minutes into the flight, our petite Japanese attendant glided down the aisle through Business Class. She bowed to *Mr. Mothballs* and totally ignored me—and I was here first. *I made a note of her name.*

She took his drink order, bowed, and glided back up the aisle. *Hey, what am I, invisible?* She returned with his drink, bowed, and glided away again. I stood up and called to her, but she kept gliding. *Okay, forget it.* I assumed it was some sort of cultural thing; serve the men first and then the women can have whatever's left.

Mr. Mothballs and I fought a constant duel over the arm rest. His arm was the size of my torso so I knew I wouldn't win this arm-butt thing, but I wasn't going to give in without a fight. For the next hour I flipped and flopped around in an attempt to get comfortable and tried to get *Ms. Teahouse of the August Moon* to bring me a drink. *Mr. Mothballs* had finally had enough. He heaved himself up and out of his seat and found an empty seat in the last row where he could spread out. *Thank you, Buddha. Little Ms. Geisha* continued to glide up and down the aisles with the single-mindedness of a bee to honeysuckle. All the males in Business Class, most of them Asian, seemed very contented while in her care.

A male flight attendant finally appeared and was ready and willing to serve the ladies. He was small, effeminate, and sashayed up and down the aisles like a ballerina, but his service was impeccable. He saw to it that all his ladies were fully pampered with warm, wet hand towels, bottled water, champagne, blankets and satin pillows. He served me a sumptuous soup with something-or-other floating in a delicate blue flowered Asian bowl. I was totally contented. After I was rid of *Mr. Mothballs* it was a most luxurious and relaxing flight—for a while.

As zzz's echoed off the cabin walls, I decided to put my usual fear of flying on hold and get some sleep. I certainly couldn't be the only person responsible for staying alert and keeping the plane in the air. When I finally managed to plump my pillow just right so one ear was free to hear any unusual engine noise—BANG—I heard an unusual engine noise. My heart beat out the Morse code as the pilot's voice came on the speaker: "Ladies and Gentahmin, we ah solly to repoht numbah one engine jut go out. No problem, we have sree more jut like it"—giggles. "We mut now turn back to Narita."

And turn back we did. The flight time from Tokyo to Bangkok is normally eight hours, but because we'd been in the air for only three, we had not made it to the half-way point. Had we been in the air four hours, we'd have forged ahead to Bangkok. *See what I mean about luck?*

The flight attendant announced that we'd be taken by bus to a hotel about thirty minutes from the airport where we'd spend the night and be bussed back to Narita in the morning to continue our flight on this plane—if it could be repaired in time. The bad news was we would have to claim our luggage as soon as it was off-loaded at Narita and take it with us to the hotel. If our plane could not be repaired we would need our luggage in order to board an alternate plane the next morning.

Standing in the long Customs lines and then fighting for a hole to claim my luggage pushed me to exhaustion. How I wished I'd done my wheelchair thing this time. When I finally managed to snag my suitcase, I tried to listen for someone speaking English. I needed to know where the hell I was supposed to go. With no one understanding me or answering my questions, I was a tad nervous. I made a decision to hang next to an elderly Asian gentleman waiting to claim his luggage next to me. He seemed to know his way around and I thought I'd seen him on my plane. I had to turn him loose when he slid into the Men's room. I hung around for about ten minutes then figured he might be having a bout of *Hirohito's Revenge* and left him to his misery. I headed back toward the carousel, worried that I'd miss the bus if I waited any longer. And then where would I go? I caught sight of a few people who'd claimed their luggage near me and followed them out of the airport, hopefully to the bus that would take me where I was supposed to be going.

Ten huge buses hovered at the curb. I looked for familiar faces as I stepped inside, but they all looked the same to me. It would've helped to have a redhead or a blonde among the bunch. I began to hyperventilate. What would I do if I were on the wrong bus going somewhere I shouldn't be going? The flight attendants had told us the hotel was about a thirty-minute bus ride from the airport. I decided that I'd wait for thirty-five minutes before I totally freaked out. I checked my watch then closed my eyes and prayed for a miracle. Then, I smelled him. Wafting up to the front of the bus drifted the spirits of little moths. *It's him!* I could smell *Mr. Mothballs* somewhere in this crowd and knew I was safe.

Doesn't it follow that the last on the bus should be the first off? Not! I had to fight for that right. With my rubber donut running interference, I rushed headlong into the hotel. The staff stood at the ready behind two roped-off areas with signs that read: FIRST CLASS PASSENGERS, and ALL OTHER PASSENGERS. Guess which line I entered? The clerk didn't ask for my boarding pass and I didn't offer it. I tried to look First-Classy as I took the key and headed toward the elevators. I prayed no one was chasing me.

The room reeked of opulence. Massive windows with gold-filigreed satin drapes swooped down from the ceiling. I felt like I was in a Japanese opera house. Sofas of finely woven tapestry and etched glass lamps graced the table tops. It was marvelous. Switches for the air conditioning, lights, radio, television and room service were thoughtfully positioned within reach above the headboard. Wow! Why not use them? I flopped down on the bed and pushed the room service button.

A sweet, lilting voice came over the intercom: *"Loom suvit."*

A little late-night snack and then breakfast the next morning and I'd be ready for my flight. Love this First Class status.

After breakfast—in bed—we were bussed back to the terminal. We were told our plane could not be repaired and we'd be flown on another carrier at no change in price. The glitch was that we had to go through check-in all over again. We're talking over 300 grumbling passengers here. Everyone lined up with much confusion to re-check luggage and receive new boarding passes.

After about an hour in line, my back began to ache and my legs were threatening to fold as I stood sandwiched between wool coats that smelled like wet Himalayan Sherpas with a serious lack of underarm deodorant. I tried breathing through my mouth, humming, meditating, even tried a few standing Yoga positions, but nothing helped. I was going to die right here in this line and nobody would even notice, in fact, probably just step over my inert body. It took well over three hours before all of us were boarded for our flight to Bangkok. *Where was my wheelchair when I needed it?*

Meanwhile, at the Bangkok airport, Dick sat waiting expectantly for my original 11:30 P.M. arrival the night before. I had no way to reach him. We were told that the airlines would notify Bangkok of our overnighter so we could relax for the evening. But our airlines *did not* notify those waiting for the flight in Bangkok. Dick told me later that sometime after midnight they posted "Flight Cancelled" on the monitor. Everyone panicked, he said, thinking the plane had gone down. The airport and counters were deserted save for a few janitors. Dick called the airline's Tokyo office but couldn't understand anything they said. He was completely fried after spending the night in the airport, sure that I had crashed and burned, when all the while I'd been eating happily and sleeping peacefully in my First Class bed.

**SLEEPLESS IN BANGKOK
AND PATTAYA**

45

ick looked like ten miles of bad road after sleeping on a bench at the airport most of the night. His clothes were wrinkled and he needed a shave. I decided it might be kinder not to mention my first class accommodations. It was a tortuous drive back to Pattaya. I knew the questions were coming as soon as the car turned onto the highway. "So, what's the verdict?"

"What do you mean by 'verdict'?"

"You know what I mean. When can we have sex?"

I wish he'd learn to say what's on his mind. "If you mean how long before I heal, I guess it would be up to the doctor after she examines me."

"What? Why is it up to her? You should know when it feels okay."

This was going to be harder than I thought. I didn't want to listen to him bitch and moan all the way to Pattaya, but I thought I'd better start with the *wirgin* bit and get it over with. "Look," I said, "we'll get all the answers once we see the doctor. There is a problem because she stitched me up a little too tight, so until she can examine me, we'll just have to wait." I was on a roll now, and his shocked silence buoyed me onward. "There's also the problem of the infection, and that's got to clear up before anything else can be done.

"'Anything else?' What the hell does that mean?"

"Well, like possibly an episiotomy." Okay, now I'd done it. I waited for this to sink in and the car to swerve off the highway.

"What the hell's an episiotomy?"

"It's a surgical procedure where they cut an incision to, you know, make the opening larger. Like when a woman has a baby and they need more room for the baby's head." My underwire was getting damp.

"Great. She screws you up in surgery and I have to pay the price?"

"Pay the price? My God, you act like I'm a commodity you sold and someone cheated you out of the money."

"You know what I mean." He softened. "I'm just pissed. It's been way before Christmas since we've had sex. That's too damn long! And why? Because your surgeon screwed up!"

"Dick. There are *other* ways to end this sexual drought besides penetration, you know, but you always turn those options down." I knew his answer to that one; he wanted the whole enchilada, he could forego the guacamole and salsa. He was silent. "Let's just wait until tomorrow. I'm too exhausted now to get into it and you've got to focus on your driving."

"Fat chance!"

The next day Dick dragged me to the surgeon's office without making the requisite appointment. "Is the doctor in?" Dick growled. The receptionist asked if we had an appointment. "I'm sure she'll work us in."

I took Dick's arm as we were led into the doctor's office and attempted to calm him down. The doctor walked in and sat at her desk, exuding smiles. "Goosday. You do okay?" *Wrong thing to ask.*

Dick pulled away from me and pounded on her desk. "What kind of a doctor are you? Why in the hell did you stitch up my wife like that? Did you bother to ask her if it was okay?"

She glanced over at me, then back at Dick. "What wrong? You can not do sex?"

"Right! There's not very much to 'do sex' with."

I found that a bit crude.

She smiled. "Oh, you sink she too small? You can stretch wit candle, you see. You wait. In time she be okay." She laughed and gave him a conspiratorial wink.

Now Dick's face looked like a ripe tomato. I think he expected the good doc to cry and beg his forgiveness. "What the hell's so funny about all this?" he yelled. "The only way it'll be okay is if you cut on my wife again. And that means pain. And pain means no sex. Get my point?"

Greater love hath no man.

She nodded, not sure why he was so red in the face.

"And why should she go through this extra pain because of what *you* did? You should've asked her before you stitched her up..."

"No, no," she interrupted. "No pain, no episiotomy. You stretch wit candle." She looked at Dick and winked, again. "You mut be patient."

I won't repeat Dick's answer.

After a quick peek at her handiwork she told us that she felt we should wait for intercourse until my infection was entirely cleared up— about two weeks, she guessed. I thought Dick would erupt right there on her floor. He did manage to pull himself together long enough to walk out of the office—then erupted on the sidewalk. "It's not fair," he wailed like a child you've just put in time-out. "She just does any old thing she wants and I have to pay the price."

"You have to pay the price? Has it occurred to you that I might have some pain and discomfort? Why is everything about you?"

That night the massage oil was nowhere in sight. I slept peacefully while Dick tossed and turned, eventually leaving the house, I supposed, to find some sort of relief.

It was wonderful to be back in Thailand, to all the friends I'd made and to get back to the newsletter and my beautiful orphans. I was concerned about all the crap going on at the jobsite, and I vowed to put it all behind me and try to mend some fences. As soon as I could manage it I'd set up a meeting with *Mrs. A*. I tried to keep a low profile, attending her "compulsory" meetings. I tried to fit in, but it seemed that she went out of her way to avoid me. Well, perhaps I should give her some time. I was just as happy not being under her steely gaze. I'd bide my time and when she saw that I was a model employee-wife, she might come around.

Watching Dick waiting for my infection to heal was like watching a time bomb ticking away. Dick made the two weeks seem like two years. I thought he was bad before, now he walked the floors at night bemoaning his fate. At the end of two weeks my doctor said the infection had cleared up and I could proceed with intercourse. "But, don't forget," she called to me as I left her office, "Try candle to stretch."

I knew I'd better give it a try or have to watch Dick take a knife to his wrists. I was rested and told him it was time. It was supposed to be a romantic night: bath, candles and all the accoutrements. It was a travesty. He wanted no part of the bath, bubbles or candles. There was no tenderness. Dick's idea of foreplay was unzipping his pants.

But it wasn't to be. There was no way he could enter my ten-year-old virginal vault. I winced when he tried, and pulled back with a cry. I told him that it hurt, but he was too overcome with desire—for himself. He'd waited long enough and wasn't going to be put off by my pain. "Come on," he grunted in the heat of (his) passion. "Quit pullin' away, the doc said I had to keep tryin'."

The night was a bust. We tried a few more times over the next week but the result of all these attempts caused extreme pain. I developed many small fissures that would not heal, and I cringed whenever I tried to urinate. Night after night I'd lie there next to him anticipating the fight that was sure to come when I pushed him away. Fingers of pain clutched at my chest as he continued his tossing, turning, muttering, cussing then slamming out of the bedroom. He'd apologize the next morning. He'd ask me to see it from his point. He'd been waiting so long. I had nothing to say to him. He'd get in my face with his excuses, turning me around so I could see his forlorn face. How could I not see how much he loved me and needed me.

Then, for over a week, he showed wonderful restraint, never reaching for me at night or listening for the shower—then brought up the episiotomy. I'd had that procedure when my children were born and I remembered the long, painful recovery period. "All right," I said, no longer having the energy to fight this or to see his sullen face. "But you know there's going to be at least four to six weeks wait before you can try anything, right?"

He shrugged, "Hell, it's better than nothin'. At least I have somethin' to look forward to."

Silver-tongued devil.

I had the episiotomy in the doctor's office under local anesthesia. Throughout the procedure she reminded me that I didn't really need this, all I had to do was stretch the opening with a candle. When she'd finished her handiwork she assured me that I should have no trouble now, but if it was not done to Dick's liking, then I could return.

I don't think so!

While I was recovering from the surgery, Dick was the picture of patience and caring. I wanted to believe he was sincere. I pictured him marking off the days on his calendar at work. Three weeks later and two glasses of wine to relax, we attempted it again. As he pushed, my muscles—despite the wine—went into self-defense mode and tightened, trying to alleviate the pain that would surely come. But this night, no amount of tears or logic could dissuade him from his objective. When I told him it wouldn't work, that he was hurting me, it fell on deaf ears. He kept pushing, telling me he was just following the doctor's orders—stretch, stretch, stretch.

Obviously the episiotomy was not large enough, and I was not going to be torn open by a man who had no compassion. I knew now it was no longer an act of love, but of lust, and we both knew it. I screamed at him as I pushed him away. "Stop it! Get away from me. Don't ever touch me again!"

He jumped up, grabbing his pants as he went. "You don't have to worry about me touching you again!" I heard the front door slam. I cried myself stupid; not for him but for the mess I'd gotten myself into. I prayed he'd find a little bargirl to relieve himself—and me.

Hold on, I kept telling myself. Bide your time. As soon as my son gets hired over here, I'm gone.

SERMON ON THE MOUNT

46

In the month-and-a-half that I'd been home it seemed strangely quiet. Dick had had no run-ins with the boss or client. I attended the wife's meetings and there'd been no confrontations. *Mrs. A* seemed to make it a point to snub me. Ordinarily, that would be just fine by me, but I knew I had to make my move soon. It was now time to keep the vow I'd made at the hospital and apologize to her. I'd made a deal with the big guy in the sky: get my son over here and I'd drop the newsletter and become a Stepford Wife.

I was doing my morning ritual of green tea and writing in my journal when I caught sight of *Mrs. I-Walk-and-Pray-for-all-Sinners* setting off for her morning walk with some of the company women. I rushed to catch up with her. When she spotted me she offered a hateful look then began singing a gospel tune without acknowledging my presence. I took a few quick steps and planted myself in front of her. "We need to talk," I said, trying to sound non-threatening. "Can you stop for a minute?" My heart began to pound in my ears so loudly I was afraid she'd hear it. She motioned for the others to continue on without her.

Mrs. I-Put-Out-Burning-Bushes squared up for the confrontation. I gave her the podium to read off her commandments. She was loaded and ready to fire, anticipating this very moment. "I've decided, prayed on it even, after talking to my sow-ces, that it's high time ah straightened you out."

"Wait." I said. I wanted her to know I was here for a peace treaty. "I just want to clear things up between us. I don't want accusations and threats. I'm willing to admit I was a bit strong-willed, but…"

She glared at me without saying a word.

"Okay." I said, "Let's hear it. At least I'll have a chance to defend myself. You seem to have convicted me without a jury trial. I really didn't mean to cause any problems." I hated the whiney sound to my voice.

She squared off her bony shoulders, glared at me, and let fly: "Numbah one. You and foah ladies used a company van to go to Bangkok without owah pah-mission."

"But we did ask…"

"Just like you did on that honeymoon thing of yoahs."

"We did ask…" I tried to interrupt her but she continued to spew her lava.

"Numbah two. You had the tah-merity to plan a Christmas potluck without owah pah-mission."

"Wait, I…"

"Numbah three…"

"Stop!" I screeched. "I need to rebut these things one at a time. Please."

She stopped, barely able to conceal her smirk, knowing the jury had voted for the death penalty.

"You and your husband were stateside when the ladies talked about going to Bangkok. It wasn't just me. Several of us made that decision. We were told to call *Mr.-Second-in-Command.* He said there was no problem and arranged a van for us. So you see? We did get permission."

"That's unacceptable," she sniffed though her thin pointed nose. "He is not and nevah has been *next* in chaage. He is second with the client, *not next in chaage!*" she said between clenched, overly-white laminates.

"Okay. I didn't know that, and obviously neither did he. But at the time we thought we had gone through the right channels. Can't you see that? But, I *did* ask you about the Christmas potluck and you said you'd be out of town that weekend, did you not?"

"Ah wasn't told anything about that."

"Told? I came to your house and spoke to you directly. Don't you remember?"

"Ah do not."

Oh God, this was not going as I'd planned. I had flashes of Dick and me sitting on a curb holding tin cups.

"Okay," I backed down. "I regret all those misunderstandings." *Liar!* "But I didn't *intentionally* go over your head. And as for the van to Bangkok, who are we supposed to ask when you two are out of town?"

She ignored my question. "There is something else."

"Go on," I said, masochist that I was, "what?"

"You..." she paused dramatically, happy that I'd given her more time for past grievances, "...deliberately invited those *men* from the ship, knowin' full well it was against owh company rules."

"Sailors."

"Whatevah."

"*I* invited no one. The chaplain asked us to host the boys. Why do you just assume it's me who plans everything? It was a group decision from all of us at the complex. We all agreed it would be wonderful to have them with us on Christmas Eve."

Again, "Ah have mah sow-ses."

I lost it. My humble resolve began to drain away. "For God's sake," I said in a much higher and louder voice than I'd intended, "I'm so sick of hearing about your sow-ces. It's like we're living in a communist country with KGB behind every palm tree. I've *never, ever* been on an overseas job where this has happened." I could feel my heart beating against my eardrums. My pulse was racing. I was blowing it. I had to back down. My son's sad face appeared before me. *For the love of God, calm down, you idiot!*

"It has nothin' to do with spies. It has evra-thin to do with deliberately breakin' company rules." By now she was crowing and speaking as loudly as I was.

"Breaking company rules? Is it written in the contract that we can't invite sailors to our homes? Why do we constantly keep hearing of new rules?" Her eyes were fixed just above mine, as if reading a Bible verse on the brim of my sun visor. "My God!" I spat. "What was the harm in inviting those sailors? They were young men who wanted to spend Christmas in a family setting instead of the bars." I was going full blast now, letting go of all my frustration and I couldn't stop. "You have a son. If he was in a foreign country wouldn't you be happy if he had the chance to spend the holidays with people from home?"

She didn't stop me. I saw a look of complete satisfaction cross her face and I wanted to karate chop her freshly botoxed chin. She remained wrapped in a silent smile while I ranted. I could've sworn I saw a few yellow canary feathers protruding from the corners of her mouth. I kept going, unable to stop. "It wasn't *my* idea to host them, but I was all for it. Joy to the World, you know? That sort of stuff."

I waited for her to get it. The lights were on but there was no sign of life.

"And what do you mean by 'deliberately breaking company rules'?" I prodded. "I think you owe me an answer. I've never heard those rules. Are they written in some sort of memorandum? On your golden tablets? Was Dick told of these rules on his orientation?" *Give it to her good*, my self-destructive self prodded, *you've waited long enough for this chance.*

She didn't attempt to interrupt me. She remained smirking, her satisfaction expanding like yeasty dough in a warm kitchen. "I didn't know we had to have your permission to have a party on our own pool deck. Why do you make it so hard for us?"

I saw a look of sheer joy flash over her face at my last question and I knew she was ready with her ace in the hole. "Foah yoah infoh-mation," she began, spreading out the DNA samples for the jury to consider, "these ah company homes. Bought and paid foah by the company. You absolutely *do* need owh pah-mission to use them foah a pahty."

"What?" I couldn't understand what she'd just said.

She repeated it again, more slowly, as if talking to a child with a learning deficit. "You *must* have owh pah-mission to entertain on these grounds..." she paused here, opening the bombardier doors and aiming her bomb at me, "...because, you see, mah deah, it is *not* yoah pool deck or yoah home. They belong to the company." She smiled now. She'd finally brought out her "company policy" rules—rules she knew could not be disputed.

I could feel my resolve flowing out of me like water from a cracked radiator. I dropped my head and tried to swallow this new bitter pill of information. She had me. She really had us. What could I do? She was the French Revolution, I was Marie Antoinette.

I turned to leave, to get away from her miserable rules and the hatred oozing from her pores. I was beaten and we both knew it. I stopped and turned back. I had more questions that needed answering. I might as well get them from the horse's mouth. "Are these rules available for all employees or are they hidden in some stateside vault? Why is it that no one ever mentioned anything about our homes not being ours? Why did they tell us these houses were ours for the two-year project?"

My posture and voice showed submission and she seemed to grow a foot taller as she knew she'd won the mud wrestling contest. She let me continue while forcing her joy behind clenched lips. "Evra-one was given a contract to read be-foah being hired and it definitely *is* written in the contract. Maybe *you* should have read it thoroughly be-foah yoah husband signed on."

I stared open-mouthed at her. She was truly smirking, enjoying this? I figured if I was going down with the ship I might as well fire off one last volley. "One last question, please. I'm curious, as are most of the wives, why you have so many rules? We aren't even employees of the company. And…" I added with a hateful emphasis, "…neither are you!"

Now I'd done it. I'd stepped over the fragile line in the sand that kept us apart with our dueling swords. She studied me for a minute or two, her face red and blotchy. "You *will* obey owah rules *or else!*" she added with vehemence as she turned on her immaculate Nordstrom's tennis shoes, leaving me to take another volley—and I had to take it. I couldn't let it go at that. I wanted her to say it, to repeat her threat—the one she'd let fly at the ladies meeting in front of my friends.

"Or else what?" I shot back, not wanting to hear it, but knowing I needed to.

She took a few steps, then turned back to face me. Her cheeks and neck were now spotted with red pools, like an acute case of Rosacea. "You will follow my rules," here she pointed an arthritic finger in my face, "*or you are outta here!*" She spat this out with such venom that her pseudo Southern accent deserted her, suddenly sounding like a Cajun fish monger.

Okay, there it was. I got it.

I walked back to my house and fell into a heap on the sofa. I cried for all the stupid things I'd done while under her watchful eye, things that I now doubted myself about. I cried for my son because I knew now he'd never be called. All his dreams, as well as mine, had been reduced to dirt under her feet. I thought of the many times I'd been ready to leave Dick, his sullenness, his hatefulness, but I'd held on hoping that my son would get here before I lost my mind.

I knew it was just a matter of time before the end came, and I felt the clock moving too fast.

THE PINK SLIP

47

My days were spent in dread, waiting to see what *Mrs. A* had planned and the fear of the September tax burden that we would face if Dick was fired. My nights were miserable. The nights of planning sex was a thing of the past. The bad days—make that horrible nights—were when Dick was turned down and his ego overshadowed all sense of self-restraint. I wondered what Pon thought of the yelling, doors slamming and cursing coming from our bedroom at night.

The newsletter was my escape, a guardrail to keep me from going over the edge. It was the one place I could go to at night without having to sit and look at Dick's sullen face.

Two weeks passed, strangely quiet and deathly still, like motionless air before a tornado. Then it struck. Dick stomped in from work and slammed the door. His face was pinched in anger as he flung some papers on the table. "It fuckin' happened."

"What?" I asked, feeling a chink in my armor.

"They found a way to get us outta here."

His words clattered like buckshot around me. I knew this was coming but was still unprepared. My heart clinched and my legs felt wobbly. I saw the pain on his face and my heart softened. I dropped to the kitchen chair for support and forced myself to speak. "How can they do that when you signed a two-year contract?" My voice sounded weak and whiney. I was sickened by it.

"That bastard can do anything he wants—and he did."

Dick sat down and I put my hand over his. As much as I had hated him during our nighttime fights, I now felt compassion for him. "I'm sorry. I know it had everything to do with her hatred of me."

"No, it wasn't just you. I had some shit going on at the jobsite. I didn't tell you the whole story. I was hopin' it'd blow over. I found a few places where someone tried to save money usin' inferior products when they knew it wasn't up to spec. I didn't want to accept it. I complained to the old man about it and he said not to worry, he'd take care of it. But I knew he wouldn't. My name was on the line. I had to sign for that shit and I wasn't gonna take the heat when someone complained down the road."

"What do you mean? What did you do?"

"I went over his head and told the client what I'd found and the client went to the old man. Nothin' was ever said to me but I knew somethin' was comin' down—and it sure as shit did."

I hated to see him so whipped. "Okay. If you were in the right, this can be fought. Did you document it?"

"What the shit good would that do me? The old man used some other excuse I can't do nothin' about. He covered his ass."

Mr. JB had managed to find just the right wording to put on Dick's pink slip. It smacked of deception. They were happy with his work, the client was happy, but because of a "slow-down," they thought it best to cut back as soon as possible.

"But if the client is happy with your work and you know there's no slowdown, how can they justify it?"

"How the fuck do I know? But I do know they're not chasin' me outta town like they've done to other employees. I'll stay and sue the bastards before I run home with my tail between my legs."

I knew much earlier that my son would never be called, and I'd heard nothing from the women who were checking on jobs with their husbands. The hope I'd held on to for so long had evaporated. My worst nightmare was taking place and I couldn't wake up and make it stop. I had to stop and rethink what was going on in my life. I hated the *Evil Duo* but I had to agree with Dick. I would not be told I *had* to leave the country. However, the consequence of having no money in a foreign land, and no work visa was a daunting thought. Staying here and flipping *The Bosses* off with a law suit gave me reason to smile. But staying in a marriage that was doomed gave me reason to pause. There was no way I was going to continue in this relationship, but now was not the time to tell him. I would bide my time and try to help him through this nightmare; as long as he could hold out until September he'd be okay tax-wise. I'd stay until he found a job and then, regretfully, leave this country that I had come to love.

The money had been great and Dick liked his job. The house, maid, car and driver were wonderful perks, but at such a huge price. We were spied on, talked down to and worst of all, told what to do with our private lives—inside and outside our home. I'd rather starve than live like that—well, maybe just eat a little less.

I mentally drew up a pro and con list: what had we gained versus what had we given up by coming here? Dick had given up a very comfortable job teaching golf, but of course he could go back to it. I had leased out my condo for two years and given my car to my sister. I had married a man with problems I'd not bargained for, someone I really didn't know, yet I felt responsible for his job loss. Had I not been here he might still be employed. Yet, he had his own demons to confront: his sexual addiction, sullenness and moods of depression. And by his own admission he'd done the unthinkable by going over the boss's head to the client. Now he felt he was paying for it. Somehow, we had to come together in this crisis. I felt empathy for him and he seemed to take on a gentler attitude, as if we were fighting the world together.

He offered to call my son and tell him that the job offer was no longer a reality. I sat by him as he talked to Dale, crying, knowing how much my son was hurting. The dream was over for all of us. But as a mother, the thought of your child hurting is devastating. He'd get over it in time, of course, but I knew I'd never forgive myself for causing him this disappointment.

When Dick finished, I took the phone. I told my son not to give up, that I had several people putting out feelers for a local-hire job. Would he still be interested? He said no, that a local-hire job would mean lower pay, and he couldn't afford to pay for his family to fly over, and would not come without them. A local hire did not come with perks such as airfare, housing, extra pay, driver, and all the reasons that would persuade someone to work overseas. He said he'd had the feeling for a long time that this would never happen, even though he hoped it would.

I guess I knew in my gut that he'd probably never really had a chance; that the old bastard had only used him as a carrot to get Dick on the job. It hurt nonetheless. And I'd done it again. My normal cockeyed optimist thing, hoping that this time, for once, my gut feelings would prove wrong. I'd also caused some heartache along the way.

Dick and I talked it over long into the night. He would look for a job. I had an obligation to do the PILC newsletter and I would honor it. We made a decision. They wouldn't run us out of the country. We still had the tax obligation and would stay until September, five more months, when the 333 tax deferred days would be up. If he'd found a job by then, all the better. We poured ourselves a drink and said a eulogy for our old life. I wondered if I'd have the money to leave by that time. I couldn't think of it now. I'd worry about it later.

Dick began handing out resumes to other construction companies in town. He was surprised when he had no response. Thailand in the 90s was considered the Mid East of the 70s—there was enough refinery work to keep oil companies busy for another decade. We had an uneasy feeling about it.

A few weeks after Dick's termination, a friend and staunch ally of mine—the wife of the man we thought was *Second in Command*—telephoned with some distressing news. Her husband had overheard a conversation at work between *Mr. JB* and some of his cronies. Supposedly he'd put the word out to other companies in the area to blackball Dick. It all made sense now why Dick hadn't heard back from anyone, even though they'd seemed so interested in hiring him during his interviews.

That was the last kick in the face. Dick made some phone calls and caught a flight back to the States. He'd found an attorney who loved hearing about every last inflammatory and slanderous word that came out of *The Evil Duo's* mouths. According to the lawyer there was a law in the California state code called "The Queen-Bee Statute" which was written exactly for our kind of situation: "...a wife who influences her husband's attitude toward one of his employees and causes dissention/termination in the performance of the employee's job..." Made sense to me—she definitely influenced her husband. Dick also had a timetable and work schedule for the project. It showed the job was picking up speed rather than slowing down.

Our company friends mysteriously became out of touch. I supposed it was that guilt-by-association thing again, not wanting to get on the *Boss Lady's* shit list. I guess keeping food on the table does take precedence over old friendships. I didn't blame them—much. I was amazed at the control she could wield over them. *Didn't they have backbones?*

Beth, *Mr. Second-in-Command's* wife, and a golf buddy of mine, had a weekly card game at her home that I attended on a regular basis.

After we were expelled from the "Garden of Eden"—company housing—Beth called to invite me, the outcast, for a game of cards. I was shocked that she had the guts to do this but delighted, nonetheless. Her husband worked for the client and was not employed by Dick's company, which gave her some leeway. Her house sat right next to *The Evil Duo's*. I remarked to Dick later that night that I'd seen *Mrs. How-Dare-You-Have-a-Life-Here* peeking out from behind her French lace curtains as I all but skipped up Beth's driveway: *Kiss my grits, lady*. We wondered how long it would be before the doo-doo hit the fan, and if so, what would her manure of choice be. We didn't have long to wait. It squeezed through the fan blades the very next morning. Beth phoned me with some disturbing news: "My husband just called me," she said. The minute I heard this I knew the manure had been launched. "He said we had a direct order from *Mr. JB* that we couldn't speak or associate with either of you."

"Oh my God, Beth!" My legs went limp. "How can he give you that kind of order? Your husband doesn't even work for his company, he's employed by the client."

"I'm sick about this," she said sadly. "*Mr. JB* said Dick was suing everyone connected to the jobsite; the boss, the client, and he said my husband's name was listed on the suit as well."

"Stop! You can't be serious! Why would we do that? Dick did start a lawsuit against the *The JBs*, and the lawyer said he had to name the client, but your husband's name was never even discussed. Why would it be?"

"Because my husband's second-in-command under the client, I guess. I can't talk anymore. I just wanted you to know that I'm sorry the way this all turned out. I hope you can understand our position."

"Wait!" I shouted. "Did your husband ask to see the papers? I mean actually read it to see if his name was listed?"

"I'm not really sure. I just know he called and was quite upset."

"But how can he just take *JB's* word for it? Everyone knows he's manipulative. How can you believe a word he says?"

"I don't know but for now we're very concerned about this mess and I have to say goodbye."

Click!

I cried for a while and then typed Beth a letter. I had to put it in writing to let her know we were suing only *The Evil Duo* and the project company. I begged her to ask her husband to actually read the lawsuit papers. I then walked to her house and put the letter in her mailbox, hoping the *Evil Wench* was peering through her curtains so I could flip her two birds. She was truly a psychiatrist's dream in the field of control. She just couldn't let it go. It wasn't enough that she had instigated the termination of Dick's contract, she had to sink her control sword deep into my chest as well. What had I done? I met some great ladies, joined them in some activities, and volunteered to do their newsletter. Where was the sin? I walked home with a pain in my heart. I put down on paper everything Beth had said and mailed off a copy to Dick's attorney. I'm sure as he read my letter he started counting his retirement money. Then I sat down and cried.

I never saw Beth again.

LIFESTYLE CHANGES

48

When Dick returned from the states he was revved up about the lawsuit. The lawyer had told him he had a slam-dunk case and just to sit tight and wait for the money to pour in. That sounded a bit strange to me.

"'Sit tight'?" What does that mean? Like maybe you'll get your job back?"

"Hell, no! I don't want that damn job back. I just want the money for the shit they caused me."

"When did he say you'd hear something?"

"Didn't know. Just said to sit tight, so I'm sittin'"

"Yes, but in the meantime shouldn't you be looking for work?"

"Yeah, right, after the old man screwed me with every company in town?"

Dick began drinking more in the evenings, telling me it was because he needed to get his mind off his problems. He was under a lot of pressure, he said, and it helped him sleep. He needed to find employment but he didn't seem to be looking too hard. Since he'd heard about the old man and his black-balling scheme he seemed to lose interest in looking.

"You'll find one," I told him. "Not every company is going to take the old man's word as gospel. Don't you think somebody might get suspicious about this? Maybe just give you a call to talk about it?"

"Naw. It's been too long. If they were gonna' call me, it would've happened."

By now our nights together were quiet. Dick would retire before me, while I worked on the newsletter. I'd wait for him to fall asleep before I ventured in. Sex was not discussed. Other things had taken precedence. I think it was a mutual feeling that we didn't need any more problems. I did wonder if he had found relief with a bargirl, but I really didn't care, as long as he didn't reach for me. I worried about his depression, but I was sure as soon as he found a job he'd be fine. He had to find one. September was still five months away—a long time to be unemployed.

We were given only two weeks to vacate company housing. We pulled some money from our dwindling savings account and found a reasonable lease in a quaint Thai house in Na Klua, not far from Pattaya. Of course I had to take Pon with me. She offered to work without pay as long as she could stay with me. I was happy to have her, but told her I'd pay her a small salary until Dick found a job. It wouldn't be much.

Pon told me this would be her last job. She had worked for expats well over twenty years, she was good at her job and she knew it, but she was tired. Her dream was to some day move in with her sister who lived somewhere in Texas, but she'd not heard from her in years. We sat down with a map of Texas and I tried to jog her memory by calling out city names. Nothing sounded familiar to her. If she couldn't find her sister, she said, would I sponsor her to come to the States? She said she'd work for me until she died. How I loved this woman. "If you come to the States with me, I'll wait on *you*." She had served her time as far as I was concerned.

An official at the Immigration Department told me that Pon would need a family member to sponsor her, and without any information on her sister it was probably not going to happen. He also informed me that the quota on Thais coming into the U.S. was very low, and the probability very slim. I sized her up for a duffle bag ride home on the plane with me. But knowing Pon, she'd crawl out and start straightening up the cargo hold.

The house in Na Klua was adequate, but would probably not be featured in *Architectural Digest*. The rooms, though sparsely furnished, were large, bright and homey. Bamboo fans kept the bedrooms and living room comfortable. The furniture, though sagging and well-used, was also bamboo with cushions of brilliant colors depicting the tropics and birds in flight. It was obvious that a Thai family were the last occupants as the mattresses were of the concrete variety. Tile, being the choice in most Thai homes, though worn, glimmered throughout the house thanks to Pon's special care.

Two large bedrooms were at the back of the house as well as a tiled bathroom with ample room for shower, sinks and commode. Sagging shutters adorned the extra-wide windows throughout the house giving it a feeling of rugged openness.

The kitchen was decorated in Early Goodwill décor and sad, gray linoleum covered the floor. The table, circa 1950s yellow Formica, with chrome trim, was added by our generous landlady; most Thais have no need for them, sitting on the floor is their preferred place for repast. The table had three functional chairs, and the fourth one, missing a leg, was repaired by Pon using Silly Putty.

The kitchen was larger than that of our company house, which added to Pon's delight. It had sufficient room for all of her culinary delights. I was actually able to cook right beside her. When I wanted to prepare a Thai meal she'd take me on the back of her motorcycle to a local grocer. I'd follow her around the aisles and point to things I needed for my recipes and she'd put them in her cart. This was the first time I'd been inside a Thai grocery store. It was alive with unidentified smells that nearly knocked me over; some fishy, others flowery, as well as unknown herbs that delighted my senses. After I'd pick out what I needed for my recipe, she'd have me wait outside while she paid. "Too mut *baht* foh *falang,*" she'd say. Bless her. She was always looking out for my *baht.*

The house was built in the '40s and showed signs of neglect, but I loved it. It smacked of character and charm. If it weren't for the small lanes that meandered through the area, I would've believed I was in the middle of the rain forest. There seemed a quaint air about it to me; a Bogart-Bacall film setting. I pictured Peter Lorre stepping between the darkened palms, stopping to light a Chesterfield in the moist tropical setting.

It didn't take long to put the place in order. As soon as I received my own teak furniture from the company house I was right back into my Suzy Homemaker mode. Seeing and smelling that beautiful teak wood made me feel like everything would somehow work out.

Our yard was vast with radiant tiles encircling a large patio. Palm trees of every variety and multicolored native flowers grew in thick profusion. Green foliage and flowers with sugary smells added to the intoxicating effect. I'd wake early to watch as slivers of sunlight spilled onto the flowers, lacing the air with sweet perfume. In the evenings I'd sit on the patio as mauve threads of twilight settled over me. I'd close my eyes and listen to the sounds of the night

Our neighbors were mostly Thai with a smattering of expats dotting the area. A charming open-air bar stood at the end of the housing lanes. Pool balls could be heard clacking together, along with music and laughter. The customers were not of the ilk we saw at the beach bars. They were locals—men trudging home after hours in the hot sun to sip a cool one and enjoy the music. There was also a restaurant attached to the bar that served sumptuous Asian food. Next to the bar sat an open-air massage and acupuncture clinic, which welcomed customers on a walk-in basis. I knew that the doctor and I would be on a first-name basis with my aching body.

We were far enough from Central Pattaya to do away with the noise of the bargirl scene and accompanying hoopla. With the Thaïs being such happy people, the soft laughter and music coming from the bar wasn't annoying, and on most nights it lulled me to sleep.

"Free at last, free at last…" as someone famous once said. For the first time in months I felt free. I could leave the house and not feel someone watching my every move. We could have guests on our patio and not be chastised because they were from "another company." Gone were worries about when the axe would fall. No more ringing phones to inform us we'd broken a commandment.

We adopted a little puppy from a departing expat. A dainty, playful eight-week-old apricot poodle we named Wani. *Wan* is Thai for "sweet" and Dick tacked an "i" on the end because he said "Wan" sounded Mexican and, after all, she was full-blooded Thai-French. She became my shadow. I couldn't walk through the house without tripping over her. Before taking a step, I'd have to first look down and make sure I didn't crush her. She'd curl up on my lap when I'd sit to read, or whine to get up on the bed at night and curl up on top of the blanket covering my feet. She even had the nerve to whimper when I'd turn over, like I might be disturbing her sleep. But It was obvious Pon would rather I'd brought home a stuffed toy from Beach Road. One of Murphy's Law tenets is if you don't like animals they'll stick to you like glue. Pon constantly had to shoo little Wani out from under her feet, then make a great show of pretending to dust dog dander off herself and the furniture.

After our fall from grace I decided to make some drastic changes. If I really wanted to adopt this *mai pen rai* attitude, I needed to change my outlook on a lot of things. With the Buddhist mentality that I wanted to espouse, why did I fret about so many things? All around me were sweet Thai faces, smiling and accepting their lot in life, and here

I was fretting over everything from sex to spatulas.

For one thing, why should my hair style mean anything to me? That would be my first change. I did what I'd threatened to do when I first arrived; cut my hair. I'm not talking cut as in trimmed. I mean cut as in all gone. About as close to a little boy's cut as you can get. Cutting my hair had a lot to do with the amount of time I spent styling it. I was fed up with my ritual: wash, blow-dry, curl, perm, color, cut, wash, blow-dry, yada, yada, yada. Why was I going against the grain when I could just wash, air dry, and walk?

A few of my friends decided to have a girl's get-away weekend in Bangkok. As all three of the ladies wore their hair very short, I felt I'd be right in the swing of things and much cooler with it all gone. I had innocently mentioned to them before we left that I'd threatened to cut my hair for decades. The battle cry was heard, the war was waged and I did it. I said "Take it off"—and the stylist did. Looking in the mirror at the salon I saw an unfamiliar person staring back at me. I was shocked at all the face I saw. My friends whooped and hollered, yeahed and high-fived about my great haircut. They told me I looked years younger. It was all very encouraging until one of them said, "It's about time you cut that mop. You always looked like a barmaid to me." Bless her tactless heart.

Dick was furious when he saw my hair or lack thereof. He said I looked older, that I had no right to do this. He said that *I knew* he loved long hair. Since he'd had to cut off his ponytail for safety issues on the job, he was enthralled with my long hair. I suggested he let his grow back if he loved long hair so much. This went over well.

My puppy, Wani, had a haircut too. I deposited her at the local grooming parlor and asked for a "puppy cut." When I returned for her she looked twenty years older and I felt like I'd lost my baby. She was given a "mature cut" and looked ridiculous. I now had to reassess my girlfriends' oath of my youthful looks. If my precious Wani, only six months old, had lost most of her hair and looked decades older, what must I look like?

We found three filthy, nasty, bloodsucking tics on little Wani—and one on me. The little scumbag hadn't burrowed in completely, but I think he planned on taking up residence in my scalp. I first noticed it when I scratched my head. I felt what I thought was a small scab, scraped it, and found some blood on my fingernail. I thought I'd probably bumped my head on something, a regular occurrence with cupboards and shelves built for short people. I asked Dick to check it, pointing to what I thought was the scab. "Can you see it? I just picked at it and I think it's bleeding. Is it a scab?"

"Shit!" he yelped. "That's not a scab, it's a fuckin' tic. "

Maybe it *was* time to go home.

The day we vacated company housing, Dick had to turn over the company car and driver, much to his regret. He now needed a car to get around town and job-hunt. I tried to veto that idea. With traffic as crazy as it was, why would anyone want to subject themselves to that type of danger? But Dick couldn't live without wheels. After a day of shopping he returned home with the cheapest thing he could rent. You'll notice I said "thing." It was a tiny European piece of metal called a Mira that tried valiantly to pass itself off as a car. It had bucket seats and a dashboard, but that's where the similarities ended. It didn't fool me. This was a motorcycle with a piece of aluminum foil stretched around it, four Tiny-Tot tires and an engine struggling to evolve from a lawn mower.

Dick drove all over the city and I feared for his life. I considered calling our life insurance agent in the States to make sure his was current. I would have nothing to do with that Tin Lizzie. I had my own transportation, thank you very much. I could hop on the back of a motorcycle taxi and head for town or anywhere I wanted. I felt much safer with a Thai driving. I did present a rather comical picture I'm sure, sitting sidesaddle, tennis racket, beach bag and purse balanced precariously on my ever-expanding lap, hoping the driver wouldn't turn a corner too quickly.

Dick began by tooling around our neighborhood in the Mira to try it out. I suggested he get used to it before he set out for the deadly highways. He thought he drove just fine, but I still worried about that thin piece of tinfoil wrapped around him. After a few weeks of his acclimating to the roads, I did go for short lifts around town with him, but only because he coerced me by offering a shopping trip. When I rode with him my colitis reared its ugly head just backing out of the driveway. The armrests became frayed and dented as I hung on for dear life. The floorboard on my side quickly gained two permanent size eight-and-a-half shoe imprints.

A big problem for any expat who drives in Thailand is one of the Buddhist beliefs. If an accident occurs it must be the *farang's* fault—even if caused by a Thai—because we are here, therefore *we* must be the reason for the accident. If we weren't here, there would have been no accident—*mai pen rai.*

Dick decided to take a Thai driving test and get his license. He was flummoxed when he found there was no such thing. He did need an international license, but an exam wasn't required to obtain it. So, as they say, "When in Rome." He began driving just like the natives. He'd cut in front of oncoming vehicles, turn the wrong way onto one-way streets, and pass cars on the shoulder with speeds of up to 100 kilometers per hour. The only thing Dick lacked—the most important, I felt—was the *mai pen rai* attitude. Tolerance was not his long suit, in fact, he was void in it. As he careened through town he'd mutter, "What the hell does that guy think he's doing?" or "I'd like to know what makes them tick," or "Dumb shit," or "Why, I otta..." as well as other such phrases. Of course he said he was just doing this for my benefit, to get a laugh. Ha!

Dick was told not to worry about a court date if stopped for a traffic violation. All he needed was 200 *baht* neatly folded and ready to palm over to the policeman—without question. Everything was then forgiven and you were on your way again—*mai pen rai*. For my near fatal accident, the truck driver who nearly killed us was fined 400 *baht* on the spot and drove away unencumbered by a ticket or lawsuit. Our driver was also fined 400 *baht*. The reason? He was there.

Speaking of police, these gentlemen certainly didn't seem to aspire to a macho image and exercised their calling very casually. We saw no police cars in Pattaya when we lived there. I had to chuckle when I saw cops rush around town on motorcycles—two to a seat. Somehow this was not a fear-inspiring image.

Dick had reason to talk to the police on one occasion when he thought his wallet had been stolen. He had absentmindedly left it in the car while stopping to have a tire changed. Later, driving home, he reached for his wallet in the console where he usually kept it. It was not there. He was sure that the two boys who'd worked on his car had lifted it. He complained to the manager, who questioned the boys, who both denied seeing a wallet. Two policemen arrived—on one motorcycle— and grilled the boys. They then asked Dick if he wanted to press charges. "Absolutely!" They told Dick to follow them to the station and to bring the boys with him.

Yes. TIT! This Is Thailand—love it or leave it. Where else in the world do you get to transport the bad guys to jail in your own car so you can press charges?

As Dick followed the police to the station, his foot hit something lumpy under the floor mat. He reached down and found the wallet, crammed between the floor mat and the gear shift. He drove back to the tire shop, dropped the boys off and apologized to them and the owner.

Mai pen lai," said the owner. "Boys say no take, I believe."

FUN AND GAMES

49

N ow that we were on our own and not under the mantle of a company for our visas, we were required to leave the country every three months and reenter as the law stipulated. This entailed getting our passports stamped and showing a country exit for the required two days. If this was not strictly adhered to, we could be deported and heavy fines would be forthcoming.

We took the first of such trips to Singapore shortly after our move to Na Klua. Singapore was immaculate and incredibly beautiful, but so expensive. I wondered how the natives could afford to live there.

Craving American food, we were directed to a Tony Roma's rib joint. We were ecstatic and ate with abandon. That is until they brought us the bill; $105 Singapore ($93 American) for two barbequed ham sandwiches and two ice-teas. Our ecstasy then turned to prudence and we decided that the Chinese restaurant by our hotel looked pretty good for dinner—and certainly would be much more ethnic. That bill for a dish of rice, *moo goo gai pan*, peapods and beef, and two beers was $60 Singapore—that ended our ethnic search. The next day I noticed the cute little push carts along the road and agreed they didn't look so bad after all—as long as we didn't look at the things doing the breaststroke across the top of the soup bowl.

The Chinese and their ancestors, who settled in Singapore with the Malay about 200 years ago, were scrupulous in their care of this beautiful island. I could understand why when I heard the rules for the island: A heavy fine would be imposed if anyone so much as dropped a cigarette butt on the sidewalk or street. It was illegal to bring gum into the country, and even illegal to chew it while there. Caning was a definite deterrent for keeping the city immaculate, which also kept the taggers in line. No graffiti was evident, no slums and no squalor. It was unbelievable. We took the subway system across the island; such a smooth and picturesque ride. The subway cars were pristine. Not a scrap of paper on the floor, no graffiti, not even in the underground subway stations—without guards or police on duty.

As the plane landed back in Bangkok, Dick admitted it was now time to buckle down. He would find a job, get rid of his funk and hopefully life would get easier.

Besides my days at the orphanage and doing the newsletter, the PILC kept me busy with fun and games. They had something going on every day of the week, from helping the needy—which I felt was soon to be me—to sports and card games. Along with golf, one of the groups that I tentatively signed up for was bridge. I assumed it had to be a pretty easy game because so many "old people" took part in it. I decided to show up and try my hand at this easy game. I'd been playing cards since I was ten years old. I was one hot card shark. How hard could this game be?

When I arrived at the bridge room the ladies were taking their seats. Not wanting to appear as though I didn't know what the hell I was doing, I sat at the first empty seat I found. Two ladies, seated at the table were chatting animatedly and seemed not to notice me. I sat there with a practiced look of calmness. A few minutes later a cranky-looking elderly lady walked up and put her purse on the opposite chair. I smiled. "Hi, my name's Dodie, I'm new here." I offered my hand as she studied me over the rim of her bifocals. Her face was an intricate map of cracks and crevices, and her mouth turned down like a pair of parentheses on either side.

"Oh?" she said, like she'd expected someone else. I assumed I'd passed her bifocal test as she extended her bony hand. "I'm June. I guess we're partners." She sat, picked up the cards and began to shuffle. "Do you play any conventions?"

"Huh?"

"Conventions, you know, Jacoby transfer, Blackwood, Stamen."

"Ah," I glanced around the room looking for a familiar face. "Ah, well, I'm kinda new at this, in fact, real new." I tried to chuckle but instead a raspy sound escaped my lips.

She frowned and her thin, white eyebrows joined in a look of distaste.

"Just tell me what to do and I'm sure I'll catch on fast."

"Directress!" screeched the octogenarian. "We have a problem here."

"We do?"

"Of course we do," she sniffed. "Have you ever played bridge?"

I looked around the room. Well-coifed, white-haired heads popped up from their game as the room became catacomb-quiet. Cards were held in motionless hands as eight pair of eyes landed on my heated face. I felt like I'd unwittingly bitten into a jalapeno pepper. "No," I whispered much lower than I'd meant to, "but I…"

She stood looking down at me, all four-foot-three inches of her. "Well, I never!"

Needing to gain control of the situation from this tiny, scary lady, I stood and said a tad louder than I'd meant to: "Well, gosh. How hard could it be? I mean, really? I'm a card person. I'm willing to learn."

I looked around for some sort of encouragement, hoping to hear: *Hey, give her a chance. We all had to start from scratch.* Nothing! Everywhere I turned I saw looks of disapproval mixed with disgust. I excused myself, put on my dark glasses and slunk out. *Geez, what grouches!*

I grudgingly asked around for someone to teach me this so-called "hard" game. I found a teacher in a lovely French lady named Muriel, a tennis buddy of mine, who knew the game "Eeensite and owt." She offered to teach me the fine art of bridge. "You come to my house, Doteee, and I wheel teach you zee right way, yes?" *Why do the French always end every sentence with a question?*

"Great," I said. I knew it wouldn't take very long. I was a card person, after all.

Ha! She sat me down for five hours, twice a week. Every time I made the teensiest mistake she'd swat my hand with a ruler. "Non! Non! Non! Leesen to what I zay, yes?" There's that question again. Ouch! She'd smack my hand when I'd forgotten somzing she'd taught me four hours earlier. "You must zink of theez as learning a foreen lankuage, yes?"

"Oui!"

"Okay! Now! What deed I just zay to you?"

Oh *merde*! I wondered why I wanted to learn zees game.

Muriel gave me a bridge computer game to take home and work on—or else—and then released me from school. I used the *Grand Slam* game for practice and took lessons from Muriel twice a week, determined to ride back into that card room on a silver steed, proclaiming for all to hear: "Seven-No-Trump!"

I was hooked on the game by the second lesson. I do have an addictive personality, I suppose, but I also found it very brain-aerobic and I needed all the help I could get in that department. Also, I reasoned that in about twenty years, when I turned sixty—who's she kidding—I'd be able to play a nice docile game of golf and then settle down to bridge with a bunch of gray-haired dowagers. Much to my dismay, I had to admit that it was a "hard" game.

The weather in Pattaya fascinated me. I learned to watch it like a meteorologist. The best weather for us *farangs*—cool, clear and dazzling—came in November and continued on through February— great for golf and tennis, and just being alive. Then the temperature slowly crept up on us like a thief in the night, bringing the humidity along with it so that by March we knew our fun was over out of doors. This continued until sometime in May; the worst time to be on the course, and made playing golf a good way to stroke—literally. However, it was a great time for indoor card games and shopping. June to October drenched us with monsoons—nearly the total amount of rain for the entire year fell at that time. Some days it rained harder than others, but seldom got to the batten down the hatches point. It was, however, heart-stopping humid and a good time to stay indoors and read a book. Then miraculously we found ourselves heading towards the wonderful month of November, when the weather began to change ever so slowly and before we knew it, it was time to hit the links again. Throughout all the rain, humidity, heat and cool breezes, the sky could change from azure to steel blue, then prison grey to charcoal, then back to steel blue again—all in the span of thirty minutes. With the changing shades of blue, green and greener from jungles to mountains to fairways—it was simply *brilliant,* as my Brit friends would say.

Tennis was another activity I took up again. I'd played the game for a few years, but after being introduced to the addictive game of golf, I'd let my racquet gather dust in the garage. Now, here in paradise, I looked forward to playing again, often two or three times a week. After the games the gals would hook up at an outdoor restaurant, a heavenly resort on the ocean that could easily have been on a travel poster. In the center were two beautiful infinity pools with a step-down into the sand and beyond that the luminous ocean. It was mesmerizing. The owner only required that we purchase a drink now and then while playing cards. He insisted we stay as long as we liked. After our activities, we would use the hotel's shower facilities, order lunch by the pool and start a serious game of bridge while the waiters brought us a moveable feast—anything we desired. Such decadence! We played until someone yelled "Uncle" and we knew it was time to go home.

THE MAGNIFICENT CADDIES

50

Pattaya has dozens of pristine golf courses. Some were not as elegant as I'd played stateside, but what set them apart was the price and availability. We seldom had to reserve a starting time. On the weekends there might be one or two threesomes in front of us, but during the week it was pretty much empty. The price for a round of golf ranged from $20 to $25—with a caddie and cart thrown in. I've never met a golf course I didn't love, but here in Pattaya, from the Pro shop to the caddies, I felt welcome and was treated with smiles and helpfulness.

On the rare occasions when only two of us gals could get together for golf we'd laughingly prepare ourselves for what was sure to come if the course had a tournament going. We'd be paired with men.

Men! Bless their hearts. They're so predictable, aren't they?

Case in point: On one particular day the course would be taken by a tournament later in the day, so the starter asked if we'd mind hooking up to make a foursome with two guys already on the first tee. As we approached, we saw one of them hit a short, chili dip tee shot and was caterwauling as he slammed his club back into his bag. When they saw us walking up to the tee box, they looked like we'd caught them with their members hanging out. We could smell their fear and we understood it—it was not altogether unfounded. Men do get nervous when women approach, dreading to have to play this "man's game" with the opposite sex. Other than their wives, when pressed to do so, most men would naturally prefer to play with the boys, whereas women have no problem playing golf with men. Most times, the guys are much more fun than women, and so helpful. They of course know exactly what you're doing wrong, and they have no problem telling you how to correct your take-away, your release, your coil, your stance, your follow-through, your hair-do. But, hey, don't get me wrong, they're such great guys to help us poor little gals.

The two guys on the first tee were the epitome of southern gentlemen—right out of Dueling Banjos. "Hey there, sweet little thangs. How'd you and your girlfriend there like to play on ahead of us?"

"Are y'all sure you don't mind?" my friend from Texas cooed.

"Shee-it, we ain't in no hurry. Right, Bubba?"

"Why, thaaank ya kindly sirs," she purred, as though she didn't have a brain in her head. This gal happened to be one of our low-handicappers and I was eager to see the guys' expressions when she teed-off.

"Shee-iiitttt!" they exclaimed as her ball exploded off the tee, straight as an arrow, and landed about 220 yards out. I knew I'd better hit my best drive so we could jab it to these rubes. I coiled back until my bra strap snapped, and then unloaded on a magnificent drive, well, nowhere near as far as hers, and maybe just a tad off the fairway and into the snake-infested rough, but hey, it wasn't a chili-dip. As we jumped in our cart to leave, we giggled and waved like the little goony birds they thought we were. "Y'all have a good one, y'heah?"

. But, everything considered, I do agree with the men. Women do an awful lot of gabbing, giggling, gossiping and joke telling, and I feel sorry for the poor guys who get saddled with us. Unless, of course, they might enjoy discussing PMS, what brand is the best panty liner on the market, and what's the best medicine for a yeast infection.

But, I did wonder: why weren't these men home barefoot and hosing down driveways where they belonged?

On the smaller courses some of the younger gals preferred to walk no matter the heat or humidity. I was able to walk during the cooler months, but after my bladder surgery I opted for the blessed electric cart. Also, during the worst of the weather, at 100 degrees and 100% humidity, I needed a cart to keep from disappearing in a puff of smoke. During the rainy season everyone needed a cart to beat it to the clubhouse before a lightning bolt gave our hair the Don King look.

The courses were long and difficult, with a smattering of snakes adding a little excitement to the game. We all learned to walk with an occasional look-see upwards and downwards along the cart paths and boundaries for the little slime balls. Snakes had also been seen lying in the long grass at the edge of the fairways and sometimes in the trees that lined the courses and cart paths. We gave them a wide berth. The caddies had excellent vision, which I greatly appreciated.

On one particular day as I was coming up to my next shot that was buried in the rough off the fairway, my caddie grabbed my arm and jumped in front of me. A mere four feet ahead was a very large, very ugly snake, slithering across the cart path. I shrieked and the snake scooted off under a rock, probably more terrified than I. A few days later it was the same scenario, but this time my caddie put her hand out to stop me. She pointed to a tree with some branches sagging and leaning heavily to one side. She put her finger to her mouth to shush me, took my 3-wood, jiggled the branches and dislodged a very large, fast snake that made his exit up the tree. I did have a little more respect for low hanging branches from then on.

Most of the courses did provide pull-carts for the caddies, but several courses were without such niceties. These tiny caddies, not one of them weighing over ninety pounds, would carry our heavy golf bags over their frail shoulders without complaint. I tried not to watch as a new caddie would hitch mine up and over her shoulder. Seeing that it was a woman's bag, most of them thought they could pick it up without a problem. Then came the look of amazement as they felt its heft. But, they didn't flinch; never letting on that anything was too much for them. I knew my bag was frightfully heavy but I really did need everything in there: snake-bite kit, mosquito spray, band-aids, lip balm, sun block, mirror, brush, lip pencil, lipstick, Kleenex, Mylanta, Lomotil, towels, thirty extra balls, spikes and a wrench, and socks and shoes, in case of blisters. There was also my rain gear, umbrella and a water bottle. I did tip them quite well and made sure to give their dented shoulder a good rub.

At the end of each hole my caddie would point to my score card and show me on her fingers what she thought I'd shot. Then with a questioning look she'd add, "Is ok, Madame?" before she'd write it down. Such tact! I'm sure if I'd told her I'd had a hole-in-one she'd unquestioningly have written it on my card.

Besides watching for snakes, my caddie did a myriad of chores. It's a wonder she let me blow my own nose. I worried that I might not be able to pull a club out of my bag when I eventually returned to the States.

The caddies were always four feet in front of, or behind you, and always thinking a few steps ahead of you. They would tee up your ball, hand you the right club for the distance, give you a read on the green, and keep your score. It was heaven. They would also retrieve your ball from the sand trap, rake it, and even step into the snake-infested rough to find your ball—while you yelled, "*Mai pen rai.*" In she'd go and out she'd come with the ball and a very wide smile.

Most of the courses hired only female caddies, which I assumed was because a male caddie would go ballistic listening to women chattering. One thing I know for sure—because I asked—women were far better tippers than men and the caddies always queued up for the lady golfers; they knew how to have a good time.

I discovered a medical miracle while in Thailand. Instant perspiration. I purchased an ice collar, a life-saving invention for people like me who don't perspire, whose body lacks a cooling mechanism and who faints with exertion in ninety degree weather. This miracle was a piece of terry cloth about four-by-eight inches, with a slit down the center to add crushed ice, then closed with a small strip of Velcro. After filling it with crushed ice I'd wrap the collar around my neck and as it melted, Voila! I had instant perspiration. A nice coolant for the body when one doesn't have the internal thermostat most normal people take for granted. But a price had to be paid for this luxury, and it was not without some embarrassing moments. As the ice rapidly melted down the front of my blouse I looked like a lactating mother. I could see the caddies exchange knowing glances and giggles. Their eyes really popped when, as the ice melted, I'd remove the collar, wring it out, refill it with more ice from our water jug, and replace it. *These crazy falangs*, the caddies surely must have thought, *they can't even sweat properly.*

A few things did bother me about these girls. Not only did they *not* perspire in the sweltering heat, they also covered themselves from head to toe with clothes and towels. All that could be seen of them were fingertips, eyes, nose and mouth. They had to be cooking under all those clothes. I also never noticed any of them shooing away the multitudes of pesky little critters that flew in our faces during the hot and humid weather. Could it be the aroma from the *farangs* skin that enticed the bugs? Beats me, but the caddies never seemed to be bothered by man, beast, insect or weather. They were precious, those magnificent caddies.

THE RAUCOUS BARGIRLS

51

Despite living in a town noted for its thriving sex industry and go-go bars running along Beach Road on the Golden Mile, we probably only stopped in a dozen times to meet up with friends for a quick drink and then on to dinner. I was always curious about the girls that worked there, and watched the goings on with a writer's eye. The modus operandi seemed to be the same at each place. While the *farangs* sat sipping drinks, the bargirls would stake their quarry and then start their act. Sometimes a plastic snake or monkey would be laid on the man's lap by a laughing bargirl or garlands of flowers thrown over his head. If he enjoyed the game, a petite brown-skinned, spandex-pantied girl might then plant herself on his lap. From then on the man would buy her drinks, and possibly include some of her girlfriends in the round. I thought as I watched this scene, a man would only be lonesome in this sensual paradise if he chose to be.

Along Beach Road, as well as in the Patpong district of Bangkok, bar owners hired scores of these girls to sit in the darkened bars and the doorways to sing and cajole to the walk-by traffic. The number of females employed depended on the size of the establishment. The owner's main goal was to make sure that the customer had one of these girls wrapped around him for the night. If a tourist were to leave with one of them, *mai pen rai;* the bar owner got his take of the baht first, and the bargirl got what was left, which in the '90s was the equivalent of about $10.00 a night for entertaining these gents, plus whatever tips might be included for extra services rendered. I have since done some Internet sleuthing and am surprised to see that the girls make quite a good living at these places since my residence in Thailand.

With my writer's curiosity I couldn't help but wonder what kind of homes these girls came from and why they chose this life. Were they slutty girls who looked for this type of job, or were they forced into it by family poverty, as I'd heard? I needed to know what they wanted out of life. What they dreamed of. I put the word out that I was looking to find and interview a bargirl before I left the country, one who could at least understand a little English. Word does spread quickly in expat communities, and soon I had my girl. I will call her *Bou.* I was told that she loved to talk to *farangs* and would be easy to question. The expat who'd set this up cautioned me that the bargirls are also known as appalling liars, and not to believe everything I heard.

It was close to noon on a day when the temperature and humidity were fighting each other for top billing. When I walked into the darkened bar I could see a few *farangs* slouched at the bar, some drinking, some laughing and enjoying themselves. A gaggle of girls could be seen standing around looking bored. Others were draped over the men at the bar. I took a seat near the entrance at a table where I would have enough light to write. I scanned the depressingly dark bar, lit only by a small bulb dangling from a fly-encrusted cord over the heads of the revelers. A palm frond fan circled lazily, blowing humid, smoky air into the faces of the otherwise absorbed partiers. The smell of cheap perfume, alcohol and stale cigarette smoke flooded my senses and burned my eyes.

Several girls were lounging in booths toward the back of the place, fanning themselves while others were squatting in corners gambling. How child-like they looked, as if they hadn't a care in the world and could just as easily have been playing "Go Fish." There ages seemed to vary from very young to mid-aged and beyond.

I introduced myself to Bou and said I'd like to include her in a story I was going to write about living in her country. She seemed excited at the prospect of using her limited knowledge of English, as well as trying to understand mine. Her speech was spotty at best but the gist of it seemed clear to me. If I didn't understand her, I'd ask her to slow down and begin again.

Bou was a tawny beauty with exquisite features and silken black hair that hung to the middle of her back. At first she seemed loud and coarse, talking much too fast for me. As she began to trust me her speech dropped a few decibels. I wondered if she had always talked this loud or, as I'd been told, was trained this way as a means to beckon the lonely male *farangs* inside.

The refined Thai women have a beautiful language that seems to flow out in pools of dark water. They speak as if addressing you in a church sanctuary, in sotto voice, warm and soothing like a gentle waterfall. But here, as in most of the bars, the girls spoke in the same shrill and grating manner.

Bou said she had left her village in hopes of working and sending home money to her family. She'd been a waitress in a Western restaurant in Bangkok for two years and had picked up some Pidgin English—fractured but understandable—and practiced it day and night. She told me that when she found she could make more money as a bargirl, she quickly changed careers. She said she was twenty-five, but her demeanor put her closer to eighteen.

Her raucous voice and manners belied her stature. She was less than five feet tall and slender as a pencil in her black spandex mini dress. No bust-line to speak of—most Thai women are not well endowed—but elegantly shaped legs. She had small, pouty, bright red lips and eyes the color of liquid lava. It was clear to me how some lonely man would want to spend an evening with this exotic young girl wrapped around him and think he'd died and gone to heaven.

What I'd gleaned from my Thai friends was that the bargirls were sleazy, money-hungry whores, and that no respectable man would ever be interested in them. Yet, as I talked to Bou, I got the impression that there was more to these women than that. I wanted to believe that the life of a bargirl was filled with misery, broken hearts, hope and then despair. "Love?" I asked *Bou.* "What about love? Do you have a boyfriend?"

She let out a gaudy laugh then turned to translate to her friends, who joined her in her raucous laughter. "What? No boyfriends?"

She stopped laughing. A serious look came over her face. She said no one has a boyfriend. They all believed if they waited long enough a rich *farang* would come along and whisk them off into a life of luxury—with the ultimate goal being America.

Several of her girlfriends gathered around as *Bou* and I talked. She translated as she went, while they made noises of agreement—with the standard giggle—and squealed at the mention of America. *Bou* said money was a priority with all the girls, sometimes maybe love. Each new trick could be Mr. Right. I got the picture here. The girls were giving *sex* for love and the men were promising love for *sex*.

Bou wanted to believe that the man she cared for really loved her, and she patiently waited for his return. Even though she'd not heard from him for several months, she wanted to believe he'd return and carry her away to a wonderful life. He had gone home to his "other family" she said, but he'd return. As *Bou* told me this, then translated, the girls agreed with bobbing heads. Try as I might, I didn't get a feeling of sadness from any of them. Even when *Bou* told me she had lost her heart to one special man, a man who never returned, she kept up her smiles and laughter. Another *mai pen rai* attitude to pain.

I visited *Bou* two more times before I left for the States. The more we talked, the more melodious her voice became, dropping decibels each visit. She was always happy to see me and introduced me around the bar as her "second mother." It made me sad to see her happy face, knowing it was solely painted on for her job. I worried for her because she'd often talked of death, albeit jokingly—"Why I live for? Maybe I die."

My last visit to *Bou,* a few days before I left, was especially poignant. She seemed a bit down, but soon she was back to her high decibels and coarse laughter. When I told her I was leaving, a sad look came over her face. She said she thought she was pregnant and was terrified that she'd have to give the baby to the orphanage. She had no means to raise this child and I knew that Thai culture frowned on half-breeds. I gave her the phone number of the school teacher that had helped so many girls like her and she promised to contact him. I never saw her again but I pray she made that call.

If what I'd been told about the girls being addictive liars was true, so be it. I wanted to believe *Bou* was different.

THE REGISTERED LETTER

52

In March, when Dick was terminated from his job, we realized we could not leave until September, for tax purposes. And now it was September, arriving hot and humid and heavy with rain. I awoke with a sick feeling in my stomach and tried to get my thoughts in order. Where was my life going? We had been in our second home now for five months. The tax bite we would have encountered back in the States was now toothless—we had fulfilled our time quota out of the country. But all was not well in Na-Klua. I knew it was time to go but I hated to leave this life and the friends I'd made. I had an obligation to produce a newsletter once a month and I didn't want to let the members down. My work at the orphanage was important too.

Dick hadn't found a job. In the months since he'd left the company he'd been drinking more and his moodiness caused more fights. He rationalized that since *Mr. JB* had blackballed him, why should he keep checking in at all the big companies. I suspected that most of his days were spent at bars and pounding the golf course rather than the pavement. We both knew things were not working, we just didn't discuss it. He was taking money from our savings account in the States to keep afloat, but we both knew that had to be dwindling away.

We'd been going on with our day-to-day life by politely avoiding each other and thus, confrontations. There was no more trying on either of our parts. I'd hoped he'd get his priorities straight and he was eager for me to understand the reason for his actions; the strain he'd been under, the loss of a job, and on and on.

I tried to help him get through it. I took partial blame for the loss of his job, but reading the encouraging letter from his attorney told me the lawsuit he'd filed would be enough recompense. However, I could give him no excuse for what he'd put me through in the bedroom.

Dick came home one day excited about a Thai PGA pro that lived in Pattaya who said he needed a partner to start up a golf academy. They would be giving lessons as well as golf course management. This partner-to-be assured Dick that there was much money to be made from the many Asian tourists that came to Thailand for weeks or months, as well as those from the U.S. and Europe. He said they were all looking for a better golf game and would pay any price to accomplish it. It was a wide open field and he intended to capitalize on it.

Dick's mood changed dramatically. He seemed happy heading for the golf course everyday to hook up with this man and make plans. Maybe, I thought, he might also be meeting up with a sweet young Thai girl who thought he was the end-all. It seemed he only showed signs of depression when he had a sympathetic audience—me. The golf deal sounded plausible but I felt a familiar bit of gut-clenching, that special intuition innate to women—that I'm capable of ignoring—and knew I wasn't getting the whole story. How could he possibly be someone's partner in a money-making venture when he was without money? Had he told this guy he had none? I knew he was a good golfer and could work as an instructor, but as far as opening an academy, that seemed a bit of a stretch. He had me type flyers to be dropped off at hotels and local golf courses in the area to drum up some business. I asked him how he could plan all this without a place to teach or without money. He told me not to worry about it, he had it all figured out. I'm sure he did but I'd never know the truth. I decided I'd help with this so-called "new job" but I was already mentally on my way out. I was squirreling away money for my exit.

One afternoon while Dick was out doing whatever he did, I was fast at work on the newsletter when I heard someone at the door. Pon answered it then called for me. A boy held a registered letter that needed a signature. He obviously didn't care who signed it and seemed glad that someone was there to take it off his hands. I noticed the return address was from a stateside law firm. I thought it was the lawyer who had taken the "Queen Bee" lawsuit. Inside was a thin piece of paper that I unfolded, eagerly anticipating the details from the lawsuit. But it wasn't from Dick's lawyer. It was a legal document, all right, for Dick to sign. It was an interlocutory for dissolution of marriage along with a letter from a woman who bore the same last name as his—and mine.

I dropped to the sofa to read it. I wasn't shocked, just pissed. It was as though subconsciously I had suspected this all along. The papers had been mailed a month earlier, and along with them was a tidy little letter written by his wife. She needed a signature from him to end the union—the marriage that he swore he had ended before we were married. She also asked for support; a huge amount of money and, of course, lawyer fees. The gist of the letter was that if he was making so much money in Thailand, and had never bothered to get a divorce, then she was still his wife and entitled to half of it. Actually, she was about six months too late. Evidently she didn't know that half of nothing is nothing. She said she'd heard he married someone while still married to her and that she pitied that person.

How I wished that *that person* had been anyone but me—and that I was anywhere but here with him.

I thought back to the day before we were to be married. I was packing some things when Dick walked into the bedroom. He said we needed to talk. One small thing he had neglected to tell me, he said, was that *maybe* he was *not quite* divorced from his wife.

"What? What do you mean 'not quite divorced'?"

His answer was immediate, without a hint of concern or guilt. "Calm down, don't get excited. I'll take care of it today."

"'Don't get excited?' Dick, we're packed. We're ready to leave for Las Vegas tomorrow. My whole life is going into storage. What are you telling me?"

Dick did have a way of skewing the truth and I'd seen him do it many times; to his clients, to his son or his brother-in-law on the phone and to me. It was as though everyone else had to be up front and honest, while he had cornered the market on skewing.

I was livid. We were ready to leave to get married. My kids were meeting us in Las Vegas to stand up as witnesses, and this man was now saying he thought he *might not* be divorced. It got very ugly, with me hysterical and him denying any guilt. He left, saying he was going to see a lawyer. I started unpacking. I wanted nothing to do with this man if I couldn't trust him. An hour or so later I got a call from him saying that he wanted me to talk to someone. I heard whispered voices then a man came on the line and identified himself as Dick's attorney. "*I think* everything is done that needs to be done. *I think* you can go ahead and get married."

I thought this man was probably with the firm of Dewey-Cheatem-and-Howe. He sounded sleazy and too cavalier about the whole thing, and there were way too many "I thinks" to suit me. I asked him what that meant? Was he still married or not? It's a grey area, he told me, but he felt it was just a matter of signing a few last minute papers, which he'd have Dick do, post-haste, and then everything would be legal.

"Last minute papers, my ass!" I slammed the phone down. What was I going to do now? I wasn't sure I could believe this. I called his daughter-in-law. Before I could ask her anything she had a question for me: "How can you marry someone who's still married?"

"What?" It seemed to me that I had said "what?" way too many times for one day. "Dick told me he was divorced but just hadn't signed the last papers yet. What do you mean?"

Silence.

"I just spoke to his attorney and he said Dick *was* divorced. What am I supposed to believe? Is he divorced or not?"

"Hmm. Not according to his wife." She didn't want to elaborate any further. She cut the call short, wished me well and hung up.

I remembered the day Dick took me to meet his son and daughter-in-law for the first time. I couldn't explain the feeling that I had that night, nor could I interpret the looks between the two of them, but it was almost as if they were shocked to see me, and moreover, surprised that Dick had a girlfriend. There's that woman's intuition again. Those gut feelings that I am famous for denying. When I asked Dick about it on the way home he sloughed it off as being normal for his daughter-in-law to make someone feel uncomfortable. He said she and his ex-wife were good friends. And, he said, that was just his son being his son—weird. "You know," he said, "how your kids always worry about you gettin' into a new relationship? He was probably just checkin' you out, is all."

Dick returned later that day, smiling, saying everything was taken care of. The lawyer said he was in the clear and we could go ahead with the marriage. When I told him about the phone call to his daughter-in-law, he said she didn't know what she was talking about, and that his wife was a liar. He loved me. Did I love him?

Did I? I had to think about that. I'd been newly widowed when we met. Dick was Johnny on the spot whenever I needed anything. I was hurting and he was there as my knight in shining armor. He did so much for me that I guess gratitude felt like love. He was good to me in a controlling sort of way. He was good to my kids, grandkids and friends, but I'm not sure that's a reason to say you love someone. My friends liked him: "Come on girl. Go for it. He seems crazy about you and you deserve some happiness."

"I don't know what I feel right now," I said. "I'm not able to think of love at the moment. I feel betrayed." I asked him why he didn't tell me when we first met that he hadn't finished the divorce proceedings. He did, he said. I asked him if he thought there was a chance that they'd get back together and maybe that's why he didn't finish things off legally. He vehemently denied it. "Then why did you go running off to the lawyer today? And what prompted you to tell me now—the day before we were getting married?"

"I thought I'd signed all the papers I was supposed to. I just wanted to clear it with a lawyer." There was that skewing thing again. "Look, you don't have to love me, just give me a chance. It'll all come out okay in time. Just let me take care of everything."

In his usual habit of controlling everything and everyone, Dick convinced me that it was taken care of and that we should get on with our marriage.

I really don't think there's one definition of love. I think love is different things to different people. When you're young, it's the physical attraction that gets all systems into motion; the hormones raging, the senses on fire, and of course, it feels so good it has to be love, right? As you mature, however, and you meet a new man, you want more than erotica and body fusion. You want to get to know him, find out his likes and dislikes, his ethics and beliefs. You have to see the warts and hear about the baggage. I think maybe a comfortable, relaxed feeling, along with some heavy breathing now and then could seem like love, but maybe the litmus test comes by living together; being around him twenty-four hours a day and learning his moods. I hadn't been around Dick long enough before I married him.

Moody! What an ugly word. Just like the face that portrays it. I had never experienced living with a moody person. My late husband of twenty-five years was so easy to live with that he made it impossible to put up with anything less. When my children gave me those long, pouty faces, the elongated sighs of dissension, I sent them to their rooms. No one wanted to look at those faces, I told them. When they felt like they could live with the horrible life that had been inflicted upon them, they could come back to the family room.

Now here I was, about to marry a grown man who was moody and who pouted and sulked around. I couldn't send him to his room. He wouldn't be talked out of it—and I couldn't abide it. Behind all this was his "give me sex and I won't pout" message. All those gut feelings should have been a red flag. Instead, I attributed them to indigestion and optimistically believed everything would work out. He begged, I acquiesced, and therein made another of the many wrong decisions in my life.

I let the registered letter drop to the floor. It wasn't just the letter. It was our whole relationship. I'd had a feeling deep down that something was amiss, but swept it under the rug. However, it kept surfacing like dandruff on my sholders for many months.

Dick wanted to stay on in Thailand and of course he felt that I should stay also. I, on the other hand, realized that I'd made a bad contract in the first place by marrying him while having all those reservations. I also knew that I'd pay the price for that mistake. It had been obvious for quite some time that I was, indeed, paying.

I loved the country, its people, and the friends I'd made. I had no doubt that without Dick I would have stayed longer, but now that was not an option. I had blamed our squabbling and disagreements on everything and everybody; his job, *The Bosses,* but I knew that down deep I resented him for lying to me, his "sex-or-pout" schemes and the constant bickering. I had lost respect for him. I had been foolish enough to think that things would get better. That he'd get over his problems and we'd live happily ever after. That we'd have a great adventure in Thailand that would make up for all the problems.

Oh, foolish woman, thy name is Pollyanna.

The day I intercepted the letter ended in a nightmare. I hid the letter and went to bed early with a pounding headache while he sat up drinking and sulking. When he got into bed next to me he began to rub my body. I asked him to stop. He whined, telling me how much he loved me, how he just wanted to touch me. I had quit giving in to his sickness much earlier and my peacekeeping was at its end. I tried to get out of bed but he grabbed me by the hair and forced me back down. By now I knew he was out of control. I was filled with revulsion. "Take your hands off of me?" He crawled on top of me and began slathering my face with his wet mouth. I struggled against his body as he tried to get leverage on top of me then reached down and yanked my gown up. I screamed at him to stop, that I was going to put him in prison for rape. I struggled again to get up, kicking him in the groin as I tried to push him away with my legs. He reached up and put both hands around my neck and began to squeeze. I could feel my throat tightening and began gagging. When he heard me he stopped, as if he realized for the first time what he was doing. He looked shocked as he let go of me and dropped down on the bed crying. I ran into the bathroom and locked the door, coughing and terrified, as bile burned my throat.

He banged on the door. "Let me in. I'm sorry. I don't know what happened. Please!"

I dropped down on the bathroom floor, my throat hurt and my heart pounded so fast I thought it might burst through my chest. I could hear his asthmatic sobs as he begged for my forgiveness. But I was beyond mercy. He'd crossed the line between human and animal in my eyes. I heard the bedroom door close softy but I was afraid to move. I spent the night on the bathroom floor, curled into a fetal position, waiting for dawn to come.

And I planned my exit. I'd squirreled away my passport and my open return ticket to the States at the time of Dick's termination. I'd hid them inside my suitcase where I knew he'd never look. The luggage was stored in an unused closet that Pon had locked after our return from Singapore. Now I needed to get some money from the bank, and I knew that would be a problem. The banks were not open yet, I would have to wait until he left the house.

Pon knocked softly on the bathroom door. "Mister he go now. You come out now?" She'd heard the crying and noise coming from our bedroom and worried all night long. I asked her to help me pack so I could leave.

Pon's tears fell as she helped me. "You no go," she cried. "Let mister go, not you, m*ai pen lai.*"

I sat her down on the bed with me. I reminded her of the many arguments that she'd overheard. I told her I had no *jai yen* for Dick and vice versa. "*Mai dii, mai dii,*" she sniffed, "men no good! You take me to US."

Of course she knew it could never be. We had talked about this several times in the past. How I would have loved to take her with me. To give her an easy life for a change, not leave her here to be somebody's servant until she could no longer walk. She said she'd probably return to her village to be near her son. We both cried and said in unison: "*Mai pen lai.*"

Dick returned while I was packing. I told Pon to tell him I was asleep, and locked the bedroom door. I curled up on the bed and waited to hear his car start, then closed my eyes and gave way to exhaustion. When I opened my eyes again, it was past noon, and Pon was at my door. "Mister go now, be back soon."

"Pon, can you get a taxi for me for the airport? I need to go before he returns."

She looked at me with shock. "*Mai dii*," she shook her head. "Mister come back soon."

I heard the car. I locked the bedroom door and jumped into bed. I could hear talking but couldn't make out the words. Then I heard the knock on the door. "Dodie. I'm leavin'. You don't have to stay in there all day. I'm sorry, and I know you don't believe me, but that's all I can say. I got an appointment to see a guy about the golf academy. I won't be back until late. Please come out of there."

I didn't answer. *Please go away. Just get the hell out of my life.* I could hear my ragged breathing in the quiet room. Could he hear it?

"Okay, I just wanted to tell you. I'll be back later, maybe we can talk then."

I heard the front door close. Pon was at my door in an instant. "I call my nephew. He come at eight tonight after he wok."

"Oh my God, that's too late. Can't he come any earlier? Can't you get someone else?"

"No, you be safe wit him. *Mai pen lai*. Mister say he be home late."

There was no way I wanted to talk to him again. I'd have to take my chances. I caught a motorcycle taxi to the bank and withdrew what was left. After paying Pon her salary, I had forty dollars and my Visa to get me safely back to the States. Once I'd made my exit plans, I felt a weight lifted from my chest. Everything would work out.

I walked through the house one more time, rubbing my hands over my beautiful teak furniture, smiling as its scent became a calming balm. I walked out to the patio and inhaled the beautiful smell of jungle and flowers. *Someday,* I thought, *I'll return.* I left the registered letter on the hutch.

As the taxi sped away toward Bangkok, my last picture of Pon was standing on the curb, smiling, tears running down her face and waving goodbye to the unhappy *farang*. I prayed that she would be able to move in with her son, but I felt sure, as Buddha had decreed, that she would have a much higher station in life in her next go-round.

* * *

The banging on my door awakened me. My brain was in a haze. I couldn't remember where I was. I scrambled around the room in the dark, my heart beating wildly. Then I heard him and my skin rose up in tiny gooseflesh. "Dodie, let me in!" I panicked. My hands were shaking as I tried to find the light. "I know you're in there. The guy at the desk said you were gonna take a taxi to the airport."

My heart seized as I felt the familiar tightening in my chest. How could this happen? I had taken such precautions. I knew Pon wouldn't willingly tell him where I was. I could hear him wheezing. It sickened me. "Go away. I have nothing to say to you. I'll call the police if you don't leave." I peered out the glass eye of the door.

"Just let me talk to you for a few minutes. I know I was a screw up and I know I drove you away, but I'll make it up to you. I promise." His voice had softened to a plea. I could see him in the stance he always adapted when he thought he would get his way. "I saw the letter you got from my ex today. She's a lyin' bitch. I did sign the final papers."

"Don't you get it? It had nothing to do with the letter. It was a sick relationship from the beginning, based on lies and promises. The letter just confirmed what I'd always known. After what happened how could you even want to face me."

"Please, open the door. I can't talk like this. I know. It was a mistake. I drove three hours to talk to you. Let me in."

"How did you find me?"

"Pon told me. I told her I needed to give you some money so she called the guy that drove you here."

"I don't want to see you or talk to you. You crossed the line. I hate you with such intensity that it hurts my chest. I can't go through this anymore."

"Please," he whined. "Just let me in for a few minutes. I just need to talk to you about last night. It was the booze. I didn't even know I was doing it until you choked. Please believe me. Let me in."

"It no longer matters to me what the reason was. I have to get away from you before I have a heart attack. We couldn't talk at home, why would you think we can talk here?"

"I just want you to give me another chance," he whined. "I can change. I can even find a therapist here if you want."

I felt nothing but pity for him now. The anger drained out of me as I listened to him begging, something no one should have to do. "It's over, Dick. Get on with your life. I'm going home. I'm saving myself from all this craziness."

I looked through the peep hole again while he mulled over my last words. He hit the door with such force that I jumped back afraid it would splinter. "Okay. Fuck it!"

I watched him turn, hit the wall again and stomp down the hall. I felt relief for the first time in months.

As my plane sat on the runway, I leaned my face against the bulkhead window. The glass was warm from the pervasive heat that envelops Thailand at that time of year. The humidity was closing in at a 100 percent. Droplets of moisture swirled in concentric shapes taking my tears with them as they spiraled downward into the inner workings of the plane's window.

As I looked out at the landscape I saw more than the occasional tourist. I saw beyond the tarmac to sprawling dense jungles that lay next to elegant high-rises, teeming slums next to gold and jewel-encrusted temples, high fashion shopping malls next to thatched huts.

Pornography rings and saffron-robed monks. Bargirls and homeless orphans. This is Bangkok. A city of extremes, the capital of, and largest city in Thailand—I felt its heartbeat.

Vivid memories and colorful pictures tumbled by in rapid sequence; the friends I'd made and would probably never see again. The beautiful orphans and Zac; the country and its sacred *Wats*; the banyan trees that covered the forests like giant umbrellas, shielding the plants in an ever-watchful stance; the fickle winds and torrential monsoons that can wipe out complete villages in one afternoon; the warm, smiling faces of the country and its people, with their stoicism and almost mystical strength.

The deafening sound of the jet engines jolted me from my reverie. Over the intercom the lilting trace of a Thai accent floated above us as the pilot announced we were second in line for take-off. I closed my eyes as the plane began its ascent and tried to make sense of why I had come here, how my life had changed and the reason I had to leave this beautiful country. I had no home to go to, no car and very little money. But I was homeward bound.

But I did know one thing for sure. If I'd learned anything from the stoic Thais, it was this: I would accept my life as it came from now on. Stressing, fretting, having chest pains was just a *farang* thing. I had this lesson shown to me for a year. If I didn't adopt this *mai pen rai* attitude, this acceptance, then what had I learned? What had I accomplished?

I leaned back in my seat, smiled and said a silent thanks to Buddha for his example. I won't think about this now. I'll *accept* it tomorrow.

THE END

EPILOGUE

I left Thailand a different person than when I arrived. I went there believing it was okay to "work" on a marriage, although I'd had doubts before the wheels ever left the tarmac. I pushed them aside because I wanted a trip to Thailand. I got one all right, but at what cost? As the saying goes, "There are no free lunches." Would I give up everything else I experienced and learned while there? I don't think so. I had also gained some insight about life; that all that glitters ain't necessarily gold. But I'd also made some great friends along the way, learning much from these smiling, accepting Thais.

In retrospect, as to the rules put forth by *The Bosses,* maybe I should have gone along with the pack as others had. However, I chose to stand up for my beliefs, as others had who'd been metaphorically banished to the Outer Darkness. At the very core of my being I fought against this type of control. It was contrary to everything I believed. I could neither help myself nor change my character to accept the unreasonable ultimatums of that female despot.

I learned so much about other people, their countries and cultures, that I can't imagine never having lived there or learned these truths. I have inhaled the sensuous aromas, tasted the delicious food and continue to be awestruck by the ever-evolving weather cycles of this incredible country. I have prayed in Buddhist temples. I have seen boisterous bargirls as they cavorted with the *farangs,* and seen them piously kneel in prayer at the temple. I have witnessed young monks bent in supplication for hours and have observed them laughing and watching TV as playful as young boys in the park.

Lord Buddha most assuredly blessed this beautiful and peaceful country. I believe that the uncomplaining Buddhist tolerance shapes both the lives of the people and the society of Thailand, and cannot help but touch the lives of foreigners who go there seeking asylum for their soul from a spiritually deaf world.

Thailand shares her beauty and many blessings with all foreigners, without prejudice, and calls them back in her own sensuous way. I will miss her crowded cities, polluted capital and peaceful people who accept all things in life, and her love of laughter and music.

I am eternally grateful that I was blessed to experience it.

A NOTE TO THE READER
2007

Although my story is accurate, I have changed the names and dates in some instances to protect innocent parties, and conflated several individuals into one character to protect the innocent (and guilty). Though the events depicted in my story all happened as portrayed, the dialogue was recreated through partial memory and notes from my journal written in real time.

My story takes place in the beginning of the last decade of the 20th century. It is now the 21st century and much has changed in the Land of Smiles, not the least of which is the comfort for the many expats who have made Thailand their home. Air conditioned taxis, now the favored method of transportation, have replaced the *tuk-tuks* for the least adventurous (the big sissies). A freeway now runs through the city to the airport in Bangkok, replacing the dangerous, pot-holed roads.

Along the Chao Phyraya River, which runs through Bangkok, high-end homes running upwards of $70,000, have appeared where wooden shacks have stood for a millennia, as the city rises vertically and majestically from the canal. High-rises and low-rent housing have replaced unkempt slums in the city while smooth running roads around town have helped with the problem of mobility.

Late model Japanese and American imports are now driven instead of old European cars—mostly Toyotas and Hondas. Now, automobile plants are up and running in Bangkok and foreign cars can be purchased for $10,000 to $15,000.

At the last census, sixty-three million people lived in Thailand. Depending on the time of year, and counting the surrounding provinces, some thirteen to twenty million live in Bangkok.

As for my surgeon, I believe she was competent, but just a bit over-zealous. And, most assuredly her hygiene practices could have been ratcheted up a few notches. I was also extremely unlucky in that I had the rare and unheard of "intolerant" Thai nurse. Today many people fly to Thailand from all over the world for major and elective surgery. Most do this to cut down on the exorbitant costs in U.S. hospitals. What they get in the bargain are top-notch doctors and nurses who are skilled in their field, and recuperation in one of the world's premier resorts. A network TV station reported last year on the thousands of people who flock to Thailand for elective and emergency surgery. At one hospital in Bangkok a patient reported that he'd had seven registered nurses attending him for the two weeks he was in a Bangkok hospital for heart bypass surgery. Where else can you get that kind of care? In the States you're lucky if you ever see an R.N.—unless it's pill time—as she must do all the paperwork, handing over the more unskilled jobs to her aides, who are also overworked with many patients to deal with.

As for my beautiful orphans, since I've written my story, Fr. Ray has gone home to his "Boss Upstairs" as he referred to his Lord, and he will be deeply missed by his staff, his volunteers, but mostly by "his children" as he called them. His life and the life of the children are chronicled in the biography: *"In the Name of the Boss Upstairs"* and is available through Amazon.com.

And conditions have dramatically changed for the better, as this email shows from Mrs. Radchada Chomjinda (Khun Toy), Fr. Ray's able assistant for many years:

"Since its inception in 1976 to the present year, 2006, there have been a total of 681 orphans taken in: 504 children have left the orphanage; 296 have been adopted and the remainder left for jobs or homes. Since 1992, there have been 309 deaf children taken in, and 259 have left for other homes. The orphanage also runs a school for blind children and from 1987 to the present it has taken in 362 children, of which 226 have since left. Since 1991 there have been 1,794 disabled children taken in, and 1,596 have left for other homes."

Kuhn Toy's last email to me states that things did change for the better after The *Hague Convention* was signed. Now, any child who bears Thai nationality and has a Thai ID (no matter that its mixed heritage) can be eligible for adoption if all necessary documents are available. The same thing for twins, siblings and disabled children, however, she said because they do not separate twins or siblings, it is too much of a burden for a couple to accept two or three children at one time. If a couple wants to adopt they must take all the siblings. As for the disabled, the parents might feel it's too much work, consequently not many of the disabled children are adopted.

This appears to be quite a change since my time in Pattaya, and I remain thankful to the sainted Fr. Ray and his tireless helpers who donate their time to helping these once lonely orphans.

If you care to donate to the orphanage, please go to their website at: www.pattayaorphanage.org.uk

I hope my depiction of Thailand proves useful to someone wanting to visit this beautiful country. Times and mores around the world have changed, and Thailand is no exception. The country is trying to fix things that have gone dramatically wrong with their once quiet, seductive land. I would urge anyone reading this to take the trip and make your own judgment. You will be enchanted, as are all visitors, as Thailand welcomes you with her special grace. And, you will want to return.

If not—*mai pen rai.*

DON'T MISS DODIE'S NEXT MEMOIR

"ONE STRAPPY-SANDALED FOOT AHEAD OF THE MULLAHS"

An Expat's Misadventures in Iran
Before and During the Revolution

An Excerpt Follows...

I'LL TAKE THE BUS, THANK YOU ALLAH!

Unlike the X-Generation teens of today with their hot cars and massive trucks, my generation grew up taking buses and streetcars. We didn't know any different. It was great fun. You could always find someone you knew on the bus and could catch up on the latest gossip, fret over a new pimple, or conspire how to get the attention of the new hottie in class.

Growing up in the 50s, in the midst of Norman Rockwell's America, we of the middle income families had only one car and that was used to get Dad to work to support us. Dad was gone from 8 a.m. to 5 p.m., so if you needed transportation during those hours—or even after those hours—you bused it. Or, as I heard echoing off the walls at my house, "Take the Shoe Leather Express." Now, in my adult years, I found myself returning to my earlier mode of transportation.

My first foray back into the Mass Transit System of my youth was in Iran during the 70s. My husband was assigned to a two-year contract in Isfahan, Iran, and I soon found that my fragile gastrointestinal state would not allow me to do much traveling by car after observing their Kamikaze-style of driving.

Hundreds of cars careened around town; some going the wrong way down a one-way street, or actually driving up on the sidewalk to get past a bottleneck. If the driver should hit a pedestrian or a car during this maneuver, "Insha Allah!" (It is Allah's will) and was the collective reasoning. It was the "Will of Allah" that had you standing in that exact spot—you had nothing to do with it.

There were no commercial taxis in Isfahan in the 70s. But there were hundreds of personal car-taxis. Anyone who owned a car could pick up a little extra rial (Iranian currency) by using his car for this quasi-taxi purpose, and it worked brilliantly. People would stand in the street yelling at the cars as they passed by. A driver who wanted to make a few extra rials would then slam on his brakes, skid to a stop, mindless of anyone that might be close behind—while brakes squealed and cars swerved—and impatiently wait for the people to pile in. This service continued until the car was so packed that the overflow were stuffed on top of each other and then maybe one or two more for good measure.

The first time I witnessed this I expected the new passengers to tell the driver where they wanted to go. Instead, they squeezed in and said nothing. Then, out of the blue, scaring me out of my wits, someone would shout something in Farsi and the driver would slam on his brakes again, sending all of us globing together in a helpless heap. The departing passenger would hand the driver what he thought his ride was worth, then disentangle himself from everyone and jump out, while the driver yelled at him in what sounded to me like death threats.

These drivers had a system that defied logic. I think they calculated that if one person would net them 10 rial (40 cents), then why not ten people, 100 rial—never mind that the elfin car was built to hold only four people at best. They continued to pick up passengers until the back and front seats were a mass of black-robed bodies packed together in one collective lump. The drivers even managed to count a few "worry beads" along the way. We expats always assumed that they were counting off how many hours they had left to live—one worry bead at a time.

One last experience ended my taxi-sardine stint and caused me to change my travelling mode. I was heading for home after a day at work. I had complained to my Iranian friends that the taxis just ignored me. They said I had to yell out my destination in Farsi, otherwise, they'd just keep going, taking me for a foreigner and infidel, and not smart enough to know their language.

I worked in town and needed a ride to Khane, a complex in the country occupied mostly by expatriates. I stood in the gutter yelling "Khane, Khane," as the cars sped by me. Finally a taxi skidded to a stop in front of me. When I opened the back door and prepared to get in, glaring at me were five men, two children, and one woman cloaked in black, revealing dark, steely eyes. I wasn't going to go through that again. I'd already done my time in the back seat of one of these small cars and ended up with six of us back there. Everyone was piled on top of each other, and five were in the front—one sandwiched between the driver and door, hanging out the driver's window. To make matters worse, at least for me, this was a country where most of the people believed that deodorant was a capitalist indulgence, and bathing every day was a ritual done only by capitalists and heathens. Need I say more? After a few "Encounters of a Close Kind" I decided to forego the taxi service.

I smiled and hesitated. How do I get out of this? Then she shot me the evil eye and I knew I was in trouble; that's a biggie here in the land of evil eyes. I decided to decline the ride, backed up and closed the door while the driver called down Satan and his tribesmen upon me, my offspring and anyone associated with me. He then sped off in a fog of diesel fuel and dirt.

The bus system was my only alternative. I had seen them careening through town, side-swiping a few cars as well as a few limbs of pedestrians, but still felt I'd be much safer with forty some-odd tons of steel wrapped around me as opposed to the little pieces of tin they euphemistically referred to as cars. I also felt that taking the bus would at least give me a little space, with just one available place to set an extra bottom instead of the taxi's version of five. I did notice that my extra seat was occupied only after all seats were taken—then and only then did they deign to sit next to the infidel.

Buses also had their own capacity quotients—determined by the driver. As do the drivers of the taxi-cars, Iranian bus drivers also take on more people than allowed by Allah. After every seat is filled, they fly down the highway with no standing room, and with one or two passengers hanging onto the bus—on the outside—balancing on the tire wells, as well as two passengers hanging out the open door waving to the onlookers.

Speed limits were non-existent in Iran. I worked in the city and lived in the country, approximately twenty miles from town. On a good day, and Allah willing, the bus driver could make that trip in fifteen minutes. Considering that the driver had well over thirty stops to make, and was traveling over roads that have not changed since Attila the Hun ran amok through Iran in the 4th Century—that's pretty fast.

Driving was a much more complicated science in Iran, and the drivers had to have incredibly fast reflexes as they jockeyed these huge busses into position, then know the exact instant to charge ahead, veer right or left, avoiding near misses, warding off certain death, and possibly leaving a string of inert bodies behind. I'd seen this for myself on one bus trip as we grazed a black-robed woman standing in the street. She fell to the ground, jumped up and began shaking her fist at the departing bus, yelling and howling, while passersby simply looked on, not the least bit concerned.

I knew that my bus ride to work was thumbing my nose at the Grim Reaper, but I still felt safer with more weighted metal protecting me. Every day as I boarded the bus I prayed to Allah to watch over my children after my demise.

I boarded the bus at 6 o'clock in the morning and was the driver's first passenger. I would walk to the back of the bus, take the last two-seater, and lay my purse, briefcase, and lunch on the vacant seat beside me; this ensured me a little more breathing room for at least ten more stops. As the bus began to fill, I'd remove my barriers and get ready for the onslaught of odors. I would then breathe through my mouth—bypassing my finicky olfactory glands—for the remainder of the trip. In many third-world countries the natives don't seem to opt for that "Aren't You Glad I Use Dial?" feeling. With so many different odors assailing me, I always grabbed a seat next to a window so I could gulp fresh air as much as possible.

All things considered, I still felt the bus ride much safer than driving or taxiing, that is until the day that our driver lost his gearshift.

I was the last one on the bus as I headed home from work. The seat I squeezed into was a flip-seat right by the driver. As we rounded a curve, he gunned the engine and rammed the stick shift into another gear, at which time it came off in his hands. He stared at it as if it was a foreign object. He looked at the gaping hole in the floorboard then glanced my way with a shy grin. I must have looked rather startled as he immediately tried to assuage my fear by trying to jamb the gearshift back into the hole. The problem was that we were sailing along at about 80 kilometers per hour and his attention was focused on the hole in the bottom of the floorboard while I watched the highway for signs of a collision. Every now and then he'd glance out the window, but most of his focus was on the floor.

"Aga," (Sir) I gasped, as another huge bus came bearing down on us, taking his half of the lane out of our side. He looked up just in time to swerve onto the shoulder, while our bus fishtailed two times, righted itself and jumped back on the highway. "No problem, Madame, Allah protect us." I couldn't quite get into his zone of comfort at that point, but hey, I'll take Allah anytime over a crash and burn.

Eventually I learned to just relax and trust Allah as I opened my book, traveling on the wonderful vehicle of the written word, while we soared helter-skelter through the Iranian countryside in Allah's Mass Transit System.

Dodie Cross is an award-winning freelance writer who has traveled the world writing about life in foreign countries. She spends her time between Washington State and Southern California. Look for her next book: *One Strappy-Sandaled Foot Ahead of the Mullahs: An Expat's Life in Iran Before and During the Revolution.*

Visit Dodie on her website at: www.abroadinthailand.com

To order additional copies of this book please go to:
www.abroadinthailand.com
or www.amazon.com